ON-LINE EDITING

James G. Stovall
Charles C. Self
Edward Mullins

Prentice-Hall, Inc., Englewood Cliffs, New Jersey 07632

Library of Congress Cataloging in Publication Data

Stovall, James Glen
    On-line editing.

    Includes index.
    1. Editing.   2. Journalism--Data processing.
3. Newspaper layout and typography.   I. Self, Charles C.,
1944-   II. Mullins, Edward, 1936-   III. Title
PN4784.E5S86 1984   070.4'1'0285   83-22905
ISBN 0-13-624403-3

Editorial-production supervision and
    interior design: Virginia McCarthy
Cover design: Lundgren Graphics, Ltd.
Page makeup: Steven Frim
Manufacturing buyer: Harry P. Baisley

Printed in the United States of America

10 9 8 7 6 5 4 3 2 1

ISBN 0-13-624403-3

Prentice-Hall International, Inc., *London*
Prentice-Hall of Australia Pty. Limited, *Sydney*
Editora Prentice-Hall do Brasil, Ltda., *Rio de Janeiro*
Prentice-Hall Canada Inc., *Toronto*
Prentice-Hall of India Private Limited, *New Delhi*
Prentice-Hall of Japan, Inc., *Tokyo*
Prentice-Hall of Southeast Asia Pte. Ltd, *Singapore*
Whitehall Books Limited, *Wellington, New Zealand*

This book is dedicated to the following people because of their love, patience and understanding:

Sally Stovall

Jefferson Stovall

Amelia Self

Natasha Self

Lara Self

Nicholas Self

Penny Mullins

Julie Mullins

Sarah Mullins

Marc Mullins

Andrew Mullins

CONTENTS

1

EDITING AND THE NEWS ORGANIZATION

At the heart of every news organization lies the work of the editor. Editing is judging, deciding, directing. It is the core around which all other divisions of the newspaper function. Every division, from reporting to management, production to circulation, functions to make editorial judgment possible. News organizations are the manifestations of the editorial judgments that guide them.

This power to establish the tone and shape of a publication makes the work of editors the most critical and important single factor in the success or failure of the news organization. That is why the principles outlined in this book are so important. These principles will help you function better as an editor and make decisions that will lead you to a successful news organization at whatever editorial level you occupy.

Yes, there are editorial levels. Executive editors make decisions that provide general guidance for the functioning of the news organization. Senior editors make decisions affecting the way individual divisions of the news organization function. And junior editors and copy editors make the decisions on individual pages, stories, and headlines which determine how the publication will look on a daily basis.

Every editor must understand the purpose of the publication, the nature of the organization's audience, and the personality the publication tries to project. These things provide the criteria for all of the individual judgments that editors must make at all levels of the news organization.

Every editor must also understand the relationships among the major divisions of the organization. Therefore, we will begin by reviewing the major units of the typical newspaper organization here and outlining the editorial functions within that organization.

THE NEWS ORGANIZATION

News reporting and news processing take place within the framework of a news organization. The framework of the organization generally includes:

1. An administrative division, which is concerned with the financial viability and health of the organization. One of the major functions of this unit is supplying the materials necessary for the other divisions of the publication to do their jobs. This division is also concerned with the maintenance and replacement of equipment and the introduction of new equipment and technology.

2. An editorial division, a product division, which is concerned with the production of the main product of the organization, the news.

3. A business division, a support unit which is concerned with making money through circulation, advertising, and auxiliary sales of job printing, reprinting, and other services.

Editorial decision-making involves directing each of the major divisions of the news organization and setting its objectives and goals. The business division generally is separate from the editorial direction from the administrative division.

In this book, we are primarily concerned with the second division, the editorial side of the publication.

THE EDITORIAL DIVISION

The people who work in this division may be put into the following categories.

1. Senior editors, who are concerned with planning the publication, supervising the various staffs, and selecting and designing the editorial portions of the paper.

2. Reporters and writers, who are concerned with identifying news and information sources, contacting the sources, taking material from the sources, and writing it in acceptable newspaper formats.

3. Copy editors, who edit material written for publication, layout the daily news package, write headlines, select photographs, and perform other duties to prepare the editorial matter for publication.

4. Backshop crew members, who prepare the edited copy for publication by supervising the typesetting and reproduction of photographs and who run the other machinery involved in reproducing the paper.

Senior editors head the editorial division. Groups within the editorial division are almost always headed by a senior editor or, in the case of the backshop crew, by a craftsman with a junior editor assigned to act as liaison between the reporters and copy editors and other units within the editorial division.

REPORTERS

Reporters provide the newspaper with much of its essential content. Reporters encounter many problems in the task of delivering news stories to the editor and the editor should remember this when handling the copy. The editor's job is to help the reporters produce superior copy.

Reporters and photographers identify and gather news from stored sources, personal sources, and environmental sources. The news reporting process may be described in the following way.

News gathering involves (1) identifying the event, problem, or issue which creates news, (2) asking investigative questions aimed at exposing the nature, the character, the extent and the importance of the event, problem or issue, with the use of the five W questions (who, what, when, where, why, and how) as guides, (3) selecting and finding the sources most likely to provide useful answers and explanations, and (4) recording the answers and information gathered. The accuracy of this material is verified both at the time it is gathered and again when the news story is written.

The sources of news and information include:

Stored sources are classified into basic newsroom references, including clippings, directories, almanacs, yearbooks, and encyclopedias; general library references, an enlargement of the newsroom references, including indexes, bound publications, books, and a whole assortment of references available in most public libraries and many newsrooms; and specialized references, such as law and science libraries and stored information at such sites as city government and other public agencies. In other words, anything that is already written down may be considered a stored source.

In addition to their use in backgrounding or preparation, stored sources are used to provide verification and to serve as core information in the form of statistics, comments in reports, revelations in findings, expert explanations, and historical antecedents.

Personal sources are persons who are involved in news or who can be used as references and verifiers of certain information. They may be (1) the main performers or adversaries, (2) the onlookers or secondary sources, (3) the persons qualified to comment on news situations, and (4) those who form opinions about what is going on or who lead the opinions of others.

Environmental sources encompass the information which reporters may gather without the help of personal or stored sources. For instance, environmental sources may be (1) the physical characteristics of the news event, such as the arrangement of material things such as cars in an accident or the physical elements of slum housing; (2) the social aspects, the way the principals in an event organize themselves in relation to each other, and (3) the psychological aspects, or how the principals, onlookers, etc. behave in the situation, whether angry, happy, sad, tense, or whatever.

News writing involves (1) reducing the bulk of the information gathered into what may be useable for news stories, (2) judging the relative importance of the information, (3) rechecking the information for accuracy, and (4) writing the information into proper news story forms. The inverted pyramid is a basic organizational form, but features, backgrounders, broadcasts, and other journalistic efforts require different forms.

Reporters may be grouped according to the types of copy they produce: local and area copy, wire copy, and departmental copy. Local and area reporters are supervised by the city editor or the area or state editor, wire reporters are supervised by the wire service chief or bureau chief, and departmental reporters (writers) are supervised by the various departmental editors, such as the financial or business editor, the farm or industrial editor, the home and family editor, the sports editor, and the entertainment editor.

The copy may be further categorized as:

1. Straight or spot news stories which include the formal and highly factual accounts of news situations and issues. These stories are usually written in the inverted pyramid form or some variation of this structure and are developed from assignments or beats. They also include such events as fires, bank robberies, murders and assaults — the unexpected and the immediate.

2. Developing stories, also written in straight news fashion and including coverage of continuing news situations written against a deadline, such as court trials, hearings, and extended spot situations. These stories may include new leads and inserted news material.

3. Compiled stories, which include the combination of reports from local or area reporters and wire stories. These may include stories on severe weather conditions and other national and regional stories which have local angles.

4. Feature stories and sidebar stories, which include human interest stories, profiles, and articles that highlight the colorful, the unusual and the dramatic aspects of the main story.

5. Investigative or depth stories which include penetrating reporting of a news situation and which are written either as single stories or as a series of stories.

6. Background or analysis stories, which include interpretations of news situations, critical reviews of social activity, columns and advice, editorials, and other special departmental stories.

THE COPY DESK

Many of the day-to-day editorial decisions are made by the copy editors and other junior editors who shape the paper so that it fits the guidelines set by the senior editors. The copy desk is supervised by the copy chief or the wire editor (the telegraph editor) and is staffed by copy editors or copyreaders or by desk editors.

The processing and packaging of the day's news is handled through (1) a universal copy desk, where all copy except departmental copy is processed; (2) separate desks, where local, area, and wire copy is processed; or (3) some other combination, which may include the reporters.

Universal copy desk. This desk is usually supervised by a copy chief or slotman (or wire or telegraph editor). This editor gets all copy, even though some of it may have been examined initially by the other editors. The copy chief determines how the budget of news, with the exception of the major news, will be distributed through the newspaper and designates the appropriate length, headline size, and type for the copy.

The copy chief is assisted in his task by copy editors, who do the bulk of the editing, and by a makeup editor, who does the final fitting of the copy in the reproduction department.

Separate desks. The editors in charge of the separate desks perform essentially the same tasks as the copy chief but, for their own type of copy and for their own pages, on instructions from the copy chief. The wire desk may also be responsible for Page 1.

Other combinations. The reporters may process their own copy, handling the copy as the copy editor does, with instructions on length, headline size, and type from the desk editor in charge.

BACKSHOP CREW MEMBERS

The "backshop" is the name given to the part of the paper's staff which prepares the paper for publication and prints it. This unit is supervised by a production chief and staffed by composers, typesetters, paste-up people, photographers, and pressmen. These people convert the processed and packaged news copy into a publishable form. The technology these people use can be hot type, cold type (photo-composition), or a combination of these; stereotyping or platemaking; and direct impression, offset impression, or some other printing system.

Editors must know many of the skills of the backshop, even if exercising such skills is not part of their daily duties. They need to know how the machinery works and how much time it takes for certain processes to take place. They need to know what technology the paper has available and how that technology can be used to the fullest extent. This knowledge is important because editors and backshop crew members have to work closely together to get the paper out on time. Each group must communicate effectively with the other. Both groups must maintain a sense of professionalism which allows them to function under circumstances which are often tense and difficult. For an editor, an intimate knowledge of a backshop's people and machinery is a must.

THE EDITOR'S DUTIES

From the top executive editor to the newest copy editor, certain duties are common to the process of editorial decision-making. The executive editor's decisions are of wider scope, but they involve the same kinds of activities. These may be grouped into three types of activities: (1) news planning, (2) news packaging, and (3) news processing.

News planning involves (1) making assignments to cover the news through the scheduling of reporters, photographers, and other newspaper personnel; (2) anticipating and preparing for the day's budget of news through the coverage of assignments and through the wire news schedule; (3) deciding what news is likely to demand prominent display and what the display may entail; (4) informing the production department of the potential copy load and any special production handling that may be needed; and (5) determining the amount of news copy space that is available and how it will be dealt with.

News packaging involves (1) sorting, selecting and scheduling stories and illustrations that result from the day's coverage and from the wire service budget; (2) placing those stories and illustrations in the appropriate pages and indicating how they are to be displayed; (3) designating the appropriate length of each story and the size and type of headline to be provided by the copy editor; (4) designating the size of accompanying illustrations and cutlines; and (5) distributing the earmarked stories and illustrations to the copy editors.

News processing activities include news editing, news headlining, news illustrating, and news compiling. News editing involves (1) examining the story for gaps in facts and weaknesses in background, for style errors, and for faulty grammar, spelling, and punctuation and correcting them where necessary; (2) checking the accuracy of names, addresses, dates, places, and other facts and checking legal implications, attribution, and fairness and honesty; (3) determining whether the story is clear, active, readable, and interesting or needs recasting, rephrasing, or tightening; (4) cutting the copy to the size indicated by trimming words, sentences, or paragraphs as needed; and (5) indicating any special typographical treatment, such as subheads or boldface type needed for the display of the story.

News headlining includes (1) determining the type of headline, the number of columns, the size of type, and the headline count; (2) summarizing the main point or essence of the story accurately in as few words as possible; and (3) making sure those words are clear, active, readable, and interesting.

News illustrating includes (1) sizing the picture or illustration accompanying the story, (2) writing the cutline, and (3) designating any special treatment for reproduction or handling.

News compiling includes (1) combining wire stories and illustrations from different news services into a unified story and display; (2) combining wire stories with locally produced stories and information and with illustrations into a unified story and display; (3) combining developing stories, whether wire or locally produced or both, into a unified whole and illustrating them ,when possible; (4) combining and rewriting stories from correspondents and other contributors into a unified whole and illustrating them, when possible; and (5) inserting background information into wire stories or locally produced stories as needed.

CONCLUSION

It is important for every member of a news organization to understand all of the functions of that organization and to realize how he or she fits in. Editors in particular need to have this understanding, since their jobs are likely to bring them into contact with many other parts of the news organization. Editors have many management decisions to make, and in order to make them effectively, they must know their organizations thoroughly.

The above description of the parts of a news organization has been given in somewhat abstract terms so that it may apply as widely as possible. Every news organization, while containing the basic units described, has a unique structure to suit its personnel, traditions, and physical settings. The effective editor will learn as much as possible about the special qualities of a particular organization.

2

THE EDITING PROCESS

The basic procedure of editing is reading a piece of copy, correcting technical mistakes (spelling, grammar, punctuation) and other problems of the copy, and making a judgment about the suitability of the copy for publication. In doing all this, editors have several options: they may decide the copy can be published with few or no changes; they may ask the reporter to rewrite it to add new facts or to give it a new emphasis; they may delay its publication for a more appropriate time; or they may decide the copy or the subject matter is not the kind that should go into their publication and may "kill" or "spike" the copy.

An editor is generally the first reader of the story after it has been written (the first, we would hope, of many). The editor of a story is in many ways its most important reader, because it is the job of editors alone to make copy presentable to readers. If they do not do this, no one else in the editorial process will.

This chapter discusses some of the basic tools and procedures of editing a story. The emphasis in this chapter will be on hard copy editing — editing with a pencil on typewritten copy. Much of what is said about the editing process, however, applies to the next chapter on electronic editing. The procedure is really the same; only the tools are different.

TOOLS FOR HARD COPY EDITING

The tools of an editor are ones with which we are all familiar: pencils, eraser, paper, scissors, and glue. A typewriter may also be required for rewriting or headline writing. For headline writing the editor will also need a head count guide, and for layout and picture sizing, picture wheels, dummy sheets, and pica poles (a printer's ruler) are necessary.

In addition, an editor will need certain reference materials, such as a stylebook, a dictionary, a thesaurus, a city telephone directory, an atlas, an encyclopedia, and an almanac. These reference materials will be discussed more fully later in the book, but they should be mentioned here. Good editors consider a dictionary and stylebook essential to their work.

Another tool an editor needs is a set of copy editing symbols. These symbols are used to correct copy in a standard and understandable way. One of the major purposes of hard copy editing is to prepare copy to be sent to a typesetter. The copy should be edited so that it is as clean and easy to read as possible. Sloppily edited copy is much more likely to provoke mistakes by a typesetter — mistakes that can be embarrassing and costly.

Sets of copy editing symbols may differ slightly according to the custom of the publication. Whatever set is preferred, it is essential that a set of copy editing symbols be learned quickly by the student so they can be used easily and accurately.

All of the discussion up to this point has centered on the physical tools, but mental tools are clearly the editor's most important possessions. The brain is the only real tool an editor has. If an editor doesn't use that tool, all the physical aids in the newsroom won't help.

Editors must have agile minds. They must have a wide assortment of facts and concepts they can call up for instant use. They must know history and literature. Their knowledge of grammar and punctuation must be thorough. They need not necessarily be expert spellers (although it certainly helps), but they must be able to spot and question possible misspellings. They should know their communities geographically and socially. They must know where to get information as much as a reporter does, and many editors spend a good deal of their time developing their own sources.

Editors must be able to find mistakes and to question what they do not understand. If an editor does not understand something in a story, there will be few readers who do. Editors must also be able to spot errors in logic or lapses in common sense. They should be wordsmiths, people who not only know how to use words precisely but also have a feel for the language and a love for good writing.

In addition to all of these traits, editors must have in their heads a clear idea of what kind of publication they are producing. They must know what is and what is not appropriate, what similar or opposing publications are doing, and the ins and outs of their own operation. Editors must edit with readers in mind, and to do that they need some information on who the readers are and what they expect from the publication.

The editor described here is not superhuman. In fact, many such editors exist on many publications. But they did not become editors of high caliber overnight. For most, it took years of hard work and concentration to acquire the tools of a good editor. And for all such editors, maintaining and adding to those tools is a matter of constant effort. Students who wish to become editors must begin now by sharpening their skills and expanding their knowledge and sensitivity.

NEWS VALUES

News in our society is built on some traditional news values. Beginning students need to understand these values, for they are the basis on which journalists decide whether or not an event is news. Millions of "events" occur in our society every day. Only a few of those events are selected by editors, and at least one of the following criteria must be present for an event to be classified as news.

Impact. Events that affect people's lives are classified as news. The event itself might involve only a few people, but the consequences may be wide ranging. For example, if Congress passes a bill to raise taxes or if a researcher discovers a cure for a form of cancer, both actions will affect large numbers of people. They would have impact, and they would be considered news.

Timeliness. Timeliness is a news value common to almost all news stories. It refers to the recency of an event. Without the element of timeliness, most events cannot be considered news. For example, a trial that occurred last year is not news; a trial going on right now may be news. How much time has to elapse before an event can no longer be considered news? There is no specific answer to that question for every case. Most events more than a day to a day-and-a-half old are not thought to be news. (Look in today's newspaper and see if you can find a news story about an event that occurred two days ago.)

Prominence. Prominent people, sometimes even when they are doing trivial things, make news. The president of the United States is a prime example. Whenever he takes a trip, even for purely personal and private reasons, his movements are covered in great detail by the news media. The president is a prominent and important person. Anything he does is likely to have an impact on the country, and people are very interested in his actions. The president is not the only example of a prominent person who often makes news. Movie stars, famous politicians, advocates of social causes — all of these people make news simply because they are very well known.

Proximity. Events close to home are more likely to be news than the same events elsewhere. For example, a car wreck killing two people on a road in our home county is more likely to be reported in the local news media than the same kind of wreck a thousand miles away. We are interested in the things that happen around us. If we know a place where something goes on, we are more likely to picture that event and have a feeling for it and for the people involved.

Conflict. When people disagree, when they fight, when they have arguments — that's news, particularly if one of the other news values, such as prominence, is involved. Conflict is one of the journalist's favorite news values because it generally ensures that there is an interesting story to write. One of the reasons courtroom trial stories are so popular with newspaper readers as well as with television watchers is that the central drama involves conflict — two competing forces each vying to defeat the other.

The bizarre or unusual. That which rarely happens is sometimes considered news. There is an adage in journalism that goes something like this: "When a dog bites a man, that's not news; when a man bites a dog, now *that's news*." These events, though they may have relatively little importance or may involve obscure people, are interesting to readers and enliven a publication. For example, it's not news when someone's driver's license is revoked (unless that someone is a prominent person); it is news, however, when a state department of transportation revokes the license of a person called "the worst driver in the state" because that person has had twenty-two accidents in the last two years.

Currency. Issues having current interest often have news value, and events surrounding those issues can sometimes be considered news. For example, a panel discussion of doctors may be held in your community. Normally, such a discussion might not provoke much interest from journalists. If the discussion topic were "The Morality of Abortion," the news value of the event would change, and there would likely be a number of newspaper, radio, and television journalists covering it. Issues with the value of currency come and go, but there are always several such issues being discussed by the public.

A news writer must make decisions about the events to be covered on the basis of these news values. News values should be used in deciding the kind of information needed for a story and in helping the writer organize the story so that the most important and most interesting information gets to the reader in the most efficient manner.

GATHERING THE NEWS: FIVE W'S AND ONE H

A journalist gathering information or writing a story tries to answer the following six basic questions for the reader.

Who. Who are the important people in the story? Is everyone included so that the story can be accurately and adequately told? Is everyone properly identified?

What. What is the major action or event of the story? What are the actions or events of lesser importance? A journalist ought to be able to state the major action of the story in one sentence, and this should be the theme of the story.

When. When did the event occur? Readers of news stories should have a clear idea of when the story takes place. The when element is rarely the best way to begin a story, because it is not often the most important piece of information a journalist has to tell a reader, but it should come early in the story and should be clearly stated.

Where. Where did the event occur? Journalists cannot assume that readers will know or be able to figure out where an event takes place. The location or locations of the event or action should be clearly written.

Why and How. The reader deserves an explanation of events. If a story is about something bizarre or unusual, the writer should offer some explanation, so that the questions the event raises in the reader's mind are answered. The writer also needs to set the events or actions in a story in the proper context. Reference should be made to previous events or actions if they help to explain things to the reader.

EDITING PROCEDURE

An editor should ideally be able to read through any story at least three times. Sometimes, of course, there isn't time enough to do that, but in this section we'll assume that for any given story, the time does exist. Here's how that time should be used.

The first reading of any story should be a fairly quick one. This reading allows the editor to get the "feel" of the story — to find out what it is about and to spot any major problems that are readily identifiable. The editor should note the story content and structure. This first reading may be all an editor needs to realize the story should be given back to the reporter for rewriting. As much as possible, editors should do first readings as if they know little or nothing about the subjects. This, of course, is the position of the average reader on first reading the story.

If the editor deems the story good enough for the rest of the editing procedure, the second reading should take place much more slowly. It is on this reading that the major editing is done. Accuracy, clarity and brevity are the major goals of the editor (see Chapter 6), and it is with these goals in mind that one should follow the checklist below in editing any story.

The lead. The editor should pay particular attention to the lead. It is the most important part of a story. A good lead will get the reader into a story; a bad lead will send the reader somewhere else. Does the lead convey the most important information of the story (if it is a news story)? Does it give the reader an accurate idea of what the story is about? Does it raise expectations in the reader that will not be fulfilled by the story? Does it emphasize the proper facts? Does it need to be updated or localized?

Story structure. After the lead has been dealt with, the editor should be concerned about the organization of the story. Is the story put together in a logical manner, especially with regard to the lead? Facts should be given in a manner that will satisfy the reader. Not all of the facts can be given at once, nor should they be. The story should develop in a way that allows the reader to understand the information the story is attempting to convey. The editor's job is to make sure that happens.

Completeness. Every story should have all the facts necessary for the reader to understand the story. While reporters and editors must make certain assumptions about the reader's prior knowledge, these assumptions cannot be carried too far. For instance, if an editor is dealing with a city council story, he or she cannot assume that the reader has read last week's city council story and remembers what happened then. If some action the council takes is a follow-up to action taken the previous week, the story must explain that.

Another area of completeness that is often overlooked involves the failure of a story to provide all of the facts the reader is led to expect. A story might talk about a new day care center that is opening up. The reader, particularly a parent who might want to use the day care center, would want to know what hours it plans to keep, what age children the center will accept, and how much it will cost. Stories without such facts are incomplete.

Grammar, spelling and punctuation. A knowledge of grammar and punctuation and knowledge of how to use a dictionary are basic tools an editor must have. No editor will survive without them. Words must be spelled correctly, and grammar and punctuation must conform to standard rules of English usage. The editor who consistently allows incorrect grammar and misspelled words into a publication is failing on the most basic level, and there is no way in which such a publication can gain credibility (see Chapter 4).

Style. Every publication should have a set style, and every editor should see that stories conform to this style. Most newspapers use Associated Press style and supplement this with a local stylebook. Style should not be a straightjacket into which an editor forces every piece of copy; rather it should be a help to writers and editors in achieving accuracy and consistency in their copy (see Chapter 5).

Objectivity. Is a story fair? Has the reporter attempted to gather all points of view? Are the facts slanted toward a particular opinion? Many feel that objectivity is an unattainable goal. Yet it remains a goal of American daily journalism, and the editor is the best insurance that this goal is being actively pursued.

Names and titles. Journalists should be particularly careful in the handling of names and titles, and editors must make every effort to ensure their accuracy. Names which have unusual spellings should always be checked, and editors need to remember that even the most common names may have uncommon spellings (as in Smith, Smyth, and Smythe). Nothing should be taken for granted when dealing with a person's name. There is no quicker way for a publication to lose credibility than by misspelling a name.

Titles, too, need special care. Formal titles should be correctly stated; they are extremely important to the people who hold them. Titles should also be descriptive of the jobs people have. If they are not, editors may consider adding a line of job description in the story if this will clarify things for the reader. (See more about the checking of names and titles in Chapter 6.)

Taste, tone, and mood. A hilarious story about a car that flips over two or three times and bounces around a road isn't so hilarious if two people were killed in the wreck. Editors should make sure that their stories convey the proper tone and mood and accurately reflect the facts of an event. In deciding about taste, an editor will often have to weigh the importance of the facts and people in the story. For instance, when a president goes to the hospital for an operation on his hemorrhoids, an editor will have to decide whether that situation is important enough to merit a story. There are no ironclad rules governing taste, tone, and mood; there are only editors who have the sensitivity to make thoughtful and logical decisions.

Quotes and attribution. Editors have a number of things to look out for here. First and foremost, are the quotes in a story accurate? Only the reporter will know this, but if something in a quote doesn't ring true, the editor should ask the reporter, "Did the person really say that?" Editors should also watch for partial quotations — those single words and phrases with quotation marks around them — and should ask themselves if they are necessary. Will the story mean just as much if they are taken out? If so, they probably should be eliminated.

All direct and indirect quotes should be attributed, and the attributions should be clear. There should be no doubt in the reader's mind about who said what in a story. A final note about attribution: there aren't any good substitutes for the word "said." Other words which can be used to indicate that people said something (explained, stated, pointed out, etc.) have specific meanings and should be used only when what the speaker says fits with the meaning of the word. Editors should not go to great lengths to find substitutes for "said" anyway. It is an easily understandable, unobtrusive word that can be used repeatedly in a story.

Triteness and clichés. Even the most common news stories should have some freshness about them. Editors need to be sensitive to the fact that some words and phrases are being overused in their respective publications, and periodically they should attempt to change their habits. "Dead on arrival," "straight as an arrow," "very," "quite," "really," and "actually" are all words and phrases that can easily show up too many times in a publication.

Transitions. Few things contribute more to the clarity of a story than proper transitions. Readers should be able to follow the development of a story easily. Each succeeding part of a story should be tied to a previous part of the story. Readers shouldn't be jolted by some totally new subject in the middle of a story. An expanded discussion of transitions can be found in Chapter 6.

Wordiness. A story should not be one word longer than necessary in order to maintain accuracy and clarity. Most reporters, especially young ones, use too many words. Editors should be on the lookout for such expressions as "a total of," "as a result of," and "at this point in time."

Repetition and redundancy. Speakers who use the same words over and over quickly become boring; so do writers. English is a language with a large variety of words easily understood by most people. Reporters and editors should take advantage of this variety and make sure they don't repeat major nouns, verbs, or adjectives in one sentence or paragraph.

A redundancy is a phrase in which the same meaning is transmitted twice. Redundancies make writers and editors look foolish. "A dead corpse," "we should not forget to remember," "apathetic people who don't care" — all are phrases in need of editing.

Libel. Watch the way people are described and quoted in a story. Will a person be held up to public ridicule because of this story? Will someone's position in the community be damaged? Is it possible that anyone will be deprived of livelihood because of the story? Remember that not only people but companies, associations and products may be libeled. Editors should be particularly careful when a story deals with illegal, immoral, or unethical activity and should make sure that what the story says is correct and that the reporter has made every effort to write a complete story. More about libel can be found in Chapter 11.

Obscenity. Different publications maintain different policies on printing obscenity. Not too long ago, "hell" and "damn" were regularly expunged from a story; today much stronger language finds its way into many publications. At this point in the editing process, it is the editor's job to see that the policies of the publication are carried out. If no such policy exists, one should be developed that takes into account the goals of the publication and the sensibilities of the readers.

After completing this second reading, checking on all of the above items, and making necessary corrections, the editor should read through the story a third time. This should be a rapid reading to make sure the story is coherent and complete. The editor should check the copyediting marks to make sure they are easy to follow and should also make sure that all of the necessary typesetting commands are written on the copy and that anything not to be typeset is circled.

EXERCISES

EDITING SYMBOLS

The following is a standard list of editing symbols which you should learn as quickly and thoroughly as possible.

Indent paragraph	⌐The president said
Take out letter	occas⌢ionally
Take out word	the ~~red~~ hat
Close up words	week‿end
Insert word	take it⸝run *and*
Insert letter	encycl^o^edia
Capitalize	president washington
Lower-case letter	the /President's cabinet
Insert hyphen	up‿to‿date
Insert period	end of the sentence ⊙
Insert comma	He said⸝"I'll stop
Insert quotation marks	the⸜orphan" quote
Abbreviate	the (United States)
Spell out	(Gov.) Sam Smith
Use figures	(one hundred fifty-seven)
Spell out figures	the (3) horses
Transpose letters	pejo⌒rative
Transpose words	many |problems|difficult
Circle any typesetting commands	(bfc⸜lc)
Connect lines	The car wreck⸝xxxxx
	⌐injured two people

EDITING SYMBOLS

The story below contains numerous errors and will allow you to practice using the basic editing symbols. No major editing needs to be done to the content of the story. Make sure the story conforms to AP style.

A 66 year old Junior College instructro from Hamblen won the masters' title in the State Open Checkers Tourney at a Nashvillee motel Sunday.

Hix Davenport who teaches electornics at Central state junior college out-scored fifteen opponents in the top division to cap the victory in the American Checker Federation Tournament.

His prze was 75 dollars.

In the secondary division — the majors' division — Luke Moane of Westville, Iowa was the top winner, bringing home $40.

"It's fun to play the game mostly, said Holley. "I like to win, but you cant aways win. I just enjoy playing the game."

The tourment drew 41 contestants

EDITING SYMBOLS

The story below contains numerous errors and will allow you to practice using the basic editing symbols. No major editing needs to be done to the content of the story. Make sure the story conforms to AP style.

WARSA, Poland (AP) — Hellmeted riot police swinging long batons briefly clashed with youths shuoting "Long Live Solidarity during a tense Monday standoff at a meorial march commemorating bloody riots twenty-six years ago in Poznan, witnesses said.

About 300 youths fled from a crowd of about 4,000 workers who gathered at a huge memorial cross in central Poznan, erected to commemorate scores of deaths injuries during the 1956 rioting there.

The clashes ended quickly however, as hevy trucks and water cannon surounded the marchers, who had wal ked quietly about 1½ miles to the cross fro the Cegielski heavy equipment factory where the 1956 began.

EDITING SYMBOLS

The story below contains numerous errors and will allow you to practice using the basic editing symbols. No major editing needs to be done to the content of the story. Make sure the story conforms to AP style.

BARABOO, Wis. (AP) — Hunters over the weekend kiled 14 racoons at the International Crane Foundation, wheree the animals have been xxxattacking rare birds. Foundtion administrater Joan Fordham said Baraboo hunters Willard and jeff Giese and Matt Kannenberg shot 7 raccoons Friday night and more seven Sunday night.

Department Of Natural Resources game warden Dennis Jameson helped organise the hunt after raccons, unffazed by electric fences traps and nylon netting spread over the pens, killed three rare birds in as many nights last week.

The raccoons victims included Tex a rare whoping crane who became something of a celebrity because she pxxformed the crane mating dance with foundation director George Archibald before her 1st chick was born last month.

Foundation spokeswomen Sue Rogers said the hunters believe there may be as many as 50 raccoons in the nearby woods. Berrys have not yet ripened and the raccoons may be getting desprate for food she said.

EDITING SYMBOLS

The story below contains numerous errors and will allow you to practice using the basic editing symbols. The story is not particularly well written and you may want to make it read more smoothly. Make sure the story conforms to AP style.

Flooding due to last nights rain storm, has damaged sevierely consturction work on the citys' newest radio station.

WXXg, which was secheduled to go on the air next month, has had it's air date moved back at least a mont, according to station spokesman Linda Rival.

Miss Rival, who is also one of the station's co-owners and has been advertised as planning to be one of the station's diskjockeys, said the floods severely damaged the interiro of the station and knowked down the half-completed towar.

"We haven't detemined the full extent of the damage, said Miss Rival, but I's sure its going to be bad."

She said the station would be delayed at least a month in going on the air.

The flooding was caused by some heavy rains that feel throughout the state earlier in the weak. Several homs and businessses in the area of the station known as Flat plains was reported damaged.

REWRITING THE LEAD

The story below has a lead which needs rewriting. Read the story and think about what facts you would want to include in the lead. Rewrite the lead and whatever else you think needs rewriting and edit the rest of the story. Make sure the story conforms to AP style.

Rev. Madison Holcomb, leader of the right wing God and Country political action group, spoke to a crowd of about 200 people last night who were gathered on the steps of the First Baptist Church.

Rev. Holcomb, of Kry Largot, Florida, spoke on a variety of topics, including abortion, the nuclear alms race and the current efforts of his God and Country group to boycot television programs which are sexually implicit.

"Abortion is a sin against God and a sine against man," said Holcomb, as the crowd cheered and waved signs, some of which said, "Save the Unborn" and "Abort Abortion." "A child is a human being from the moment of contraception, and that child has rights. The most basic right he has is the right to live."

Holcomb said that while he detests the thought of having to use nuclear weapon, American should remain a leader in this regard. "The Russians cannot be trusted to reduce their nuclear arsenal," he said, "so we cannot afford to reduce ours."
Holcomb praised the efforts of his God and Country group in their fight against sex on television by saying, "There's too much sex on television, and we've taken a stand against it," he said. He said those efforts were having an affect and mentioned the fact that several shows from the last season which they have been bouycotting have been cancelled.

Even though Holcomb previously reported his group had raised more than 55 million dollars last year, he said at last night's meeting that they were short of money. "We are in dire straights," he said. If you don't give, the Lord's work won't get done."

REWRITING THE LEAD

The story below has a lead which needs rewriting. Read the story and think about what facts you would want to include in the lead. Rewrite the lead and whatever else you think needs rewriting and edit the rest of the story. Make sure the story conforms to AP style.

INVERNESS, Scotland — Stories of the Loch Ness monster have fascinated residents and travelers in this remote area of the Scottish highlands for more than a 1,000 years. Now theree is yet another story to spur the interest of Nessie buffs.

The latest "siting" of the monster may have something different -- pictures. While many have claimed to have seen the monster, few pictures of it have every been produced. The most famous is one taken by a London dentist in the 1039's.

Now, it seems, there may be another. Lonnie McKenzie, a crofter near Inverness, reported last week that he had seen the monster clearly and had watched it swim along the lock for several minutes. What he didn't report then but did reveal yesterday was that he had a camera with him.

"I didn't want to say anything about the camera," he told a reporter for the Inverness Gazette yesterday, "because I didn't want people to get too excited about it. Acually, I'm a pretty good photographer."

McKenzie said that he had film in the camera at the time and thought the condidtions for taking a picture that day were pretty good. There were some low hanging clouds, he said, but generall the air was clear.

The film, he said, was in a secret location and is now being developed. He won't say who is developing the film or where it is.

What is certain is that if the pictures do indeed show the Loch Ness monster, Lonnie McKensie is sure to become a rich many. Two of London's largest selling newspapers, the Daily Mirror and the Sun, have already begun a bidding war for rights to publish the photographs, and sources say the price has gone over $150,000 so far.

REWRITING THE LEAD

The story below needs considerable rewriting. Read the entire story and think about what facts you should include in the lead. Rewrite the lead and whatever else you think needs rewriting and edit the rest of the story. If any important information is missing from the story, you should ask your instructor to supply it. Make sure the story conforms to AP style.

A Red Cross official said Saturday's State-Tech football game was the worst in terms of heat exhaustion cases in at least 27 years.

The victims were treated by volunteer medical personell in Memorial Stadium's three first aid stations according to red Cross volunteer Jody Johns.

At leaest 200 people were treated for heat related ailments at the game. A total of thirteen were sent to local hospitals.

The stricken fans were so numberous that medics stretched them out on the staduim concourse near the Northeast station while treating them.

Three people, one of them a heart-attck victim, were sent to hospitals before the kickoff at 1:30 P.M. central time.

Five cardiologists were on standby during the game, to prevent a recurrence of the tragedy which occurred at the 1972 game, when six people died of heart attacks.

"We haven't lost anybody since 1969," local cardiologist Dr. Russell Turner said. Turner has worked at the medical stations for local games since 1966.

Johns said only one of the patients treated at the was "obviously drunk out of his mind."

"I've never seen a game like this," he said. "The heat got to them before the booze did."

In addition to the fans, several players suffered ill affects from the record-breaking heat. Tech's starting quarterback, Billy Bob Braun, played only one inning before collapsing. Tech managed to pull through and win without him by a slim margin, however.

WORDINESS; FACTS OMITTED FROM THE LEAD

A major problem with this story is wordiness; try to tighten up the language. Another problem is that an important fact has been omitted from the lead. Remember that you are editing this for use in a daily paper which serves White Oak.

Harvey S. Baker, president of Brickline Corporation, made an announcement today that his company has chosen White Oak as the site for the company's newest plant.

Mr. Baker, whose company has 35 plants in the United States and around the world, said White Oak was chosen because of its excellent location and favorable economic factors.

"The people in White Oak and the rest of the state have been most gracious to us and have made us feel very welcome," Mr. Baker stated.

Brickline Corporation, a subsidiary of Amalgamated Industrial Products, manufactures a line of packaging products for many goods found in retail stores. For instance, the corporation has contracts to make the packaging for several brands of soap and labels for cans of soups.

Construction on the White Oak plant will begin within a month and is scheduled for completion in about a year. When operating at full capacity, the plant will employ about 300 people.

The plant will be located near the Brookhaven exit of Interstate 72 on Old Jug Factory Road. It will be on a 200 acre tract that was once part of the Queenland estate.

"We are very happy about this industry coming to our area,k plant will begin within a month and is scheduled for completion in about a year. When operating at full capacity, the plant will employ about 300 people.

The plant will be located near the Brookhaven exit of Interstate 72 on Old Jug Factory Road. It will be on a 200 acre tract that was once part of the Queenland estate.

"We are very happy about this industry coming to our area," said Patrick O'Connor, mayor of White Oak. "We are looking forward to a good relationship with them."

TRANSITIONS

In editing the story below, watch particularly for the lack of transitions. There may be other errors in the story, too. Make sure the story conforms to AP style.

A large oak tree, located on the university campus and though to be one of the oldest in the state, was severely damaged yesterday.

The storm, which knocked down power lines in many parts of the city, ocurred between 4 and 5 o'clock yesterday afternoon. and hampered the movement of rush-hour trafic. University officials believe that the high winds, combinded with the ortting interior of the tree, caused most of the damage.

The tree is believe by university botonists to be in the range of 150 years old.

The tree was partially destroyed. The damage to the tree went unnoticed until this morning when two of the major branches of the tree fell.

The tree is located between the sociology and education buildings on campus. There are many legends surrounding the tree, including one that captured pirates during the Civil War were hung from the tree.

"I don't know if we'll be able to save it or not," Charles Fancher, associate professor of biology said. "Trees like that are usually not in good shape, and we may have to just cut it down and start growing another one."

Power was quickly restored to most areas of the city last night.

REPETITION AND REDUNDANCY

The story below needs to be edited, with particular attention paid to repetitions and redundancies. There may be other errors in the story, too. Make sure the story conforms to AP style.

The state supreme court has order a local business to cease and desist selling drug related items and paraphenalia.

The court ordered the Mau-Mau Shop, located at 213 Broad Street, on the corner of Broad and Main Streets, not to sell certain itmes which have been outlawed by a recent state law while the constitutionality of that law is being tested in the courts.

The court ordered the proprietors and owners of the shop to remove various "roach clips," water-pipes, siringes and miniature little spoons from the shelves and premises of the shop.

The Mau-Mau Shop owners, Heavy Heat and Bob Beatle, have sued the state and taken it to court, saying the state law which the state legislature passed last session unduly restricts and limits their rights as businessmen.

In the initial court battle which was initiated four months ago, state attorneys argued that the shop and all others like it in the state should have to abide by the law until the court had ruled on the law. Today the state supreme court agreed.

"This is not at all what we wanted to happen," said Bob Beatle, one of the shop's co-owners. Beatle added that he thought the ruling was a distortion of the legal and judicial system.

Bart added that it was apathetic people who don't care about the constitutional rightsof others who allowed laws such as this one to pass.

OBJECTIVITY

The following story contains several examples of bias in the form of unattributed allegations, undocumented statements of fact, and word usage indicative of the reporter's feelings about the topic. Reduce the biased tone of the story by eliminating or rephrasing the offending phrases, sentences, and paragraphs. Make sure the story conforms to AP style.

BOSTON — Several top executives of the Massachusetes Transit Authority are looking for new jobs because of what they call the arogance of the new MTA chairman, Donovan Hughes.

According to sources from within MTA, Hughes's "arrogance and inacessibility" have increasingly become points of contention among top MTA executives who have been wih he Authority for most of their careers. Hughes was named MTA chair only four months ago.

"Alot of us try to see him on a regular basis and can't," one source said. "He just doesn't seem to have the time for us."

Hughes spends alot of time outside of Boston, traveling to Washington, D.C. and other places. Local newsmen have also complained of Hughes's inacessibility. They say that he has no time for them, although he has given interviews to newsmen from Washington and New York.

For instance, Hughes has been out of town every day this week. Reportedly, he was in Nashville, Tennessee, giving a speech.

Another complaint about Hughes from the inside of MTA is the way in which he conducts meetings. Sources said he often humilliates members of the staff in front of their colleges, asking them questions he knows they can not answer and then berating them for their lack of knowlege.

"Moral is getting to be very low around here," said one source.

Hughes has also ordered personnel cuts, and many executives say that they are unable to do their work properly because they simply dont have enough staff. At the same time, Hughes is reported to have increased his own staff, especially those working in the PR department.

When Hughes became chairman last spring, he conceeded that his first months on the job would be spent "learning the ropes."

"I don't know everything that I should he admitted. But he said that he was going to try to learn what he needed to know and warned that "changes would be made" in MTA's operations.

Hughes was unavailable for comment yesterday.

3

ELECTRONIC EDITING

The 1970s ushered in the use of electronic editing for newspapers. Suddenly, editors whose mechanical abilities extended no further than changing a typewriter ribbon were faced with spending tens of thousands of dollars on electronic editing systems and training staffs in a whole new method of production.

These new systems offered editors and reporters a speed and flexibilty they could never approach with hard copy editing. Without leaving their desks, editors could check on what stories had been written by which reporters, which stories had been edited by which copy editors, what stories had been sent by the wire services, and which ones had been sent to the typesetter. Copy editors could make corrections without using editing marks, they could switch paragraphs around without a pair of scissors and a pastepot, and they could update a breaking wire story — all by pressing a few buttons. They could then send the story to an automatic typesetter, assured that the changes and corrections they had made would not be subject to human error. An editor, or anyone with access to the system, could check on the progress of the story, send messages to the copy editor or reporter, or even ask for a hard copy of the story. The editor could introduce new material right up to typesetting time without retyping or inserting it manually.

Electronic editing has done more than just give the editor more control over the copy flow. The makeup editor has been given greater flexibility, too. A system enables an editor to determine exactly how long a story is; it allows cutting of the story to fit a certain space; it can set the copy using a variety of type faces and sizes. The makeup editor thus has a wide range of choices in designing the page, all as close as the keyboard.

Electronic editing systems are still evolving. Recently, systems have been introduced that enable a makeup editor to lay out a page on a VDT screen — allowing speed and flexibility unattainable previously. Some companies are even working on a system that would bypass all of the functions of the backshop — typesetting, paste-up corrections, etc. — and instead would provide a direct link between the newsroom and the press. In a related area, a teletext system that transmits parts of a newspaper directly to a home television screen is being installed in parts of this country and is already widely available in Great Britain. There are, in fact, many possibilities for the transfer of information by electronic means.

The development of electronic editing has not been without its problems, however. Editors have sometimes found their systems difficult to manage; too many people have access to the system so that the control that the editors had with hard copy editing is gone. Editors who have installed electronic editing systems have encountered numerous personnel problems, from the resistance of those reluctant to change to trouble with unions faced with the loss of jobs. Still other editors have found that the editing process has been slowed, at least initially, offsetting the gains in speed made during the typesetting process.

One of the major problems with practically all systems is what we might call the "down syndrome." When major problems occur within an editing system, the whole system must sometimes be shut off; when this happens, of course, no one in the newsroom — especially on the copy desk — can do very much work. Newsroom personnel often find themselves so wedded to their machines that when the machines break down, they are unable to do any editing.

Copy editors have experienced their own problems with VDT systems. While working at the screen, an editor must remain in a set position and does not have the flexibility to move around much. The editor may find that this work causes more eyestrain, backache, and even tension than the old method of hard copy editing. Generally, the editor may find that the work cannot be sustained for as long a period of time as with hard copy editing.

Finally, editors have found that sometimes the blessing of flexibility may also be a curse. Copy and makeup editors may find that they can do so much that they are tempted to do too much. Consequently, a good story may be over-edited because it is easier for the editor to change words and move paragraphs. Systems that make it easy for editors to set copy in a variety of widths may tempt the editors to overuse this function. A lot of different copy widths may give a page a ragged and erratic look. In these instances, the electronic editing process has hurt rather than helped the final product.

Editors should remember, then, that an electronic editing system is an extremely useful tool, but that's all it is — a tool. Neither it nor any other machine can replace the most basic of all editing tools, the brain. Good publications are produced not because of the physical tools of the editor but because of the editor's mental tools. Without an extremely inquisitive mind, a basic knowledge of a wide range of subjects and an absolute command of the English language, an editor will be unable to bring out a suitable publication, no matter what tool is used for editing.

PURPOSES OF ELECTRONIC EDITING SYSTEMS

As we have already mentioned, electronic editing systems offer some tangible advantages to the editing process. To understand these advantages, we need to take a look at some of the basic purposes of all electronic editing systems.

Capturing the original keystroke. An underlying premise of electronic editing is that when a reporter types a story, that should be the first and last time it is typed. In processing hard copy, this premise is not operable. A reporter types a story; it is then edited by an editor and sent to a typesetter, who retypes the story. Electronic editing makes this last step obsolete. A reporter types the story and enters it into the editing system; an editor then takes the story, makes what changes are necessary, and sends the story to an automatic typesetter, which does not require retyping of the story.

Greater flexibility in editing. Editors can do more to a story in a shorter period of time with an electronic editing system. They can move whole sentences or paragraphs around, insert blocks of copy where needed and delete words, phrases, sentences, or paragraphs with a simple command. An editor also has greater flexibility in choosing column widths, type sizes, leading, and fonts; again, many of these operations may be done much more quickly than in the hard copy editing process.

Greater storage capacity and filing capability. One of the real advantages of microelectronics in general is their ability to reduce the storage space required for material. By converting letters and other symbols to electronic signals, electronic editing systems allow editors to store many times more copy and other materials than could be previously. At some newspapers, editors and reporters have used this advantage to store not only stories but notes and other material used in the news gathering process. Reference material and other material used in the day-to-day operation of the paper (such as indexes, standing heads, and editors' notes) may also be kept readily available this way.

Easier access to stories and other materials for more people. With hard copy editing, there may only be one and probably will not be more than two copies of a story in existence. If an editor-in-chief or managing editor wants to see a copy of a story, he or she might have to walk over to a copy editor's desk and ask for it. If there is only one copy, no one else will be able to look at it while it is being read. An electronic editing system makes access to material somewhat easier. Anyone who has access to a terminal is able to read any story that is in an unrestricted file. Some systems allow only one terminal at a time to have a particular story, but others allow the same story to be read on several terminals at one time. In any event, paper copies of stories no longer have to be carried around for different people to see.

Increased speed and accuracy in typesetting. One of the major advantages of electronic editing systems is the speed at which copy may be set in type. Large blocks of copy which might have taken the fastest of typesetters several hours to complete may now be typeset in a matter of minutes.

DO NOT TYPE BELOW THIS LINE

```
(s-501.2

Brookwood reception/1                        SCANNED

/c{By GINA SA¤TAPPAS}/c

/c}n¤¤/c{News Staff Writer}/c

     Very rarely do you walk¤¤¤Very rarely does one walk into a high
c¤school ~~cafeteria~~ where over 300 former students are being honored
        △ cafeteria △
by their former teachers.  It happened at Brookwood High School Sun{
day, however.
     Mr. and Mrs. Paul W. Jones, now of Birminh¤gham, gave ar¤ rece{
ption at the school's cafeteria honoring any student who attended the
school between the ya¤ears of 1931 and 1951.  The Joneses taught at
Brookwood for 20 years before being transferred¤ to Birmingham.
     Mrs. Jones, then Charlotte Hereford, came to Brookwood High in
1931.  Mr. Jones came to¤¤two years later and they later married and
had one duaghe¤¤daughter, Nancy JOnes,¤¤Jones ➞ Tallahassee, Fla.
          △ now of △
     ''My parents came here during the depression -- this was a dep{
rived area.  They loved the kids l¤so much that they wanted to do
something special for them,'' Miss Jones said.
     Approximately 350 people attended the reception Sunday, and some
came from all over the state, while others came from Texas, Georgia
and Florida¤y.
     The Joneses switched the principalship of the highschool five
times while they were there..¤  Mr. Jones came as the first high sc{
hool football coach, but later became principal, while Mrs. Jones la{
ter became Tuscaloosa County School System Supervisor.
     ''We're happy with the turnout today,'' Mrs. Jones said,.  ''But
```

DO NOT TYPE BELOW THIS LINE

ALIGN FIRST CHARACTER UNDER THIS ARROW

Figure 3-1   SCANNER COPY

Scanner copy is typed by a reporter or editor using a special ball on an IBM Selectric typewriter.
This copy requires reporters and editors to learn special codes which are read by an OCR machine.

Another advantage is an increase in the accuracy of the typesetting process, in the sense that, if the system is working properly, it will do exactly what the editor tells it to do. That is not to say that the copy itself will be more accurate or less error-free. It still takes an editor to correct misspellings, mistakes in grammar, and errors in facts. The system will respond more accurately than a human typesetter will to the commands of the editor, however.

FUNCTIONS OF ELECTRONIC EDITING SYSTEMS

Despite all of the previous discussion about electronic editing systems, those unfamiliar with such systems may still be asking themselves, "Just what do electronic editing systems do?" or "What do they look like?" or "How do they work?" These are legitimate questions. All of us are familiar with a typewriter, paper, and pencil — the basic tools of hard copy editing — but not everyone has seen an electronic editing system in operation.

There are two basic kinds of electronic editing systems: off-line systems and on-line systems. They both perform the same functions although they go about doing it in somewhat different ways.

Off-line systems use an Optical Character Reader, or OCR, to get copy into the system. The copy, when it is written by reporters, must be typed on special paper with an IBM typewriter so that it can be fed into an OCR machine or "scanner," as it is often called. The scanner's "eye" electronically records the characters from the sheet and enters them onto a tape or computer disk. An example of scanner copy can be seen in Figure 3-1.

The tapes or computer disks are located in a central computer, and any story so stored may be called up and displayed on a video display terminal, or VDT. A VDT unit contains a television-like screen and a keyboard with all the letters of a typewriter and other keys for giving commands to the system. In an off-line system, editors and copy editors are likely to have VDTs that they can use for editing copy and sending it to the typesetter. Figure 3-2 will give you some idea of how this system is set up.

With on-line systems, reporters as well as editors have VDTs which they can use for "direct inputting" of copy. Instead of using a typewriter, the reporter types a story, and as it is being typed the story is displayed on the VDT screen. When the story is finished, the reporter can give the VDT a command that will place the story directly in the system's computer. The story can then be called up and edited by copy editors and then sent to the typesetter. The configuration for an on-line system is shown in Figure 3-3.

In some cases there may be no direct links between the computer and the typesetter. In these cases, the OCR scanner or the central computer produces a paper tape with lots of holes punched in it.

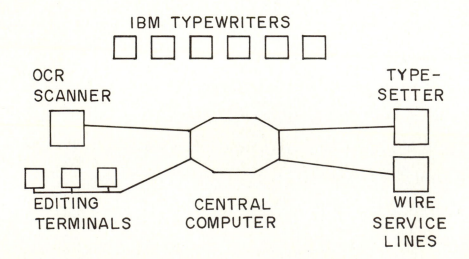

Figure 3-2   OFF-LINE EDITING SYSTEMS

An off-line editing system uses an OCR scanner to get reporters' stories into the system. The copy may then be called up on an editor's terminal for editing and typesetting.

Figure 3-3   ON-LINE EDITING SYSTEMS

An on-line editing system provides a terminal for reporter and editor. Anyone with access to a terminal may input stories as well as edit them.

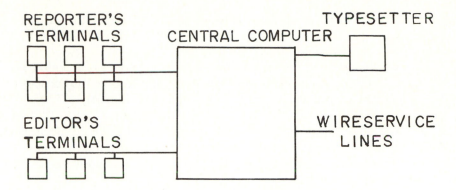

These sets of holes designate the different letters of a story. The tape must be hand-carried to the typesetter and fed through a tape reader attached to the typesetter in order for the justified copy to be produced.

In both of these systems, as can be seen in Figures 3-2 and 3-3, wire service copy can be captured directly by the system's central computer. Consequently, the clacking of the hard copy wire machine — once a staple sound for many newsrooms — has fallen silent.

Another piece of machinery which may be attached to an electronic editing system is a line printer or hard copy printer. Attached to the central computer, the line printer can produce a hard copy of a story for an editor or reporter.

The answer to "What does an electronic editing system do?" is not a simple one. The answer depends on the capacity, comprehensiveness, and flexibility of the system. Electronic editing systems can, in general, do many things; particular systems may be more limited. The following is a list of functions performed by electronic systems.

Act as a typewriter for a reporter. Stories and other copy which is locally produced may be entered into an electronic editing system in two ways, depending on whether the system is off-line or on-line. As we explained earlier, reporters may use an IBM typewriter and OCR scanner or a VDT terminal to enter copy into a system.

One variation on these methods of getting copy into a system is the set-up many newspapers have for receiving wire service copy. A direct telephone line is established from the wire service office to the paper's computer system, and the wire service copy is transmitted in the form of electronic signals which are received directly by the system. No typing or retyping of wire copy takes place in the newspaper office.

Edit copy. Most systems can do any of the things an editor of hard copy needs to have done. For instance, using the system, an editor can insert, move or delete letters, words, paragraphs, or other blocks of copy; capitalize or lower-case letters; and perform searches through copy to look for particular words or numbers and automatically make changes.

While most systems perform the same basic editing functions, different systems require different sets of commands. There is no standard electronic editing system or set of commands. If you learn how to operate one system, you will still have to learn other commands for other systems. However, learning one system is helpful because you can get an idea of how the basic editing functions work.

What a particular electronic editing system can do depends on its flexibility and degree of sophistication. Some systems perform only the basic editing functions. Others may do many more things to help the editor in handling copy. For instance, some systems have a split-screen function which allows two stories to appear side-by-side on the screen. This function is particularly useful for compiling information from two stories. Some systems have search and replace functions which help editors search through copy for words, numbers, or phrases. Generally, the more sophisticated a system is, the more expensive it is.

Store copy and other materials. A system may store local copy as it is fed into the system, automatically "capture" wire copy, compile multiple takes of wire stories, search through lists or files of material for a particular item or set of items, keep reporter's notes on file, and store other material which a newspaper may use periodically.

Prepare copy for typesetting. Systems may be programmed to set column widths, measure copy length, set type sizes and leading, center copy or run copy with a ragged right or left edge, change column widths within a story, and so on.

The copyfit function of an electronic editing system automatically tells an editor how long a story will be when it is set in type. This function must be programmed to take into account column width and type size, but if programmed properly it can measure copy very precisely.

Make hard copies of stories. Many systems are connected to a hard copy printer which will type out any piece of copy in the system. Such machines are useful because sometimes an editor or reporter will want a copy of a story before it has been typeset. The quality of this copy varies from small, hard-to-read letters to typewriter-quality printing.

Write and measure headlines. The headfit function of an electronic editing system is a very important one. This function allows editors to write headlines on a terminal and then have the system measure those headlines to see if they are too long or short. The headfit function can save the editor much time and effort in writing and counting headlines.

Help with advertisement and page layout. A system may measure and cut stories or produce a picture on the VDT screen of how a layout which an editor has drawn will look.

The term used for laying out pages with an electronic editing system is "pagination." With pagination systems, editors may "draw" their page layouts on a VDT screen rather than on a piece of paper. The system will measure stories to see if they will fit into designated parts of the page. It will also tell the editors if headlines will fit into the space allowed, and it will allow editors to fit pictures onto a page. Not many newspapers have pagination systems yet, but it is only a matter of time before they will be widely adopted.

The above material is designed to give the student a basic and general knowledge of the functions and uses of electronic editing systems. As we have said before, every system differs in its ability to perform certain functions, and editors should know thoroughly the systems with which they have to work. They should make it a point to know a system's limitations and possibilities so that the system can be used to the fullest extent.

EXERCISES

ENTERING A STORY

1. Type the following story on the VDT. There are a few spelling, punctuation, and grammar errors in the story, and you should correct them as you type. However, the point of this exercise is to get used to using the VDT keyboard, so don't be overly concerned with editing the story.

2. Enter the story onto your disk when you have finished typing.

Three classes of second-graders at Woodvale Elementary School have made use of 40 pounds of things most people would rather throw away: toilet paper cylinders, egg cartons and empty spools, and the products of the students's efforts are on display in the school's art gallery.

Caterpillars, bunnies, Easter baskets, and puppets are included in the display along with more ambitious efforts such as Jo Anna Moore's model of a steamship made entirely of styrofoam.

The art project was one component of an enviromental awareness program formulated by the state Enviromental Association in a booklet called "Recycling: Using the Unusable."

The entire Woodvale school system has adopted the program, whih includes collection of aluminum, showing film strips, and a campus clean-up day.

"The purpose is to make children more aware of the potentail value of things we normally throw away, Woodvale Principal Donna Estill said.

ENTERING A STORY

1. Type the following story on the VDT, making any necessary changes.
2. Enter the story onto your disk.
3. Make a hard copy of the story.
4. Read through the story and make sure that everything is correct and edited properly and according to AP style.

Two temperature records, one of them 78 years old, were broken in less than six and one-half hours after a frigid blast of Canadian air chilled Taylor County late Tuesday and early today.

The mercury dipped to 26 degrees shortly before midnight Tuesday at the Weather Bureau station at Municipal Airport.

The reading broke the old record of 29 degrees, set eight years ago.

Continuing its fall, the temperature hit 20 degrees at 6:25 a.m today. The mark bested the 78 year-old Nov.7 record low of 28.

The 20 degree reading was thelowest of the season and the lowest since March 5 when the mercury also hit 20.

DELETIONS

1. Type the following story on the VDT, without making any changes.

The governing board of the Student Union will induct three new members tonight at its first fall meeting.

Senior James Martin, of Route 5, Henderson; junior Bill Best, of 223 Willet Lane, Rutland; and sophomore Ellis Johnson, of 667 Oxtail St., Bainbridge have been named to the powerful Governing Board.

They will take their seats on the Board despite protests from some students stemming from the fact that no female woman student has ever been named as a Board member on the Board.

Board Adviser Pierce Daniels said no qualified woman had applied for a positon.

"We have been trying to seat a woman, but it seems that noone of the qualified ones will apply," he said.

The Board is in charge of disbursing funds for all entertainment-related activities held by the Student Union. The annual Union budget exceeds $200,000.00.

The agenda for the fall meeting includes discussion of the annual welcome-back dance and final planning for a freshman banquet.

2. In the second paragraph, delete the word "powerful" before "Governing Board."

3. In the third paragraph, delete the word "woman" before "student" and delete the concluding phrase "on the Board."

4. In the fifth paragraph, "noone" should be "none."

5. Correct the style error in the sixth paragraph.

6. Read through the story and make sure that everything is correct and edited properly and according to AP style.

7. Enter the story onto the disk under a new slug and make a hard copy of it.

INSERTIONS

1. Type the following story on the VDT.

Suzie Headacher, who taught inner-city children from a housing project about caring for small animals in limited space, today was named one of six national winners in the 4-H agriculture education program.

Headacher, 18, received a scholarship during the 60th National 4-H Congress in Chicago. The Congress opened Sunday and continues through Thursday.

Selected by the Cooperative Extension Service, Headacher and the other five winners were presented their awards by Johnson Fertilizer Company, sponsor of the 4-H agriculture education program. Awards were arranged by National 4-H Council.

"Miss Headachers' unique project illustrates to all of us the value of thinking beyond our limitations. She had the courage to conceive of a New York City where kids can see animals somewhere besides zoos, and she did something toward fulfilling that vision," the National 4-H Council President said.

Headacher was one of four state 4-H'ers who won national honors and scholarships.

2. Insert the following facts: a. Suzie Headacher's address is Route 2, Midville; b. The amount of her scholarship is $1000; c. The National 4-H Council President's name is Howie Evers.

3. Correct the style error in the fourth paragraph.

4. Read through the story and make sure that everything is correct and edited properly and according to AP style.

5. Enter the story onto the disk under a new slug.

6. Make a hard copy of the story.

INSERTIONS, DELETIONS

1. Type the following story on the VDT without making any changes.

WILSONVILLE — City fathers have gone to court to fight state officials in a zoning battle involving convicts.

Defendants in the suit are the Department of Corrections; John Willet, Carol Largess, Bob Mathews, and Clarence Copper.

The city filed suit in Weston County Circuit Court seeking an order requiring the state Department of Corrections to remove several temporary facilities for housing inmates in south Wilsonville. The suit said the tent-like units located near the National Guard Armory on U.S. Highway 322 violated city zoning ordinances.

The land is owned by the Corrections Department and is zoned for industry.The suit alleges the three units, which house some 20 female work-release inmates, were placed on the south Wilsonville property without the consent or authorization from the city council or Wilsonville Planning Commission.

Among other things, city zoning ordinances specify that no temporary structure in any district shall be used in a manner that is dangerous or otherwise objectionable to the surrounding areas.

Residents in the area complained about the "huts,", and the city council last week warned the prison system that they should be moved immediately or legal action would be taken. The warning was the second since April.

Prison officials say they were in the right because, they say, a previous court case exempted state operations from local zoning ordinances.

The city's suit says the state's structures are on lots which aren't big enough to meet minimum standards outlined in the zoning ordinances.

The suit also contends the defendants "illegally connected" the housing facilities to water and sewer lines at an existing building without the required permit from city utilities.

A hearing date has not been set.

2. Move the third paragraph so that it is the second paragraph.

3. Insert the following identifications for the defendants: State Prison Commissioner (Willet); Wetumpka Work-Release Center director (Largess); head of the state work-release program (Mathews); a department official (Copper).

4. Delete the last three paragraphs.

5. Read through the story and make sure that everything is correct and edited properly and according to AP style.

6. Enter the story under your name and a different slug on your disk.

INSERTIONS, MOVING COPY

1. Type the following story on the VDT.

A local elementary school teacher has apologized for calling a fellow instructor a "Klansman" and has agreed to pay about $2000 in court costs.

The letter of apology Tuesday from Lacey McGruder to Charles Peace avoided a Circuit Court trial of the $150,000 defamation of character suit Peace had filed.

The suit said McGruder had labeled Peace a "Klansman" and had told people he marched with the Ku Klux Klan during a demonstration in Centerville on September 8, 1979.

In addition to writing the apology, McGruder agreed to pay court costs and other expenses incurred by Peace in filing the suit against her.

in the letter of apology McGruder said she did not see Peace in the Klan march and "my statements were based on rumors that were circulating at the time and upon statements that were made by others to me. I apologize to you for those statements made by me.

"I now realize that repeating these unfounded statements and rumors hurt you personally and I deeply regret this."

2. Put an attribution in the last paragraph.

3. Insert "third grade teacher" between "from" and "Lacey" in the second paragraph. In that same paragraph, insert "a physical education teacher," with appropriate commas, between "Peace" and "avoided."

4. The correct date of the demonstration in question is November 15, 1980.

5. Move the fourth paragraph to the end of the story.

6. Read through the story and make sure that everything is correct and is edited properly and according to AP style.

7. Enter the story onto the disk under a new slug and make a hard copy of it.

GENERAL EDITING

The following story contains numerous errors in style, spelling, and grammar. Working on the VDT, correct those errors and rewrite any parts of the story which you think could be improved.

When the city coucil met Monday night in the city hall council room, several councilment reacted violently to Mayor Johnson Greene's proposed $26,000 increase in city spending appropriations for next year.

"There ain't know way we can handle that kind of spending without raising taxes," Council Member Fred Watson said.

Watson and others say they cant see why the mayor failed to suggest an increase without coming up with any additional income for the ciey.

The higher bdget results from increases in appropriations in the protection o persons and property category and in pollution contrl.

The budget includes $121,000 for protection of persons and property, $16,000 over last years budget.

This incerase was because of the installation of traffic signals at main Street and Florida ave and Main STReet and Wilson Boulevard, and the adding of personnel in the Police Department

Budgeted for the pollution inspector's office was $105,000, an increase of $8725 ovet last year.

The council also acted Monday to stop issuance of solicitation permits until it ca review and possible revise the existing ordnance.

The action stemned from an incident last week when tw cometpitive groups of magazine soliciters stated fighting in th street and were ordered to leave the city.

The council said residents have complained about "high pressure salesmen being allowed in the city.

In other business, te cuncil awarded a contract for a new police car to ogden Auto Sales Co. for $1,969 with a tradein of a present police car.

GENERAL EDITING

The following story contains a number of errors in style and logic. Working on the VDT, correct the errors and improve the logic by restructuring the story. Watch for internal agreement of facts and transition between major ideas. Also be sure to supply such missing information as the name of the state's largest newspaper.

A majority of people in the state favor the raising of Federal taxes on cigaretes and alcoholic beverages, according to the poll conducted by the state's largest newspaper.

The proposed "sin taxes" were endorsed as a means of raisng tax revenues and to discourage smoking and drinking, according to the Oct. 25-26 telephone poll of 1,598 adults in a scientific random sample.

Fifty-two per cent said they think state taxes on cigarettes should be raised, while 41% said they should not.

The 52 per cent who said cigarettes taxes should be raised broke down this way: 5 percent said taxes should be reasied to increase revenues, 10 percent to discourage smoking and 33 percent both.

Fifty-five per cent said Federal taxes on alcoholic beverages should be raised broke down this way: 11 percent said taxes should be raised to increase revenues, 9 percent to discourage drinking and 35 percent both.

The State Senate Budget Committee recently drew up a number of proposals to raise taxes next year, including one which would double the excise taxes on cigarettes, liquor, wine and beer.

The proposed increases, which Senate leaders say will be considered next year, would raise the price of a pack of cigarettes by 8 cents, the price of a gallon of liquor by $10.50, a barrel of beer by $9 and a gallon of wine by 34 cents. These increases will riase the prices of cigaretts and alcohol significatly over the prices in neighboring states.

Sixty-two percent of the poll respondents said they drink alcoholic beverages, while 32 percent said they smoke cigarettes.

People who said they smoke and those who said they drink were less likely than non-smokers and non-drinkers to say either cigarette or alcoholic beverage taxes should be raised.

The poll said single and divorced people were more likely than married people to say they smoke and drink.

Protestants were more likely than either Catholic or Jweish respondents to say they are teetotalers; and people with more education and higher incomes were more likely to say they drink.

And while people with children 17 or younger were less likely than other respondents to say they smoke, they were more likely to say they drink.

the results of the polls can vary from the opinions of all Americans because of chance variations in the sample.

For a poll based on about 1,600 interviews, the results are subject to an error margin of 3 percentage points either way because of chance variations.

GENERAL EDITING

Edit the following story.

A total of 3 men were arested on Chicagos south side yesterday at around 2:30. The charges were: posession and intent to distribute 30,000 Qualude tablets. The drugs worth is estimated at $150 thousand dollars.

Toby Willetson, a special ageant with the Federal Bureau of Investigation, said the arests were the final result of a 3-month undercover investigation by his agency and other law inforcement personnel.

Willetson identified the two as Clem Forrest, 49, of Detroit, and Newt Felton, 34, of Kalamazoo, Mich.

Forrest was arested near 6th Ave South and 23rd St. and Felton was apprehended a few blocks away.

Willetson said the mood-altering drugs were aparently brout to Chicago from Florida for sale.

In addition to the Quaaludes, two cars and two riffles were confiskated.

Felton is on federal parole in another drug case. If convicted, he could receive the maximun sentence of 40 and a fine of $240 thousand.

Forrest may be subject to a five-year sentence and a $5000 fine.

4

GRAMMAR, PUNCTUATION, AND SPELLING

English is a basic tool of the editor. Like any other worker, the editor must know the tools of the trade thoroughly — what they can do as well as their limitations. Knowing when and under what circumstances they can be properly used is vital. Above all, a worker must know how to use the tools to get the job done. The editor needs to think of language as a tool, as a means of getting a job done. The editor who cannot coherently use the English language is like a carpenter who cannot saw a straight line. The products of such an editor or carpenter will not inspire confidence; nor will they be items people want to purchase.

Unlike the carpenter's hammer or saw, however, the English language is an extremely complex tool. It has many nuances and subtleties. People spend years mastering English. There are many rules for its usage and many arguments over the propriety of some of these rules.

One thing making English so complex is its dynamic nature. English is the closest thing the world has to an international language. It is spoken and understood in nearly every part of the globe. But no central control or authority governs its use. Consequently, the language is always changing. New words and expressions come into use as others fade. Old words take on new meanings. English is mixed with other languages. Spelling rules shift with differing usage. Mankind is discovering new phenomena needing description in the language. All this makes English a difficult but exciting tool.

Editors should not be in the vanguard of efforts to change the language. In fact, an editor's position in this regard should be a very conservative one, slow to accept change and accepting it only when it improves the language and helps people communicate. Several years ago a number of editors ran into some trouble on this very point. Thinking that the spelling of a number of words was clumsy and confusing (which it is), these editors arbitrarily changed the way these words were spelled in their newspapers. "Through" became "thru," "thorough" became "thoro," and "employee" turned into "employe." Reader acceptance of these changes was less than complete, and many editors had to beat a hasty retreat.

The editor should be the overseer of the language, working to prevent changes that would degrade the language and its users and promoting its thoughtful and creative evolution.

The job of the editor, however, is not to change language but to use it. To do so effectively requires knowing the basic rules and conventions. Editors should know thoroughly the eight basic parts of speech (nouns, verbs, adjectives, adverbs, pronouns, conjunctions, interjections and prepositions), and the basic unit of the English usage (the sentence) and its two parts (subject and predicate). Not only should they have an eye for the language, they should also have an ear for it. Editors should know when things that are technically correct sound wrong. Beyond that, they should be able to recognize — and hear — the confusing phrase, the unclear sentence, and the absence of transition. They must be able to spot the confusion and illogic that are the harbingers of misinformation, inaccuracy, and a failure to communicate. Like the carpenter, the editor should use the language to saw a straight line to the reader.

That straight line to the reader is the goal of the editor. Because having people read and believe a publication is vital to the publication's life, inspiring and holding the confidence of readers is the job of the editor. The editor who does not use English correctly will annoy the reader and call the publication's credibility into question. A misspelled word will not destroy a publication, and an agreement error will not inspire calls for a repeal of the First Amendment, but too many such mistakes will convince the reader that a publication is not worth his or her time and money.

GRAMMAR

The following is not intended to be a complete grammar manual. There are many of these manuals on the market, and the student having serious problems in any of the following areas should consult one of them regularly. In this section we will examine some of the more common mistakes in grammar made by college students. These are the problems that are most likely to crop up in the writing you will be working with as an editor.

Subject-verb agreement. Singular subjects take singular verbs; plural subjects take plural verbs. A mistake of this kind most often occurs when the subject is separated from the verb by a long phrase containing a noun of a number different from that of the subject — for example, "The members of the team, which lost the last game of the tournament to its arch-rival by one point, was honored by the school." This mistake is an easy one to make and is sometimes hard to catch.

Another type of subject-verb disagreement occurs when there is a compound subject. "The man and his wife is standing on the street." Even though the subjects of this sentence are separately singular, together they are plural and should take a plural verb.

Confusion often occurs when nouns of different number are separated by linking verbs. "Disagreements of this kind is one of the army's major problems." The verb should agree with the subject, so in the above sentence, the verb should be changed to "are," since the subject, "disagreements," is plural.

Pronoun-antecedent agreement. Disagreement between pronouns and their antecedents is one of the most common mistakes made by people who write. One of the reasons for this is that such disagreements are generally accepted in spoken English. They are not acceptable in written English, however. Singular antecedents must have singular pronouns. It is incorrect to write, "The Supreme Court issued their decision today." "Supreme Court" is a singular noun even though the court is made up of nine different justices. Consequently, it would be correct to write, "The Supreme Court issued its decision today" or "The members of the Supreme Court issued their decision today." Any group of people or things referred to with a singular noun must be referred to with a singular pronoun.

By the same token, plural antecedents must have plural pronouns. "The Atlanta team and the St. Louis team had their game rained out." The "their" in this sentence refers to both teams and is correct.

Dangling participles. A participial phrase at the beginning of a sentence should modify the sentence's subject and should be separated from it by a comma. One would not write, "After driving from Georgia to Texas, Tom's car finally gave out." The car didn't drive to Texas; it was driven. We must assume from this sentence that it was Tom who did the driving.

PUNCTUATION

The apostrophe. The proper use of the apostrophe probably gives more users of English more problems than any other form of punctuation. The apostrophe can be used in a number of ways. First, we use apostrophes to form possessives, as in " Mary's hat" and "Tom's book." If a word ends in "s" or the plural of the noun is formed by adding "s," the apostrophe generally goes after the final "s," and no other letter is needed. For example, the possessive of a word such as hostess" is "hostess'." The plural possessive of the word "team" is "teams'." The plural possessive of "child" is "children's."

Even many professionals have problems when the word "it" and an apostrophe come together. Is it " its," " it's" or " its' "? Here are some rules worth memorizing. "Its" (without the apostrophe) is the possessive of the pronoun "it," as in "its final score." "It's" (with the apostrophe) is a contraction meaning "it is," as in "it's hard to tell." "Its' " makes no sense because "it" has no plural form.

Appositive phrases and commas. Appositive phrases basically follow a noun and rename it. Such phrases are surrounded by commas in almost all cases. For example, in the sentence "Billy Braun,

Tech's newest football star, was admitted to a local hospital yesterday," the phrase "Tech's newest football star" is the appositive to "Billy Braun." It is important to remember to put a second comma at the end of the appositive; this is easy to overlook if the appositive is extremely long. For example, the sentence "Job Thompson, the newly named Will Marcum State Junior College president who succeeded Byron Wilson has accepted the presidency of the Association of Junior College Administrators," needs a comma after "Wilson."

Comma splices and compound sentences. When two independent clauses are connected, they must be connected by two things: a comma and a conjunction. When two clauses are connected only by a comma, that is called a comma splice or a run-on sentence. For example, "The team won its final game, now they are the champs" is a comma splice or run-on sentence. The reader needs a conjunction to help separate the two sentences. Just as incorrect is the compound sentence with no comma before the conjunction: "The team won its final game and now they are the champs."

Commas between subject and verbs. Commas should be used to separate phrases and other elements in a sentence, but they should not be used solely to separate a subject from its verb. Obviously, you wouldn't write, "The boy, sat on the bench," but neither would you write,"The moment the train comes in, is when we will see her" or "Having no money, is a difficult thing."

Colons and semicolons. Colons should be used when the phrase or sentence before the colon anticipates the material that comes after it. For example, "There are four elements involved: gold, calcium, hydrogen, and oxygen." The semicolon should be used to separate a series of long phrases where a comma is inadequate, as in a series of names and titles such as "John Jones, Secretary of State; Jane Smith, Secretary of the Treasury; Ray Johnson, Secretary of Defense." A semicolon may also be used to separate the parts of a compound sentence when the writer does not want to insert a conjunction. "A terrible storm hit; many were killed."

SPELLING

Spelling correctly involves three thought processes: applying phonics, memorizing some words, and knowing the rules that usually apply to most words. Editors should know how to do all three. Phonics can be learned, either in early years or later. One must memorize those words that are not spelled phonetically or do not follow spelling rules. However, most words can be spelled correctly without memorization because either rules or phonetics apply to the majority of English words. Some of the rules, with known exceptions, are explained in the following paragraphs.

1. With words of one syllable or words accented on the last syllable that end in a single consonant preceded by a single vowel, the final consonant is doubled before adding "ed" or a syllable beginning with a vowel — for example, plan, planned; prefer, preferred; wit, witty; hot, hottest; swim, swimming; stop, stopped; bag, baggage; beg, beggar.

There are a few exceptions. One illustrates the impact of accent. Refer becomes reference, without doubling the R, but the accent also changes away from the final syllable when the suffix is added.

There are other exceptions: words ending in K, V, W, X and Y; also benefit, benefited; chagrin, chagrined (even though stress stays on the final syllable of the new word).

2. A final E is usually dropped on addition of a syllable beginning with a vowel: come, coming; guide, guidance; cure, curable; judge, judging; plume, plumage; force, forcible; use, usage. There are exceptions: sale, saleable; mile, mileage; peace, peaceable; dye, dyeing.

3. A final E is usually retained on addition of a syllable beginning with a consonant: use, useless; late, lately; hate, hateful; move, movement; safe, safety; white, whiteness; pale, paleness; shame, shameful. The case of nine, ninety, nineteen, but ninth is an exception. Other exceptions are judge, judgment and argue, argument.

4. Words ending in a double E retain both E's before an added syllable: free, freely, see, seeing, agree, agreement, agreeable.

5. Words ending in a double consonant retain both consonants when one or more syllables are added: ebb, ebbing; enroll, enrollment; full, fullness; dull, dullness; skill, skillful; odd, oddly; will, willful; stiff, s tiffness.

6. Compounds of all, well, and full drop one L: always, almost; welfare, welcome; fulfill and skillful. (This is really a listing of exceptions to rule 5.) Exceptions include "fullness" and occasions when a word is hyphenated (as with full-fledged).

7. I before E, except after C, or when sounded like A, as in neighbor or weigh: receive, deceive; relieve, believe.

8. A final Y preceded by a consonant is usually changed to I with the addition of an ending not beginning with I: army, armies, spy, spies, and busy, business. Some exceptions are shy, shyness, pity, piteous (but not pitiful). The AY endings are usually exceptions for example—play, played.

9. This is really not a rule but just some information about a few tricky words, which must be described as exceedingly difficult. These must be memorized: exceed, proceed, and succeed all end with ceed, but supersede ends with sede. All others with this sound end in cede. These include precede, intercede, secede, concede, accede, and recede.

Rule 9 tells you how to become a very good speller. Memorize the tricky words and the spelling "demons," and if you know both your rules and phonics, you can spell most of the rest.

FIFTY COMMON WRITING ERRORS

The following is a list of fifty common errors in newspaper writing, as prepared by the Writing and Editing Committee of The Associated Press Managing Editors Association.

1. Affect, effect. Generally, affect is the verb; effect is the noun. "The letter did not affect the outcome." "The letter had a significant effect." But effect is also a verb meaning "to bring about": "It is almost impossible to effect change."

2. Afterward, afterwards. Use afterward. The dictionary allows use of afterwards only as a second form.

3. All right. That's the way to spell it. The dictionary may list alright as a legitimate word, but it is not acceptable in standard usage, says Random House.

4. Allude, elude. You allude to (or mention) a book. You elude (or escape) a pursuer.

5. Annual. Don't use first with it. If it's the first time, it's not annual yet.

6. Averse, adverse. If you don't like something, you are averse (or opposed) to it. Adverse is an adjective: adverse (bad) weather, adverse conditions.

7. Block, bloc. A bloc is a coalition of persons or a group with the same purpose or goal. Don't call it a block, which has some forty dictionary definitions.

8. Compose, comprise. You compose things by putting them together. Once the parts are together, the object comprises or is comprised of the parts.

9. Couple of. You need the of. It's never "a couple tomatoes."

10. Demolish, destroy. They mean "to do away with completely." You can't partially demolish or destroy something; nor is there any need to say "totally destroyed."

11. Different from. Things and people are different from each other. Don't write that they are different than each other.

12. Drown. Don't say someone was drowned unless an assailant held the victim's head under water. Just say the victim drowned.

13. Due to, owing to, because of. We prefer the last. Wrong: The game was canceled due to rain. Stilted: Owing to rain, the game was canceled. Right: The game was canceled because of rain.

14. Ecology, environment. They are not synonymous. Ecology is the study of the relationship between organisms and their environment. Right: The laboratory is studying the ecology of man and the desert. Right: There is much interest in animal ecology these days. Wrong: Even so simple an undertaking as maintaining a lawn affects ecology. Right: Even so simple an undertaking as maintaining a lawn affects our environment.

15. Either. It means one or the other, not both. Wrong: There were lions on either side of the door. Right: There were lions on each side of the door.

16. Fliers, flyers. Flier is the preferred term for an aviator or a handbill.

17. Flout, flaunt. They aren't the same word; they mean completely different things and they're very commonly confused. Flout means to mock, to scoff or to show disdain for. Flaunt means to display ostentatiously.

18. Funeral service. A redundant expression. A funeral is a service.

19. Head up. People don't head up committees. They head them.

20. Hopefully. One of the most commonly misused words, in spite of what the dictionary may say. Hopefully should be used to describe the way the subject feels— for instance, "Hopefully, I shall present the plan to the president." This means I will be hopeful when I do it, not that I hope I will do it. And it is something else again when you attribute hope to a nonperson. You may write, "Hopefully, the war will end soon." What you mean is that you hope the war will end soon, but this is not what you are writing. What you should write is, " I hope the war will end soon."

21. Imply and infer. The speaker implies. The hearer infers. You may also infer general principles from a sample.

22. In advance of, prior to. Use before; it sounds more natural.

23. It's, its. Its is the possessive, It's is the contraction of it is. Wrong: What is it's name? Right: What is its name? Its name is Fido. Right: It's the first time he's scored tonight. Right: It's my coat.

24. Lay, lie. Lay is the action word; lie is the state of being. Wrong: The body will lay in state until Wednesday. Right: The body will lie in state until Wednesday. Right: The prosecutor tried to lay the blame on him. However, the past tense of lie is lay. Right: The body lay in state from Tuesday until Wednesday. Wrong: The body laid in state from Tuesday until Wednesday. The past participle and the plain past tense of lay is laid. Right: He laid the pencil on the pad. Right: He had laid the pencil on the pad. Right: The hen laid an egg.

25. Leave, let. Leave alone means to depart from or cause to be in solitude. Let alone means to allow to be undisturbed. Wrong: The man had pulled a gun on her but Mr. Jones intervened and talked him into leaving her alone. Right: The man had pulled a gun on her but Mr. Jones intervened and talked him into letting her alone. Right: When I entered the room I saw that Jim and Mary were sleeping so I decided to leave them alone.

26. Less, fewer. If you can separate items in the quantities being compared, use fewer. If not, use less. Wrong: The Rams are inferior to the Vikings because they have less good linemen. Right: The Rams are inferior to the Vikings because they have fewer good linemen. Right: The Rams are inferior to the Vikings because they have less experience.

27. Like, as. Don't use like for as or as if. In general, use like to compare nouns and pronouns; use as when comparing phrases and clauses that contain a verb. Wrong: Jim blocks the linebacker like he should. Right: Jim blocks the linebacker as he should. Right: Jim blocks like a pro.

28. Marshall, marshal. Generally, the first form is correct only when the word is a proper noun: John Marshall. The second form is the verb form: Marilyn will marshal her forces. And the second form is the one to use for a title: fire marshal Stan Anderson, field marshal Erwin Rommel.

29. Mean, average, median. Use mean as synonymous with average. Both words refer to the sum of all components divided by the number of components. Median is the number that has as many components above it as below it.

30. Nouns. There's a growing trend toward using them as verbs. Resist it. Host, headquarters, and author, for instance, are nouns, even though the dictionary may acknowledge they can be used as verbs. If you do you'll come up with a monstrosity like: "Headquartered at his country home, John Doe hosted a party to celebrate the book he had authored."

31. Oral, verbal. Use oral when use of the mouth is central to the thought; the word emphasizes the idea of human utterance. Verbal may apply to spoken or written words; it connotes the process of reducing ideas to writing. Usually, one speaks of an oral contract, not a verbal one, if it's not in writing.

32. Over and more than. They aren't interchangeable. Over is best used for spatial relationships: The plane flew over the city. More than is used best with figures: In the crowd were more than a thousand fans.

33. Parallel construction. Thoughts in series in the same sentence require parallel construction. Wrong: The union delivered demands for an increase of 10 percent in wages and to cut the work week to thirty hours. Right: The union delivered demands for an increase of 10 percent in wages and for a reduction in the work week to thirty hours.

34. Peddle, pedal. When selling something, you peddle it. When riding a bicycle or similar means of locomotion, you pedal it.

35. Pretense, pretext. They're different, but it's a tough distinction. A pretext is that which is put forward to conceal a truth. He was discharged for tardiness, but this was only a pretext for general incompetence. A pretense is a "false show," a more overt act intended to conceal personal feelings. My profuse compliments were all pretense.

36. Principle, principal. A guiding rule or basic truth is a principle. The first, dominant, or leading thing is principal. Principle is a noun; principal may be a noun or an adjective. Right: It's the principle of the thing. Right: Liberty and justice are two principles on which our nation is founded. Right: Hitting and fielding are the principal activities in baseball. Right: Robert Jamieson is the school principal.

37. Redundancies to avoid. Easter Sunday. Make it Easter. Incumbent Congressman. Congressman. Owns his own home. Owns his home. The company will close down. The company will close. Jones, Smith, Johnson and Reid were all convicted. Jones, Smith, Johnson and Reid were convicted. Jewish Rabbi. Rabbi. 8 p.m. tonight. All you need is 8 tonight or 8 p.m. today. During the winter months. During the winter. Both Reid and Jones were denied pardons. Reid and Jones were denied pardons. I am currently tired. I am tired. Autopsy to determine the cause of death. Autopsy.

38. Refute. The word connotes success in argument and almost always implies an editorial judgment. Wrong: Father Bury refuted the arguments of the proabortion faction.

39. Reluctant, reticent. If he doesn't want to act, he is reluctant. If he doesn't want to speak, he is reticent.

40. Say, said. The most serviceable words in the journalist's language are the forms of the verb "to say." Let a person say something, rather than declare or admit or point out. And never let him grin, smile, frown, or giggle something.

41. Slang. Don't try to use "with-it" slang. Usually a term is on the way out by the time we get it in print. Wrong: The police cleared the demonstrators with a sunrise bust.

42. Spelling. It's basic. If reporters can't spell and copy editors can't spell, we're in trouble. Some ripe ones for the top of your list: It's consensus, not concensus. It's restaurateur, not restaurnteur. It's dietitian, not dietician.

43. Temperatures. They may get higher or lower, but they don't get warmer or cooler. Wrong: Temperatures are expected to warm up in the area Friday. Right: Temperatures are expected to rise in the area Friday.

44. That, which. "That" tends to restrict the reader's thought and direct it the way you want it to go; "which" is nonrestrictive, introducing a bit of subsidiary information. For instance: The lawnmower that is in the garage needs sharpening. (Meaning: We have more than one lawnmower. The one in the garage needs sharpening.) The lawnmower, which is in the garage, needs sharpening. (Meaning: Our lawnmower needs sharpening. It's in the garage.) The statue that graces our entry hall is on loan from the museum. (Meaning: Of all the statues around here, the one in the entry hall is on loan.) The statue, which graces our entry hall, is on loan. (Meaning: Our statue is on loan. It happens to be in the entry hall.) Note that "which" clauses take commas, signaling that they are not essential to the meaning of the sentence.

45. Under way, not underway. But don't say something got under way. Say it started or began.

46. Unique. Something that is unique is the only one of its kind. It can't be very unique or quite unique or somewhat unique or rather unique. Don't use it unless you really mean unique.

47. Up. Don't use it as a verb. Wrong: The manager said he would up the price next week. Right: The manager said he would raise the price next week.

48. Who, whom. A tough one, but generally you're safe to use whom to refer to someone who has been the object of an action: A 19-year-old woman, to whom the room was rented, left the window open. Who is the word when the somebody has been the actor. A 19-year-old woman, who rented the room, left the window open.

49. Who's, whose. Though it incorporates an apostrophe, who's is not a possessive. It's a contraction of who is. Whose is possessive. Wrong: I don't know who's coat it is. Right: I don't know whose coat it is. Right: Find out who's there.

50. Would. Be careful about using would when constructing a conditional past tense. Wrong: If Soderhelm would not have had an injured foot, Thompson wouldn't have been in the lineup. Right: If Soderhelm had not had an injured foot, Thompson wouldn't have been in the lineup.

EXERCISES

GRAMMAR AND PUNCTUATION PROBLEMS

Correct the errors you find in these sentences either by copy editing or by rewriting the sentences. Underline your corrections. When you find a sentence that is correct, place Corr. before it.

1. Although Drake was not expected to give UCLA much of a battle, everyone got their money's worth when the Uclans barely pulled it out, 85-82, in the NCAA semifinals.

2. Each one of the Miss Teen-Agers were judged on their talent, their poise and their personality.

3. The couple was married in 1966 and were divorced in 1967.

4. Each team was splitting their ends wide.

5. The North and the South each have six backs and six linemen which have been drafted by the NFL.

6. Everybody in the stadium was on their feet and screaming for a home run.

7. The library has been increasing their stack of books since their move to the new municipal building a year ago.

8. Any one of the three vice presidents is qualified to handle their job.

9. He told James that he was responsible for the error.

10. The losing team ate their dinner in silence.

11. Washington and Oregon each have won six games and lost two.

12. The mayor presented Nano Scarborough and myself to the governor.

13. Anyone who wants a personalized license plate should send in their application by April 15.

14. "If any player on this team thinks I'm too strict in regard to training rules, they can turn in their suit right now."

15. Any one of the national civil rights leaders were available for consultation, according to the Massachusetts senator.

16. At least three farm products contain this strong fiber, and they can be made into fabrics resembling gossamer silk.

17. It's a first down for the Tigers on its own 28-yard line.

18. Cherry nearly came to blows with Axton after he had protested the nomination of Afelbaum.

19. His proposition will be submitted to the board, and it is likely that most of the members will agree with him.

MORE PROBLEMS

Most of the errors in these sentences are in the uses of relative pronouns. There are also some misplaced relative clauses. Correct the errors either by copy editing or by rewriting the sentences. Underline your corrections. Some of the sentences are correct; place the abbreviation Corr. before each of them.

1. The epidemic has struck more than 60 persons, at least 11 of which have died.

2. He distributed the rat poison throughout the barn which he had bought that morning.

3. To the question of whom looked good in line, Walker replied with a warm smile: "I can't remember all of their names right now, but there were seven of them."

4. The senator pointed out that in September a vice-presidential candidate had not been named, and that voters could only express a preference for the nominee's running mate," whomever he might be.

5. One of the constructive things that has come out of the meetings of the delegates is that some of them are determined to eliminate these redtape obstacles.

6. Who do you think State's quarterback will be?

7. He refused to state, did he not, whom the new employees would be.

8. The President declined to comment directly on the case of the undersecretary, whom the Attorney General says was promoted by his predecessor.

9. There are at least seven men who's integrity is to be investigated.

10. Maurice Stans, who former President Richard Nixon chose as Secretary of Commerce, is a colleague from the Eisenhower days.

11. With Dietrich Fischer-Dieskau, famed German lieder singer, was his new bride, Christina Purgell, whom he met during a 1967 U.S. tour.

12. One player who you can depend on to make the NCAA Tournament All-Star team is Will Soloman of Drake.

13. One player who is sure to be placed on the NCAA Tournament All-Star team is Will Solomon of Drake.

14. They will seriously consider the mayor whom they regard as "a terrific Republican property."

15. Regardless of who is chosen, the majority of the board members promise to support him.

16. It was Rod Steiger, Academy Award winner, whom they wanted to meet.

17. He swore that he would see to it that Haideman "got this important part."

18. The chairman of the Board of Regents is leading the fight over who is going to run the university--the board, the legislature or the student militants.

PRONOUN USAGE

Underline the correct pronoun.

1. No matter how you look at it, it was (she, her) whom they opposed.
2. My sister, who is two years older than (I, me), is much less hopeful.
3. Everybody stood erect except Dick and (I, me).
4. None was better prepared for the profession than (he, him).
5. Jack can play ball as well as you or (I, me).
6. We considered (she, her) to be the best actress in the company.
7. It must have been (he, him).
8. If I were (she, her), I would get a permanent.
9. None was more kind than (she, her).
10. You have lived here longer than (we, us).
11. It was (she, her) they considered last.
12. I must admit, between you and (I, me), I failed that last test.
13. The club sent three members to represent it--Tom, Don, and (I, me).
14. (Who, Whom) are they asking?
15. Nobody can be as lucky as (he, him).
16. Everybody had supposed it was (he, him) who threw the rock through the window.
17. For you and (she, her) to walk twenty-five miles would be tiring.
18. It is always (I, me) who gets severely punished.
19. Why were you counting on (they, them) to bring the cake?
20. Jack asked Mary rather than (I, me) to go to the show.
21. (Who, Whom) did it seem would be nominated?
22. The army sent three men to the conference--General Dans, General Bixby, and (I, me).
23. The campus policeman swore it was (they, them) whom he had seen.

USING VERBS CORRECTLY

In the following sentences underline the correct form of the verb.

1. A burglary ring of Dallas youngsters (lead, led) by a 9-year-old boy faced juvenile delinquency charges Monday.

2. Yesterday Patrick Welch (led, lead) the St. Patrick's Day parade.

3. Suddenly the children (sprang, sprung) from their hiding place and (sung, sang) "Happy Birthday to You."

4. He charged that the commissioners had not (payed, paid) him the stipulated fee.

5. H.L. Hunt (strove, strived) hard to accumulate his first million.

6. He dived in and (drug, dragged) the body of the (drown, drowned) girl from the creek.

7. The ground was (froze, frozen) over and one pipe had (burst, bursted, busted).

8. The Johnsons (use, used) to live in San Jose.

9. The boy's body (hanged, hung) there for almost an hour before it was removed.

10. After questioning the youth for nine hours, the detectives (rang, rung, wrang, wrung) a confession from him.

11. She could have (sung, sang) "Yes, We Have No Bananas" and (drawn, draw) an ovation.

12. Carol Farmer had (sewn, sewed, sowed, sown) on a dress all day and her husband had (sewn, sewd, sowed, sown) about 25 acres of wheat.

13. The candidate for Place Four seemed to have his two opponents soundly (beat, beaten).

USING VERBS CORRECTLY

Correct the verb forms in the following sentences. If the sentence is correct, please note by writing Corr. in the margin.

1. My son rushed into the room, grabs his coat and goes dashing down the hall.

2. A few minutes elapsed; then as suddenly as the storm appeared, it disappeared.

3. It has been very cold since we are here.

4. I am waiting for this dance for three weeks.

5. When we entered our cabin, we found some thief made off with our supplies.

6. I expected to have gone to Richmond for the holidays.

7. On Saturday I discussed with Kelpert the material which he presented to the committee on Friday.

8. From 1934 until now he was director of the Community Hospital.

9. After some discussion we decided that real happiness did not lie in material things, but in the qualities of the spirit.

10. All the roads were blocked because the snow had fallen.

11. Unfortunately, we found that your credit rating is not up to our standards.

12. Can I go to the concert tonight?

13. I intended to have seen you about the exam.

14. He is studying French for several years, but he cannot say a word of the language.

15. When Judy appeared, she was dressed in a filmy blue dress. In a few minutes the doorbell rings and in comes Stanley.

16. People in white seem to be everywhere in the physicist's laboratory, but no sound is heard.

17. When the respirometer started, the surgeon nods to the nurse and she hands him the instruments.

PREPOSITIONS AND CONJUNCTIONS

In the following sentences, circle the preposition and underline the prepositional phrase.

1. Anderson worked in a London advertising agency.
2. Before sundown, all the men had returned home.
3. Many private fortunes were founded on privateering.
4. Quickly, the thief glanced down the long dark hall.
5. I heard about your very unusual problem.
6. These shirts are made of very fine imported domestic materials.
7. Four hundred thousand people passed through the turnstiles that year.
8. The chicken rode off perched on the rear bumper.
9. He replied, off the record, that he had voted to have the restrictions removed.

Circle the conjunctions in the following sentences.

1. The woodsman was angry because someone had stolen his traps.
2. Spot the frogs with your flashlight; then shoot before they jump.
3. Whenever a pocket of air shook the bomber, the tailgunner shouted over the intercom, threatening the pilot with court martial and announcing repeatedly that he was going home.
4. Although I am a heavy sleeper, I awoke with a start when the lightning flashed, and I rushed to the window to see what had happened.
5. As he came in the door, he said he would whip any man in the room.
6. He goes golfing three or four times a week, but his game never improves.
7. The price that he wanted for the house was too high.
8. We ate ham and eggs.
9. We left the party early because we were tired.

AGREEMENT: PRONOUNS AND ANTECEDENTS

In the blank before each sentence mark an X if there is an error in the agreement of pronoun and antecedent.

.....1. A person at all times guard themselves against slanderous tongues.

.....2. Someone has been here and left her calling card.

.....3. The sonnet was introduced by Wyatt and Surrey. They were love poems of fourteen lines.

.....4. Needless to say, everyone who invested in that stock lost their money.

.....5. If one becomes discouraged, you lose interest.

.....6. Everyone of the veterans was responsible for their own lodging.

.....7. When anyone is irritated, it is best to let him alone.

.....8. Every pilot returned safely from their dangerous mission.

.....9. Bernie told his partner that he was a failure.

....10. Everyone was dressed in his best and glad to be at the party.

....11. They were told that all of the men would have to wait their turn.

....12. Each of the dogs entered in this race has won his share of trophies.

....13. We enjoyed our visit to the Bar X Ranch very much. They were extremely hospitable people.

....14. The one or two members of the class who raise their hands answer most of the questions.

....15. Either my sister or her roommate may miss her bus.

....16. Neither of the two secretaries had brought their lunch.

....17. Each of the horses entered their stall.

....18. Neither of the boys would admit that he had missed school.

PROBLEMS IN WORD CHOICE

The following exercise is designed to check your ability to distinguish between commonly confused words, such as "accept" and "except." Choose the correct word in each sentence.

1. (except, accept)

    I...............your invitation; everyone will be there...............Jane.

2. (advise, advice)

    Will you give me some...............? I...............you to sell your mining stock.

3. (effect, affect)

    Although that drug has a powerful..............., it did not...............me.

4. (affected, effected)

    At last the prisoners...............their escape.

5. (affective, effective)

    George had an...............manner of speaking.

6. (already, all ready)

    At last the men were...............to go.

7. (altogether, all together)

    The grandchildren were...............that Christmas.

8. (already, all ready)

    Sally had...............gone when I arrived.

9. (altogether, all together)

    There has been...............too much whispering.

10. (angel, angle)

    An...............appeared to him in a vision and said, "Please hand me a right-...............triangle.

11. (capital, capitol)

    We looked up at the dome of the................

12. (capital, capitol)

    Pierpoint supplied the...............for the project.

13. (capitol, capital)

    The president discussed the conflict between...............and labor.

14. (Course, Coarse)

    ....gravel was used as a base for the street.

15. (compliment, complement)

    The squad had its full...............of men.

16. (coarse, course)

    You know, of...............,that this is foolish.

17. (compliment, complement)

The press paid the actress a high.................

MORE WORD CHOICE EXERCISES

Choose the correct word for each of the following sentences.

1. (statues, statutes, statures)

   More and more...............are being written each year.

2. (angles, angels)

   Scholars debated the question of how many...............could stand on the point of

a   pin.

3. (except, accept)

   No one can go...............Charles.

4. (dessert, desert)

   The old prospector was lost on the...............

5. (accept, except)

   Everyone was there...............Smith.

6. (your, you're)

   Let me tell you that...............wrong about him.

7. (Its, It's)

   ....paw was caught in the steel trap.

8. (principle, principal)

   The...............announced the new appointments to the teaching staff.

9. (council, counsel)

   My uncle gave me good...............about leaving school.

10. (Whose, Who's)

    ....car are you driving?

11. (prophecy, prophesy)

    No one can...............with certainty what will happen in the East.

12. (loose, lose)

    I do not think he will...............by trading in his old car.

13. (capital, capitol)

    The old man was formerly a guide employed at the...............

14. (already, all ready)

    We found, to our sorrow, that they had...............gone.

15. (course, coarse)

    The old miner brushed his hands through his...............hair.

16. (lose, loose)

    The mechanic found that a nut had come...............

17. (capitol, capital)

    The group of businessmen started the bank with less than a million dollars in

    ....

18. (stationery, stationary)

    The clown stood...............on his hands.

19. (respectively, respectfully)

    The committee..............submitted its annual report.

FURTHER PRACTICE: WORD CHOICE EXERCISES

Choose the correct word for each of the following sentences.

1. (farther, further)

     He chased the ball...............than I chased it.

2. (farther, further)

     He pursued the subject...............than I pursued it.

3. (alright, all right)

     That is...............with me.

4. (among, between)

     The money was divided...............four players.

5. (among, between)

     The money was divided...............two players.

6. (affect, effect)

     A charming...............was produced.

7. (implies, infers)

     Farming...............early rising.

8. (implied, inferred)

     Since he was a farmer, we...............that he got up early.

9. (Regardless, Irregardless)

     ....of the consequences, we intend to go.

10. (Leave, Let)

     ....it stand the way it is.

11. (less, fewer)

     He had...............men than in the previous campaign.

12. (than, then)

     It looked more like a robin...............a heron.

13. (from, than)

     Robins are different...............sparrows.

14. (tortuous, torturous)

     A winding road is................

15. (tortuous, torturous)

     A painful ordeal is................

16. (the most unique, a unique)

     It was...............balancing act.

17. (perfect, most perfect, very perfect)

     The balancing act was...............

18. (very, awfully)

    This is a...............difficult assignment.

19. (better, best)

    Which is the...............of the two sentences?

    (1)Soulwise, these are trying times.

    (2) Times like these try men's souls.

20. (laying, lying)

    Do you have a copy of the graduate catalog...............around?

21. (good, well)

    He does extremely...............in mathematics.

22. (real, really, very)

    It was...............good.

23. (like, as)

    He dresses...............I do.

POSSESSIVES

Write the singular possessive of each of these:

1. the boy........coat
2. Gray and Perry........shop
3. John Keats........poems
4. Holmes........mansion
5. his wife........property
6. the puppy........ball
7. a hero........welcome
8. the princess........escort
9. a witch........broomstick
10. the notary public........sign

Write the plural possessive of each of these:

1. witch........broomsticks
2. child........toys
3. Holmes........autos
4. hobo........shoes
5. mouse........tails
6. fox........tails
7. farmer........ magazines
8. woman........dresses
9. alumnus........newsletters
10. the Charles........reigns
11. policemen........beats

USING POSSESSIVES

Rewrite or correct the errors in the following sentences—or improve the expressions.

1. The Clinton Dad's Club will hold it's first Dads and Sons banquet Tuesday night.

2. "I don't mind you making a few popsicles in the freezer," the mother told her daughter.

3. The union gave 48 hours notice before striking, and the strike was settled in one hours time.

4. Leslie did not bother with the smallest deers antlers, but he had the two largest deers antlers mounted.

5. This coat is your's, but Harry is not here.

6. The two Harry's suits look alike.

7. This one is our's, but who's is that?

8. Ellis met Quarrys' second-round rush with a sustained attack. Ellis's hard right to the stomach made the challengers knees buckle.

9. The Volunteers new coach would make no comment concerning his teams prospects.

10. Although he said he could do a good days work, he was unable in three days time to show he could do the work satisfactorily.

11. Prospects of them being written into labor law were considered gloomy today.

12. Give him two tablespoonsful every four hours.

13. The men servant's quarters were searched.

14. She could not bear the thought of Elmer gambling.

15. Please sell me a quarters' worth.

16. She is a friend of Janes.

17. Fans are looking forward to State meeting with Tech Saturday.

18. You must watch your p's and q's.

19. In the poll there were 42 yes's and 51 noes.

In the following sentences choose the correct word by underlining it.

1. To (who, whom) should the letter be addressed?

2. (Who, Whom) will be selected for the chairmanship?

3. Do they know (whose, who's) putting up the money?

4. That is State's star player, (him, he) with the taped legs.

5. The coach is removing his star player, (him, he) with the taped legs.

6. Do you remember (who, whom) it was (who, whom) won the Nobel Prize in 1966?

7. Do you think that (we, us) men can do anything about women's fashions?

8. Garets is the only man here (whom, who) I know very well.

9. It appears to be Douglass (whom, who) was injured in the play.

10. Only John and (me, I) are to blame.

11. (Who, Whom), then, would the tax hurt?

PUNCTUATION: GENERAL

Insert the correct punctuation.

1. We may divide the poems into three classes narrative lyric and dramatic.
2. Stumbling toward the telephone I wondered who would be calling me after 11 30 p m
3. At any rate this much can be said The Council is not the vital organ it is supposed to be
4. Within two hours we had a strange variety of precipitation rain hail sleet snow
5. Promptly at 8 15 p m the minister began his sermon by quoting John 20 21
6. Whos going to do the dishes
7. On Thursdays the childrens department doesnt open
8. They havent said the property is theirs
9. Theyre not coming to see Freds new house
10. That boys one of the worlds worst at what he's doing now
11. I didnt go to sleep until after 2 00 a m
12. He makes ladies hats and childrens coats
13. All her thoughts were centered on one objective marriage
14. In 1803 Thomas Jefferson said We have seen with sincere concern the flames of war lighted up again in Europe"
15. Blair regarded the demand for popular rights as a king might regard it as a mode of upsurpation
16. The three causes are as follows poverty injustice and indolence
17. Intercollegiate athletics continues to be big business but Robert Hutchins long ago pointed out a simple remedy colleges should stop charging admissions to football games
18. There is one strong reason why gambling should not be legalized gambling establishments always attract gangsters and criminals

PUNCTUATION: CONNECTIVES

Insert the correct punctuation.

1. I do not say that these stories are untrue I only say that I do not believe them

2. I had hoped to find a summer job in the city however two weeks of job hunting convinced me that it was impossible

3. The loan account book must be sent with each monthly payment otherwise there may be disputes as to the amount still owing

4. The *Daily World* though officially a Republican paper handled the story with scrupulous if disdainful objectivity but many of the supposedly Democratic papers to everyone's surprise played up all the scandalous aspects of the case

5. The committee consisted of Webster the president of the bank Elton the bank manager and the mayor

6. Supplementary material will be found in W.D. Taylor *Jonathan Swift* Ricardo Quintana *The Mind and Art of Jonathan Swift* and Bernard Acworth *Swift*

7. As a reward for his services to his country the Duke was given pensions special grants and honorary offices and a fund was created to erect a memorial in his honor

8. From the high board the water looked amazingly far away besides I was getting cold and tired of swimming

9. There are no set rules which an actor must follow to become proficient in his art however there are certain principles regarding the use of mind voice and body which may help him

10. When Lord Warwick desired with great tenderness to hear his last injunctions Addison told him "I have sent for you that you may see how a Christian can die"

USING APOSTROPHES

Insert the apostrophes as necessary in the following sentences. Many of the errors in these sentences have to do with the use of apostrophes in possessives, but there are also other types of apostrophe-usage errors.

1. Its true that Robert Thomas car was found shortly after it was stolen, but its fenders were smashed and its tires were missing.

2. The presidents secretary has ordered a three-weeks supply of carbon paper.

3. Womens fashions change every year — to everyones satisfaction but their husbands.

4. After working with this company for a years time, you are given a two-weeks vacation with pay.

5. This book is Hans, whose collection of dime novels numbers over a thousand items.

6. Tex McCready, Associated Studios leading western actor, was a childrens and juveniles favorite during the 1930s; his income wasn't far from a hundred thousand dollars a year.

7. Dr. Daniels wouldnt have spent his whole years leave trying to establish the Ellins Brothers theory if he hadn't been convinced of its validity

8. Its too bad that the city of Newbridge cant keep its streets in the condition of those of the wealthier suburbs such as Glen Ridge.

9. The Stevenes aren't at home this month; theyre visiting their relatives in Florida and won't be back until Christmas.

10. Count to 10,000 by 2s.

11. Cross your ts and dot your is.

12. There were suggestions that the mens uniforms be modified.

13. It isn't the cough that carries you off; its the coffin they carry you off in.

14. Dickens novel is a very famous one.

15. Dobbs hand contained only two sevens and two fives and he wasnt confident when he called the bowers ten-chip raise.

16. Nickels next two books weren't reviewed favorably, but they turned out to be popular as clubwomens choices.

17. Who will administer the citys policies?

18. Who will administer the cities policies?

19. The cat is lying on its back, but I can't tell whether its dead or not.

20. Her ladies hats are famous throughout the nation.

21. This pencil is Charles, not Marys.

22. The garages roof sloped sharply.

23. Robert Burns poems are favorites of ours.

24. In spite of its reputation, Hughes restaurant is not popular with the students; its too expensive.

25. Don't take Keats poem too seriously.

26. In our reading of Shakespeares *A Midsummer Nights Dream*, Theseus part was read by the teacher.

27. The mens dormitories are always open, but the womens dormitories close at midnight.

28. The Davises car was parked on our driveway, right behind Travis hot rod.

29. Dont take anyone elses word for it.

30. My brothers boat was not working, so we borrowed a launch belonging to the Willises.

31. It used to be thought that *Titus Andronicus* was Thomas Kyds work, but scholars now agree that its Shakespeares.

32. His Us were like Vs, and his 2s like Zs.

SPELLING

The story below contains several spelling errors. Edit the story to correct those errors and any others you may find in the story. Make sure the story conforms to AP style.

State Bureau of Investegation Director Johnny Jolly told frustrated residents of West Greenville he couldn't give them details on the slayings of four young people in the last year.

But details were just what 200 townsfolk asked about during a town meeting with Jolly and two other investegating officials Thursday night.

Jolly would not answer when Connie Russell, 22, asked wether the killer was a local person.

"Everybody in this town is just terrified to live normally," Russell said. "I can't go to the grocery store without carrying a revolver. I've become really dependant on that gun."

The first of the four victims was Central High School cheerleader Beth Harris, 16, who was last seen walking to school on May 1, 1981. Her fully clothed body was found tied with a wire to a basketball goal at an abandoned house. A nickle was taped to her forhead.

The charred remains of Jeff Toumey, 15, of Ripton, who was visting in West Greenville, were found in a garbage can July 15, 1981. He was last seen walking along a road to a friend's house.

Billy Henderson, 16, was abducted from his bedroom while vaccuuming his carpet August 1. His body was found in an antequated automobile a week later after an intensive search by law enforcement officers and volunteers.

Carol Ann Bellows, 19, vanished from a soroity sister's parked car September 4. Her nude body was located only 300 yards from the cite.

Peters said all four killings are definitely related. The Bureau of Investegation has produced a psycological profile of te killer, Peters said, but he would give no details on the profile.

The director also refused to answer questions on whether anything had been taken from the bodies that might identify the killers or on what the causes of death were.

Jolly did answer a question by a woman who wanted to know what law enforcment officers were doing about a prediction from a local psycic.

"She said it would happen again," Mrs. Bertha Nunne said.

Peters replied, "We're not in the habit of following psycics."

SPELLING

The story below contains several spelling errors. Edit the story to correct those errors and any others you may find in the story. Make sure the story conforms to AP style.

Eighth-grader JoLinda McSpadden, daughter of Mr. and Mrs. Percy McSpadden, Route 3, Pineville, won the county spelling bee yesterday by spellling "hemmorage" correctly when her rivals could not.

First runnerups in this year's contest were Terri Callaway, daughter of Mr. and Mrs. John Callaway, 16 Baker St., and Nancy Wood, daughter of Mr. and Mrs. Arnold Wood of 3701 Oakdale Road. Both girls successfully spelled "epiphany" to gain a tie for the second spot.

JoLinda, a student at Maplewood Junior High, was the first runnerup in last year's contest. She will go on to compete in the state contest next month in the state capitol.

The two first runnerups are seventh graders at Highland Junior High.

Jane McMillan, an English teacher at Maplewood and coordinator of this year's contest, said more than 300 students entered the three-day competion. She called the contest "an extremely succesful one."

"Many of the words we used this year were much more difficult than ones we have used in years past," McMillan said.

She pointed out that many of the contestants successfully spelled words like "pantomime," "liquify," "naphtha," and "questionnaire." JoLinda, she said, outlasted a number of good spellers.

"I believe that JoLinda will do quite well in the state bee. She is very composed young lady who is not upset even when she is being hurried, giggled at, or otherwise harassed. That quality of coolness frequently works better than the agression shown by some contestants," McMillan said.

SPELLING

The story below contains several spelling errors. Edit the story to correct those errors and any others you may find in the story. Make sure the story conforms to AP style.

The spinal menigitis outbreak which has plauged the valley area for two weeks is apparently over.

State health department officials have verefied reports that only one person with a confirmed case of the disease is still hospitalized in Greendale.

"We are absolutely delighted to report that 11 of the 12 Greendale residents who were struck with menigitis have been released from Community Hospital," Tommy Beans, deputy assistant to the head of the health department, said yesterday.

The remaining patient, 11 year-old Bonnie Johnson, had her firist symtoms several hours after a family outing to Vinson park and the nearby national forrest campgrounds last Monday. She became the seventh person admitted to the local hospital for spinal menigitis treatment in only 10 days. Her illness was complicated by a chronic resperatory problem, but physicians say her condition is good and that she will be released within days.

A number of neighboring counties have experienced a rash of menigitis cases this month. In Billson County, where 15 pre-schoolers were hospitalized in one week, two deaths have been atributed to the ailment.

Billson County Sherrif Ed Willis said he had no idea where the epidemic originated.

"We've checked out a number of possibilities, but I don't really think we are going to figure out where it began. I'm just happy that it's over," he said.

A total of 55 cases have definitly been treated at five area hospitals since March 1. Isolated cases have been reported in other parts of the state.

Beans said reports of futher cases at area schools are false. He added that it is important for the menigitis patience to take care of them selves.

"Good food and rest, with only a moderate amount of exercize, should take care of the weakness that follows menigitis."

SPELLING

The story below contains several spelling errors. Edit the story to correct those errors and any others you may find in the story. Make sure the story conforms to AP style.

A local man remains puzzelled today over the mysterious disappearance of his automobile.

Billy Hendricks, 21, of 227 Fern St., said he drove to a supermarket near his home yesterday at around 2:30 p.m. to buy steaks for a neigborhood cookout. On leaving the store, he was "absolutely astonished" to find his dark blue 1981 Ford Fairmont missing.

"I wasn't in that store for more than five minutes. I can't imagine how anyone could have stolen it. I had locked the car, and I had my keys with me. It was really an embarrasing situation to be in, standing there with my mounth hanging open in surprize," Hendricks said.

Although police assigned to the case have questionned local residents and others who were in the area at the time of the incident, they have practiclly no leads.

Sgt. Tommy Wilson, officer in charge of the investegation, said he has "little to go on.".

"It could have been anybody from a profesional auto hustler to a kid out for a joy ride to some prankster friend of Mr. Hendricks. When you're dealing with an occurrance as strange as this one, you can't really rule out any possibility," Wilson said.

Wilson said he and his officers are constently working with police from all over the state on cases similar to this one.

"We keep tabs on various people who occasionnally deal in 'hot' cars, and one of them will inadvertantly make a mistake sooner or later. We can hope that one of those mistakes will get Mr. Hendricks' car back for us. And we do have other sources of information to depend on, informents in the car business who keep eyes and ears open."

5

STYLE AND THE STYLEBOOK

English is an extremely diverse language, giving the user many ways of saying the same thing. For instance, 8 or eight o'clock, 8 a.m., 8 A.M., eight a.m., and eight in the morning may all correctly refer to the same thing; a reference may be made to the President, the U.S. president, the President of the United States, and so on. All of these references are technically correct, but which one should a journalist use? And does it really matter?

The answer to the first question is governed by journalistic style. Style is a special case of English correctness which a publication adopts. It does so in order to promote consistency among its writers and to reduce confusion among its readers. Once a style is adopted, a writer won't have to wonder about the way to refer to such things as time.

Journalistic style may be divided into two types of style: professional conventions and rules of usage. Professional conventions have evolved during years of journalistic endeavor and are now taught through professional training in universities and professional workshops. The rules of usage have been collected into stylebooks published by wire services, news syndicates, universities, and individual print and broadcast news operations. Some of these stylebooks have had widespread acceptance and influence. Others have remained relatively local and result in unique style rules accepted by reporters and editors working for individual news organizations.

For example, a publication may follow the Associated Press and United Press International stylebook and say that AM and PM should be lower-case with periods: a.m. and p.m. The writer will know that a reference to the President of the United States is always simply "president," lower-cased, except when referring to a specific person, such as President Reagan.

Likewise, the reader will not be confused by multiple references to the same item. Unconsciously, the reader will expect the style that the publication uses. Consequently, if the reader uses a college newspaper regularly and that paper always refers to its own institution as the "University," upper-cased, the reader will know what that means.

Similarly, a reporter may follow the usual convention in newspaper writing and write the sequence of time, date, and place of a meeting despite the fact that it may seem more logical to report the date before reporting the time.

Having a logical, consistent style is like fine-tuning a color television. Before the tuning, the colors may be there and the picture may be reasonably visible. Eventually, however, the off-colors and the blurry images will play on the viewer's mind so that he or she will become dissatisfied and disinterested. That could cause the viewer to stop watching altogether. In the same way, consistent style fine-tunes a publication so that reading it is easier for a reader and offers few distractions from the content.

Beyond that, the question may still remain: Does style really matter? The answer is an emphatic "yes!" Many young writers think of consistent style as a repressive force hampering their creativity. It isn't. Style is not a rigid set of rules established to restrict the creative forces in the writer. Style imposes a discipline in writing that should run through all the activities of a journalist. It implies that the journalist is precise not only with writing but also with facts and with thought. Consistent style is the hallmark of a professional.

Editors are the governors of the style of a publication. It is their job to see that style rules are consistently and reasonably applied. If exceptions are allowed, they should be for specific and logical reasons and should not be at the whim of a writer. Editors should remember that consistent style is one way of telling readers that everything in the publication is certified as accurate.

WIRE SERVICE STYLEBOOKS

Several years ago, the two major U.S. wire services negotiated agreement on the basic rules of style found in their two stylebooks. As a result, the Associated Press and United Press International now publish stylebooks that are in fundamental agreement on the basic rules of style. This has resulted in widespread adoption of these rules by newspapers around the United States. Since the Associated Press has published its stylebook in a form commonly available to students in universities around the country, we shall refer to that stylebook in this section of our discussion. Keep in mind that this style is now held in common with UPI and is accepted by many newspapers nationwide.

Most publications base their style on that found in the Associated Press Stylebook. Here are some representative problem areas and some advice generally taken from the Associated Press Stylebook.

Capitalization. Unnecessary capitalization, like unnecessary punctuation, should be avoided because it slows reading and makes the sentence look uninviting. Some examples: Main Street, but Main and Market streets. Mayor John Smith, but John Smith, mayor of Jonesville. Steve Bradley, executive director of the State Press Association. (Note lower case title after name, but upper case for State Press Association, a formal name and therefore a proper noun.)

Abbreviation. The trend is away from alphabet soup in body type and in headlines, but some abbreviations help conserve space and help to simplify information. For example: West Main Street, but 20 W. Main St. The only titles for which abbreviations are called for (all before the name) are Dr., Gov., Lt. Gov., Mr., Mrs., Rep., the Rev., Sen., and most military ranks. Standing alone, all of these are spelled out and are lower cased. Check the Stylebook for others.

Punctuation. Especially helpful are the sections of the Stylebook dealing with the comma, hyphen, period, colon and semicolon, dash, ellipsis, restrictive and nonrestrictive elements, apostrophe, and quotation marks.

Numerals. Spell out whole numbers below 10, and use figures for 10 and above. This rule applies to numbers used in a series or individually. Don't begin sentences with numerals, as a rule, but if you must, spell them out.

Spelling. In journalism a word has but one spelling. Alternate spellings and variants are incorrect (because of the requirement of style consistency). Make it adviser, not advisor; employee, not employe; totaled, not totalled, traveled, not travelled; kidnapped, not kidnaped; judgment, not judgement; television, not TV, when used as a noun; under way, not underway; percent, not per cent; afterward, toward, upward, forward (no s), vs., not versus or vs; vice president, not vice-president. Check the Stylebook or a dictionary for others.

Usage. Comprise means to contain, not to make up: "The region comprises five states," not "five states comprise the region" and not "the region is comprised of five states." Affect means to influence, not carry out. Effect means a result when it's a noun and means to carry out when it's a verb. Controller and comptroller are both pronounced "controller" and mean virtually the same thing, though comptroller is generally the more accurate word for denoting government financial officers and controller is better for denoting business financial officers. Hopefully does not mean it is hoped, we hope, maybe, or perhaps — it means in a hopeful manner: "Hopefully, editors will study the English language" is not acceptable usage of the word. Good editors use fad expressions because readers do, but they do not use them as crutches, and they should know when they are using them.

Ages. Use numerals always: a 2-month-old baby; he was 80; the youth, 18, and the girl, 6, were rescued.

Dates. Feb. 6 (current calendar year); in February 1978 (no comma); last February.

Dimensions. He is 5 feet 9 inches tall; the 5-foot 9-inch woman; 5-foot-9 woman; a 7-footer; the car left a skid mark 8 inches wide and 17 feet long; the rug is 10 by 12. The storm brought 1 ½ inches of rain (spell out fractions less than one).

JOURNALISTIC CONVENTIONS

A strong sense of professionalism has developed in journalism during the 300 years of its history in America. With this professionalism has come a powerful tradition of conventions in journalistic writing. As with rules of style, these conventions are known to trained journalists and used by them to communicate things about their stories to readers. Most readers do not think about what these conventions are when they read the newspaper, yet most regular readers of newspapers know these conventions and what they indicate about the judgments made by editors and reporters.

The conventions include both the basic structures of the stories and the individual ordering of facts and even words within sentences that regularly are used in certain types of stories.

Inverted pyramid. The inverted pyramid is the structure most commonly used for the modern American news story. For the editor, the inverted pyramid structure means two things: Facts should be presented in the order of their importance, with the most important facts coming at the beginning, and a story should be written so that if it needs to be cut, it may be cut from the bottom without loss of essential facts or coherence. The inverted pyramid is certainly not the only acceptable structure for the presentation of news, but its use is so widespread that if it is not used, the facts of a story must dictate the alternate form used by the writer.

Types of stories. The news values discussed in Chapter 2 make it incumbent that editors cover and give importance to certain types of stories. These kinds of stories are handled so often that a set of standard practices governing how they are written has been established. For instance, the disaster story must always tell early in the story if anyone was killed or injured. Another example of this routinization of stories is the obituary. Newspapers develop their own styles for handling obituaries, and some even dictate the form in which the standard obituary is written. For instance, the New York Times has a set two-sentence lead for an obituary: "John Smith, a Brooklyn real estate dealer, died at a local hospital yesterday after a short illness. He was 55 years old."

Other types of routine stories are those concerning government actions, the courts, crime, holidays, and weather. Part of an editor's job is to make sure that the paper covers these kinds of stories fully and that it covers other stories which have become important to the community which the newspaper serves.

Balance and fairness. One of the basic tenets of American journalism is fairness. Journalists should attempt to give all people involved in a news story a chance to tell their sides of it. If an accusation is made by a news source concerning another person, that person should be given a chance to answer in the same story. Journalists should not take sides in a controversy and should take care not to even appear to take sides.

Writing and editing a balanced story means more than just making sure a controversial situation or issue is covered fairly. In a larger sense, balance means that journalists should understand the relative importance of the events they cover and should not write stories which overplay or underplay that importance. Journalists are often charged with "blowing things out of proportion," and sometimes the charge is a valid one. They should make sure that they are not being used by news sources and being put in a position of creating news rather than letting it occur and then covering it.

The impersonal reporter. Closely associated with the concepts of balance and fairness is the concept of the impersonal reporter. Reporters should be invisible in their writing. Not only should reporters not report their own views and opinions, but they should avoid direct contact with the reader through the use of first-person (I, we, me, our, my, us) or second-person (you, your) pronouns outside of direct quotes.

Reporters and editors inherently state their opinions about the news in deciding what events they write about, how they write about them, and where they place those stories in the paper. No journalist can claim to be a completely unbiased and objective observer and deliverer of information. Yet stating opinions directly and plainly is generally not an acceptable practice. Even for a reporter to include himself with the readers is not a good idea. For example, the following lead is not acceptable because of its use of a first-person pronoun: "The Chief Justice of the Supreme Court said yesterday our legal system is in serious trouble." There may be someone reading this story who makes no claim to the United States' legal system, and the reporter should write for that person as well as all who do.

Reliance on official sources. Much of the information printed in a newspaper comes from what we might call "official" sources. These sources are those which are thought to have expertise on the subject being written about, not those who may merely have opinions about the subject. An example of this reliance might be found in a story about inflation. A journalist writing a story about inflation would probably use information from government reports and the studies and opinions of respected economists and influential politicians. These would be the "official" sources and they would have a large amount of credibility with the reader. An "unofficial" source might be a homemaker, who would certainly have an opinion about the effects, causes, and cures of inflation but who would not have information which would be credible in the mass media.

Young journalists often make the mistake of relying on these unofficial rather than on official sources of information. They interview people who have opinions about news events, such as their roommates, rather than those who can provide information to support an opinion about a news event. Use of official sources means that when a source is quoted in a story, it should be readily apparent why that source is used. Joe Johnson, a college student from Beantown, is not going to have much credibility even in a story about resistance to draft registration laws. However, Joe Johnson, the leader of the Draft Registration Resistance Movement, will have high credibility in the story.

Attribution and quotes. Journalists should make it clear to the readers where information has been obtained. All but the most obvious and commonly known facts in a story should be attributed. Editors should make sure that the attributions are helpful to the reader's understanding of the story and that they do not get in the way of the flow of the story.

A number of journalistic conventions have grown up around the use of indirect and direct quotes. First, except in the rarest instances, all quotes must be attributed. The exception is the case where there is no doubt about the source of the quote. Even then, editors should be careful. Second, journalists disagree about whether a direct quote should be the exact words a person speaks or the exact meaning the quoted person intended. Most of the time, people's exact words will accurately express their meaning. Sometimes, however, a journalist must chose between accuracy of words and accuracy of meaning. Finally, direct quotes in news stories rarely include bad grammar even if the person quoted used bad grammar. Quoting someone using English incorrectly can make that person appear unnecessarily foolish and can distract from the real meaning of the story. In a news story, a journalist usually cleans up bad grammar in a direct quote. (Feature story writers may choose not to follow this practice.)

These conventions are important ones for journalists to observe if they are to gain the respect of their readers and colleagues. They should not be looked upon as arbitrary rules which must be followed at the expense of accuracy and clarity. Rather, they are a set of sound practices which are extremely useful to journalists in the process of deciding what to write and how to write it.

EXERCISES

STYLEBOOK

Using your AP Stylebook, make the following sentences, expressions and words conform to AP style. Use proper editing symbols.

1. The former president of the Columbia Broadcasting System is Frank Stanton.

2. transcontinental, reelect, transsiberian, reexamine

3. Some Scotch people live in Mountain City, North Carolina.

4. five, ten, twelve, two and a half percent

5. The People's Republic of China is the largest country in the world, with over 800,000,000 people.

6. Margaret Chase Smith use to be the chairperson of the committee.

7. breakdown, fullfledged, infighting, Indo-China

8. Joseph P. Kennedy, Jr., was the president's older brother.

9. The instructor has a PhD in journalism.

10. Rank the following titles from one to five with the highest as one:

........Sergeant

........Major

........Colonel

........Major General

........Captain

11. The train is arriving at ten P.M. tonight.

12. The Pontiff, John Paul the Second, speaks several languages, including english, french and german.

13. William faulkner won a Nobel prize in literature.

14. like-wise, pre-historic, post-operative, holdover

15. The Labour Party lost the last election in England.

STYLEBOOK

Make the following sentences conform to AP style.

1. Jane Smith, age three, won the tricycle race. her aunt Mrs. Joyce Jones was her sponsor. Miss Smith lives at 201 north 8th Street, Prairie, S.D. Ms. Jones lives at 28th Pl., NE, Prairie, S.D.

2. The Southeast Region History Division (S.R.H.D.) of the Association for Education in Journalism (AEJ) will haost a Colloquium Friday and Saturday, January 27-28, 1978 on Journalism History at the Downtown Ramada Inn in Tuscaloosa, AL. The Event is expected to be attended by eighty to one hundred participants from the southeast.

3. The couple have 10 dogs, 6 cats, and 97 hamsters. None of the pets have been inoculated against rabies. The vet locked them up in 2 4 bedroom houses and said he would send them even further away next time.

4. The faculty advisor said: "Your 1st class begins at 8:00 A.M.." "Please make," he added, "an effort to get to class on time". "Shall we call it a 'gentlemens agreement'"? the prefessor continued.

5. The churches program was to collect girl's clothing boys toys and childrens' furniture.

6. The rock and role group also played music from the Gay' 90's, the Class of '65 and the "Roaring Twenties."

7. Attending the meeting were Bill Ray, Athens; Jack Smith of Columbus, and Joe Jones, of Dayton.

8. She hoped to fulfill her ambition of becoming a navy nurse after basic training in San Diego cal. She would then be equiped more formerly to do her job for the U.S.

9. Miss Hepburn, the screen's unchallenged "First Lady", is the first performer of either sex to win three Oscars for best actress.

10. I waved at the girl, who was standing on the corner. (One girl was.)

11. I waved at the girl, who was standing on the corner. (She was not sitting on the curb.)

12. After a quiet vacation in the midwest the young Marine Biologist was ready for his trip to the Antartic Region.

13. The President called in Atty. Howell to help to arrange his meeting with Atty. Gen.

Griffin Bell at three o'clock in the afternoon; with the Pope at 7 in the a.m.; and with the Joint Chiefs of Staff at 12 noon. He will discuss "Law and Order" with Mr. Bell; "Peace In The Middle East" with Paul; and the communist party with the Chiefs.

14. On Mothers Day the City Commission will visit the Capitol in Montgomery, view a project at Halsted and marks streets, and board the flag ship of the Seventh Fleet.

15. He "jumped" 1:25 meters after declaring he "wouldn't budge."

16. They ate dinner with their daughter, Suzy, and her husband David. (They have only one daughter, and she has two husbands?)

STYLEBOOK

Using your AP Stylebook, make the following words and sentences conform to AP style. Use proper editing symbols.

1. co-operate, preelection, pre-heat, preflight, pre-dawn, postmortem

2. The Reverend Johnny Milton led the Easter services at 4:30 A.M. this morning.

3. Flowers adorned either side of the altar at the Brown-Morris wedding.

4. Bronson's Co., Incorporated, is opening a new factory near Wilsonville next month.

5. 8:00, 8 o'clock in the morning, 12 noon, 12:00 p.m., 1:36 A.M.

6. Over 50,000 people attended the midsummer All-Star baseball game.

7. Bill Brody, the school's best runner, placed 22nd in the Regional Track Meet this year; Howard Wilson, a freshman, was 1st.

8. The French Army and the U.S. Army joined forces today in an effort to keep the peace in war-torn Lebannon.

9. Mix the ingredients in a ratio of 12-1.

10. A 12-to-one majority in the voice vote expressed the widespread approval of the bill.

11. Karl Teague, Dean of the College of Arts and Sciences, will address the graduating class at 11:15 in the morning.

12. freelancer, duffle bag, sister in laws (plural), t-shirt

13. The Gross National Product rose significantly in January, 1979.

14. The case in question is now in Federal District Court.

15. I found my material in the "Encyclopedia Britannica," in "The Autobiography of Lincoln Steffens," and in several magazine articles.

16. The U.S. is comprised of 50 states.

17. The company is headquartered in Albany, New York.

18. The council meeting will include a discussion on what to do about replacing deteriorating city sewage.

19. Howard Willet will be teaching History 222 and a graduate seminar in Political Science this fall.

20. Both the Nobel Peace prize and the Nobel prize in Chemistry were won by Americans.

STYLEBOOK

Edit the following copy to conform to AP style:

1. The dept. expects an increase of seven % in all items between seven cents and 11 cents, the Manager said.

2. Fire swept through the complex at Lindley and Shaw Streets at 2:00 A.M. Sat. morning.

3. Accident average in industry each day in the US is 55 killed, 8500 disabled, and 27000 less seriously injured.

4. He proposes the Government employ the poor and unemployed at good wages, raise the present $1.60 cents an hour to $2.00, and raise other benefits like workmen's compensation.

5. Temperatures dropped five degrees in the ease to pull the average down to a cool seventy-three degrees.

6. Five other republicans voted with the Senator.

7. The house passed the 12 month extension but senate democrats balked

8. "We had the problem of a five year old boy in a candy store," said Mr. Armstrong.

9. Others named to the committee were James Ahern, Police Chief of New Haven, Connecticut, Erwin D. Canham, Jr., Editor-in-Chief of the "Christian Science Monitor" James F. Cheek, President of Howard university in Washington, Mr. Benjamin O. Davis, public safety director of Cleveland and Martha A. Derthick, associate prof, of political Science at Boston College.

10. Harold Reagan fraternity President graduates in the Spring with a bachelor of arts in Government.

EDITING FOR STYLE

The following story contains a number of errors. Edit it according to AP style.

Judge Billy Estes has qualified to run for reelection as Circuit Judge, Place Number 3 of the the 6th Judicial Circuit in the up-comming Democratic party Primary.

He is seeking his third six year term as juvenile and family court judge. Bobby Ray Yves, Director of the state Legal Aid program, has also qualified for the position, to be determined in the September 7 Primary.

"I have worked hard for 12 years to be a good judge," Estes said. "In the juvenile court and in the family court, my concern has been on childrens's problems and needs."

Estes, an Kentucky native, was born and raised there. After having graduated from High School in '39, 11 years were spent as a railroad engineer's helper.

He got a bachelor degree in 1950 and a law degree in 1954, both are from the University of Alabama.

He has been working in the Legal Profession for twenty-eight years; five years in private practice and five as a district attorney.

He was a county D.A. for twelve years before being elected circuit judge.

He is a member of the Y.M.C.A. and the Boy's Club. He has coached Little League baseball teams for ten years and has worked with the Y's Men's Club tennis clinic for twelve years.

A World War I veteran, Estes is a member of the American Legion and the VFW.

Estes is married to the former Mary Ellen Thompson of Washington, D.C., and they have a 12-year old son, Travis.

EDITING FOR STYLE

Edit the following story. Make sure you follow AP style throughout the story.

LONDON, ENGLAND (AP)— Faced with a nationwide rail strike and walkouts that halted London subways and some buses, British commuters took to the roads in droves today, threatening nightmare traffic jams in the capitol.

Hours before dawn, roads to cities were clogged with traffic as commuters sought to beat the rush and find parking.

"It seems to me everyone has already started going into London for work. We have never experienced such traffic at night before," said an Automobile Association spokesman at 3 A.M. (10 P.M. EDT).

The Royal Auto club said that by seven in the morning, cars were backed up for 8 miles in some places and many emergency parking lots were full.

"There is too much traffic for us to identify the trouble spots," a police spokesman said.

Greater London is the workplace for 3,750,000 people, a third of the nation's 24-million-member work force. Two million passengers ride the subways every day, and 3-and-a-half million more ride buses. On a normal day, 80 per cent of workers in central London use public transport: 435,500 by subway, 411,00 by railroad, and 103,000 by bus.

The striking railroad carries two million passengers daily nation-wide.

An openended strike by the National Union of Railwaymen, kindled by a pay dispute, strangled the 11,000 mile state-run railroad network, British Rail.

Union general secretary, Shelton Walpole, predicted "total chaos" in London as commuters paralyze the streets with their cars.

The capital was already entering the 2nd week of a subway strike and some of it's bus drivers struck Sunday in sympathy with the railwaymen, one week ahead of there own scheduled strike over salaries.

The move posed the sharpest union challenge yet to Prime Minister Margaret Thatcher's three year-old Conservative government.

6

ACCURACY, CLARITY, AND BREVITY

Editors must be concerned with ensuring accuracy, seeking clarity and promoting brevity. Each is related to the other and none of these concepts can be separated from the editor's daily routine. In this chapter, we will discuss the relative importance of accuracy, clarity and brevity and point out some of the ways in which an editor can work toward including these elements in the news process.

ACCURACY

Accuracy is the most important consideration of an editor. Accuracy is the central reason for much of what an editor does. In the pursuit of accuracy a word of doubtful spelling is checked, one last fact in the story is looked up, or a source is called late at night or early in the morning when parts of a story are in question.

A reputation for accuracy is a publication's most valuable resource. Not only does it inspire the confidence of readers, but an obvious willingness on the part of editors to strive for accuracy opens up new sources of information for the newspaper and often gets the paper out of embarrassing and dangerous legal entanglements. In the final analysis, this reputation for accuracy may be the surest way to ensure the survival of the publication. One example of this which many journalism historians cite is the reputation for reliability which the New York Times built during the "yellow journalism" era. While other papers, especially in New York City, were trying to outdo one another in their sensationalism and outrageousness, the Times remained a calm, thoughtful voice which readers found they could count on. Today, the one New York paper which survives from that era is the New York Times.

No substitute exists for accuracy. Readers are notoriously unwilling to accept the very reasonable excuses that reporters are young and inexperienced, that the newsroom is understaffed or that it was a busy news day; few readers have any concept of what the pressure of deadlines can do to good reporting or editing. What they understand is that a headline did not accurately reflect the content of a story, that the capital city of their home state was misspelled, or that their child was misidentified in the cutline of a picture which included several other children. Readers won't forgive these mistakes, nor will they forget. Just a few errors are enough to get a publication in trouble, damage its credibility and demonstrate to readers that it is unworthy of their attention — and money. Like weeds in a garden, a bad reputation needs no cultivation; all it needs is a start.

For an editor, the pursuit of accuracy is a state of mind. An editor must be willing to check everything he doubts and must be willing to doubt anything. He must cast a cold eye on the work of his reporters, even those with the most experience and best reputation; he must demand an accounting from them as much as from his inexperienced recruits. He must even be willing to doubt his own knowledge and experience and must occasionally re-check what he knows to be true. Such editors may make life hard on themselves and those around them, but their efforts will pay dividends for the good reputation of the publication.

WHAT TO CHECK

Obviously, a newspaper editor cannot check every single fact in a story. (Some magazines, however, take pride in doing just that.) Time pressures will not allow an editor to do this even if the resources were available. Instead, an editor must be alert to the things in a story which are most likely to be wrong. Certain elements of stories should always raise some questions in the minds of editors, and the following is a list of some of those elements.

Names and titles. There is no quicker way for a publication to lose readers than to misspell names. A name is a person's most valuable possession; to misspell it shows an inexcusable sloppiness on the part of the writer and editor. If there is any way possible, names should always be checked for proper spelling. Titles are another element journalists are not as careful about as they should be. An editor should do his best to ensure that titles are checked and correct. Titles, of course, should conform to AP style or the style used by the publication, but otherwise they should be technically correct, e.g., they should be written as those who use them regularly would write them. For instance, most people probably think that a person who teaches at a college or university is a "professor." That title would suffice for most readers, but for those who know better, there is a vast difference between calling someone "professor" and "assistant professor." The journalist should seek technical as well as general accuracy in titles.

Numbers. Any time there are numbers in a story, bells should ring in the head of the editor — especially if those numbers add up to something in the story. This kind of error, an inconsistency in numbers, is very easy to check if the answers are contained in the story, but it is often overlooked. Unfortunately, journalism is filled with people who hate mathematics and are self-professed know-nothings about the subject. They look at numbers, and if they make any assumptions at all, they assume them to be correct. Editors cannot safely make such assumptions. They need to make sure that percentages add up to 100 and that all numbers add up correctly.

Places. Editors should be extremely careful about describing places and place names. To say that something is happening in Nashville when it is really happening in Knoxville or to describe St. Louis as the capital of Missouri or to write that Holland is part of Scandinavia can make a publication look extremely foolish. On the other hand, editors should be more precise than they normally are in pinpointing the location of places mentioned in stories.

The story's inner logic. We have already said that the numbers in a story should add up correctly. So should the facts. Readers should get a good idea of the time sequence of a story even if the facts of the story are not presented in chronological order. Questions raised in one part of the story should be answered in another part of the story. One example of this might be to say in a story, "This building is the third tallest in the state," and not mention the two taller buildings. All of the facts in a story should have a logical relationship to one another — a relationship which the reader can easily discern. Throwing facts into a story without proper transitions and outside a logical sequence presents obstacles to the reader, obstacles which can ultimately decrease his interest in a story or in the publication.

REFERENCES

Certain references will be available to you near almost any copy desk. If you find yourself in a newsroom where these references cannot be found, you should ask your superiors to provide them. Once these references are available, learn to use them efficiently. They are fundamental to doing good work as an editor. They will answer most of the common questions you will encounter, so using them should become automatic.

Five of the basic and commonly used reference are:

Dictionaries. Any person working with words will find a dictionary an indispensible reference work. A newsroom of any size should have a large dictionary for reporters and editors. Smaller dictionaries should be provided to individual editors. Dictionaries are most commonly used to help people spell words correctly, but they can have many more uses. Many dictionaries contain a gazetteer (a dictionary of place names), a glossary of foreign phrases, grammar and punctuation guides, maps, the names, identifications and life spans of famous people and a list of colleges and universities in the U.S.

Atlases. A road atlas and a world atlas are essential to a newsroom. Reporters and editors must locate places and events for their readers. It is especially important for a newpaper to have accurate maps of the area which it covers — preferably a large wall map which can be used by anyone in the newsroom. Such a map can save the newspaper a lot of time (and money) and provide another means of ensuring the accuracy of a story.

Almanacs. Alamanacs provide a wide range of information which can be easily referred to. For instance, an almanac can tell you how many people live in Boise, the members of the Baseball Hall of Fame and the way California voted in the last presidential election. One of the chief advantages of almanacs is that they are relatively up-to-date; many are published on an annual basis. Another advantage is that these annual almanacs are relatively inexpensive. A newspaper operation which cannot be persuaded to purchase more expensive reference material will usually provide an almanac for its copy editors.

Directories. The most common directory is the telephone directory, and these are usually found in most newsrooms. Telephone directories, although they go out-of-date fairly quickly, are easily used to check the spelling of names and other local facts. If a university, large industrial plant or military base is located near the newspaper, chances are these places will have their own telephone directories, and the newspaper office will need a copy of these as well. The next most commonly used directory is the city directory. Sometimes these city directories are expensive, but they are well worth the money. A city directory goes beyond the telephone directory in listing the names of the citizens of a town, their home addresses and telephone numbers, their occupations and places of business and their spouses. In addition, a city directory will have a list of all the addresses in the city, usually listed by street name and number and then telling who the occupant of that address is; a list of the telephone numbers in sequence and to whom the phone is listed; and the officers and proprietors of businesses in the community. A city directory is really indispensible to a serious news operation.

Encyclopedias. Larger news operations will probably have a set of encyclopedias available. These can be extremely useful in providing background information for stories and in checking facts of a less current nature. A good set of encyclopedias can mean an enormous expansion in the ability of the editors to check facts, but they can be an expensive addition to the newsroom. If they are not immediately available, find out where the nearest available set is located, and don't hesitate to use them when you need them.

CLARITY

Accuracy isn't enough. After accuracy, clarity must be one of the chief goals of an editor. Facts which are unclear are of little use to the reader. The English language is extremely versatile, but that versatility can lead to confusion when the language is in the hands of amateurs. Editors must be experts in the language and in the proper and clear structuring of a story. Editors must be on constant guard against writing or story structures which could be confusing to the reader.

Like the pursuit of accuracy, the pursuit of clarity is a state of mind for the editor. It must be constantly with him, and he must make sure that everything he does in some way promotes the clarity of the copy with which he is working. An editor must look at a story with a fresh mind — one that is unencumbered with too much knowledge of the subject. He must, like the reader, approach a story as one who was not there and did not see it happen and who has not talked with anyone about it. This approach is doubly difficult for an editor who may in fact know a great deal about the story's subject. Editing for clarity demands a rare degree of mental discipline on the part of the editor.

The opposite of clarity is confusion. Confusion can infiltrate a story in many ways, and it is the editor's responsibility to eliminate this confusion. The chief source of confusion is often the reporter who does not understand what he is writing about. If a writer does not understand his subject, it is highly unlikely that he will be able to write about it so that other people can understand it. Reporters rarely recognize this shortcoming, however, and it is up to the clear-eyed, clear-minded editor to point it out and to do something about it.

CLARITY IN WRITING

Clear writing is an art but it is also a skill. Expressing thoughts, ideas and facts in a clear way is one of the most difficult jobs a writer has — even though his product may read as if the clarity were easily accomplished. The mind moves much faster than we can write or even type. Thoughts can be easily jumbled and so can writing. The key to clear writing is understanding the subject we are writing about. When a writer can express his thoughts about a subject in clear terms, then that understanding has been achieved.

The following are some tips for helping writers and editors achieve clarity in their writing:

Keep it simple. Many people believe that they can demonstrate their intelligence by using complex terms (like terminology). Their language, they feel, will show others that they have mastered a difficult subject or that they speak or write with authority. Consequently, they use big words and complex sentences to express the simplest ideas.

The problem with this attitude is that people forget their original purpose for writing — to communicate ideas. Any writing which draws attention to itself, and thus draws attention away from the content, is ineffective. Writing, especially in the mass media, should be as simple and straightforward as possible. Reporters and editors should use simple terms and sentence structures. They should avoid piling adjectives and phrases on top of one another. They should do this, not in order to talk down to their readers, but to transmit ideas and facts as efficiently as possible.

Avoid all kinds of jargon — even your own. Jargon is specialized language which almost all groups in society develop. Students, baseball managers, doctors and gardeners use words that have special meaning for them and no one else. Journalists are not doing their jobs if they simply record jargon, however accurately, and give it back to the reader. Today's journalists must be translators. They must understand the jargon of different groups they cover but must be intelligent enough not to use it in their stories. Editors, too, must keep a watch out for the jargon which can slip into stories. Phrases like "viable alternative," "optimum care," and "personnel costs" must be made to mean something by journalists. They cannot simply thrust them on the reader and believe that he has done his job adequately.

Be specific. Journalists must set the stage of the story for his reader. They must make sure that the readers have a clear picture in their minds of what is going on, when it is happening, where it is happening and how it is taking place. A reporter or editor cannot assume that readers know very much about the stories they write and edit. They cannot get by with telling readers that it was a "large crowd" or a "long line" or a "beautiful girl." Stories are built on facts, little facts and big facts. Sometimes it is the little facts which will make the difference in whether or not a reader understands a story.

Readers who have not seen what reporters have seen won't know what they are talking about. One aspect of this problem occurs with the use of "the," especially by more inexperienced reporters. For example, a lead may begin in the following way, "City council tonight approved funds for purchasing the new computer system for the finance department." A reader is likely to ask, "What new computer system?" While covering the story, the reporter kept hearing everyone talk about "the new computer system," so that's what appeared in the story. Editors particularly need to watch for this kind of assumption and to make sure that readers are not left behind by what a reporter writes.

Check the time sequence. Most news stories will not be written in chronological order, but readers should have some idea of the narrative sequence of the events in a story. When the time sequence is not clear, readers may become confused and misunderstand the content of the story.

Transitions. Transitions are necessary for smooth, graceful and clear writing. Each sentence in a story should logically follow the previous sentence or should relate to it in some way. New information in a story should be connected to information already introduced. Readers who suddenly come upon new information or a new subject in a story without the proper transition will be jolted and confused. The following first paragraphs of a story about the high costs of weddings will serve to illustrate the point about transitions:

The nervous young man drops to one knee, blushes and asks that all important question.

What about all the planning involved in a wedding, from reserving the church to choosing the honeymoon site? June and July are the traditional months for making the big decision, according to Milton Jefferson of the Sparkling Jewelry Store.

Jefferson said most engagements last from seven to 16 months.

A woman sometimes receives a ring that has been passed down through her fiancee's family for generations, or maybe her boyfriend has bought an estate ring. . . .

The lead assumes that the reader will know what "that all important question" is. This assumption might be acceptable if the second paragraph followed the lead properly, but it doesn't. Instead it plunges the reader into the subject of planning a wedding; the reader has no indication from the lead that this is coming next — and what happened to "that all important question"?

In a similar manner, the second sentence of the second paragraph introduces yet another new subject to the reader, again without the proper transition. The reader is taken from a question about planning to the traditionally popular months for weddings with no connection being made between them. In addition, the attribution forces the reader to make another transition. The reader must say, "The man is a jewelry store owner. Jewelry stores sell wedding rings. The jewelry store owner is then an authority about when weddings occur."

The third paragraph introduces yet another new subject — the length of engagements. Again, the reader has no transition. Merely bombardment by one fact after another.

The fourth paragraph talks about how prospective brides attain their wedding rings. What has this information got to do with what has just been said? The writer has left it to the reader to figure it all out. The writer has said ,"My story is about weddings. Therefore, anything I put in my story about weddings is okay."

It's not just the writer's fault, however. It was an editor who let this story get into print — without having a proper consideration for the reader. Editors are just as responsible for seeing that these things do not happen as writers.

BREVITY

"Brevity is the soul of wit," according to Polonius, Shakespeare's ill-fated character in "Hamlet." Polonius was in reality one of Shakespeare's most verbose personalities. Words came tumbling out of his mouth. He went on and on. Not only was he verbose, he was boring. Polonious was one of those people you try to avoid at parties and hope you don't have to take long car rides with. He talked too much.

Publications can do the same thing. They can use too many words, piling phrase upon phrase and letting the sentences run on far after the thoughts have run out. They put too many words in the way of what really needs to be said.

Editors need to recognize when writers are being long-winded. They should remove the well-turned phrase that is unnecessary and eliminate that which has already been stated. The process can go too far, of course. Accuracy and clarity should never be sacrificed for brevity's sake, but brevity should be another major goal in the mind of the editor.

Many editors approach editing a story thinking that it deserves to be a certain length and no longer. Sometimes a writer writes 300 words and an editor wants only 200. How does one go about paring such a story down? Here are some tips:

Get to the point. What is the story about? What happened? What does the story need to tell the reader? An editor needs to be able to answer those questions in the simplest terms possible. Answering those questions is sometimes the hardest part of writing or editing, but once that is done, the writing or editing job can become much easier.

Watch for redundancies and repetitions. Redundancies show a lack of disciplined thinking. They slip into writing unnoticed, but their presence can make the most important stories seem silly. Repetition is also an indication that the editor was not concentrating on the story. Sometimes facts need to be repeated for clarity's sake, but this is not often the case.

Cut out the unnecessary words. There may be words in a story that simply add nothing to the meaning of the story. These words are hard to pin down, but a sharp-eyed editor can spot them. They are words like "really," "very" and "actually." They're simply phrase-makers, but they don't tell the reader very much.

Finally, when you have run out of things to write about, stop writing.

EXERCISES

ACCURACY AND LOGIC

Edit the following story. The story contains a number of inaccuracies and inconsistencies which you will need to correct. The list of questions after the story will help you spot some of these.

Convicted murder and rapist Jimmy Allen appeared at a news conference at the state penitentiary in the state capital tonight and disavowed all efforts to save his life today.

He said he is ending his five years of appeals and is "ready to die" for his sins.

Allen, convicted three years ago of raping and murdering the wife of a Greenback grocery store owner and then later killing her husband, lost his final appeal for a stay of execution from the state's highest court, the U.S. Court of Criminal Appeals, last week.

Since that time, Allen said at a news conference just a few feet away from the state prison's gas chamber, he has "made peace with the Lord" and is ready to pay for his crimes.

Allen is scheduled to die in the electric chair at midnight on Sunday night.

Meanwhile, David Lauver, an attorney with the state chapter of the American Civilian Liberties Union, said he was preparing another appeal to the State Supreme Court and an appeal for clememcy to the governor.

"We don't believe the state should be in the business of killing people," Lauver said. "We are appealing on the grounds that the death penalty is cruel and unusual punishment." Lauver said the Sixth Amendment prohibits that.

Allen disavowed the ACLU petitions, however, and told newsmen that he would "rather die than spend the rest of my life in prison."

John Clark, the prosecutor in the Allen case, said last night he was "glad this appeals business was over" and hoped that the execution would be carried out on schedule. "No one likes to see anyone die, but if anyone ever deserves to, this man does," he says.

Check on the following questions concerning this story:

1. What is the state capital?
2. What is the state's highest court?

3. What method of execution is used?
4. What does ACLU stand for?
5. What does the Sixth Amendment say about cruel and unusual punishment?

ACCURACY AND LOGIC

This story contains at least three internal inconsistencies. Edit the story to clear these up and to correct any other errors.

Seven years aftehr Italy's deadliest terrorist attack, the last two suspects are being freed from prison because the government has failed to win any convictions in the case.

The release today of alleged rightist extremists Giovanni Ventura and Franco Freda has remewed public debate on the problems iwth the Italian justice system and the governments ability to deal with terrorism effectively.

Forty persons, including suspected extremists from the right and left, were arrested as a result of the Dec. 12, 1869 bombing of a bank on Milan's Piazza Fontana. the attack killed 17 persons and injured about 80.

Only one suspect remains in prison - a former agent of the Italisan intelligience service who was arrested last month. Legal maneuvers, public demonstrations, three abortive trial and other complications have delayed resolution of the case and many of the defenders have fled abroad.

Ventura and Mr. Freda were oredered released after serving the maximum four years of preventive detention, benefiting from a change in Italy's bail laws that came about because of a challenge from another defendant in the case.

The two men have been allowed to live in exile on the tine resort island of Giglio.

They also have been charged with 19 other bombings attacks on trains, dempartment stores and public buildings in what invistagators said was an attempt to create choas that would promote instillation of a leftest dictatorship.

CLARITY, LOGIC, AND CONSISTENCY

The following story has problems with clarity, logic, and internal consistency. Read through the story, correct any errors you find, and try to make the facts of the story consistent and logical.

Mr. James R. Ward, 66, of 23,323 W. Fifth St., died today at Druid City Hospital after an extended period of convalescence.

Mrs. Ward, who was born in Guntrsville, Tenn., in 1910 had lived in Tuscaloosa since she moved here with her husband in 1923. She was an active member of the First Baptist Church of Northport and had worked since 1952 as an acquition clerk at the University library until she became ill last year.

Mrs. Ward's husband was born in Tuscaloosa and was a brick mason here. Mrs. Ward met her husband in Chicago where she was attending the University of Chicago. They were married Jan. 5, 1928.

Mrs. Ward is survived by her husband; three children. Donald Williamson os Westville, Tenn., Rebacka Ward of Orange, Fla., and Mrs. John Williamson of Des Moines, and three grand children, JanBill and Winston Williamson of DesMoines.

Funeral Services are pending with the Brosh Funeral Home of Tuscaloosa.

USING REFERENCE MATERIAL

You should be able to answer each of these questions or check each of these facts using the reference materials available to you in your editing laboratory or your library. What are the sources you would use to answer each?

1. How many barrels of oil did the United States import in 1977 and which country supplied most of the oil to the U.S. that year?

2. Imagine that there has been a robbery at 1611 Main Street (or any address your instructor gives you) and your managing editor has told you that your newspaper cannot get any information from the police and that reporters have been barred from the scene. He wants you to call a neighbor right now and find out all you can. Get the neighbor's name and telephone number.

3. A caller has told the city desk that he has some information that needs to be given to the public. He says he can't talk now, but that if you will call him in 30 minutes he will reveal some important information. The editor wants to know the guy's name and asks you to help. He gives you the telephone number: 752-7527 (or a number supplied by your instructor). Whose telephone number is that and where does that person live? What kind of work does the person do?

4. Where is Eclectic, Ala.?

5. What are the names of the associate professors of English at your university?

6. Jimmy Carter was the 43rd president of the United States. — True or False?

7. What year was your university founded?

8. What year was your city incorporated?

9. How many churches are in your city?

10. How many weekly newspapers does your state have? How many dailies?

11. Who is editor of the state's largest newspaper?

DICTIONARY USAGE

Choose the correct word or change the incorrect usage in these sentences.

1. About 1,954 fans saw the game (some 50 odd more than last year).
2. All of the bandits carried weapons. Between the three of them, they had five pistols.
3. After the man (confessed to the crime, admitted his guilt) the prosecutor asked him to sign a written (confession, admission).
4. The officer literally leaped up the three flights of stairs in a single bound.
5. Television is a media with more power than newspapers.
6. He was (meticulous, careful)--never too fast and never too slow.
7. The city council decided on buying the new equipment at its meeting.
8. The school board's vote is expected to be a (precipitate, precipitous) action.
9. While the total number of persons running is not known, the present incumbent is expected to be one of them.
10. The conquering army (ravaged, ravished) the city after seizing it.
11. The vice-president called him a (proven, proved) friend.
12. During almost 12 hours and for five attacks, the entrenched soldiers (repelled, repulsed) the enemy.
13. (Regretfully, Regretably) the meeting came to an end before the student reached the room with the critical information.
14. During the auto accident he recieved a broken leg, sustained a broken arm and was hit over the head with fragments of the windshield.
15. Suddenly, the eagle zoomed down upon the unsuspecting rodent.
16. Not only was the road steep, it was (tortuous, torturous) as well.
17. He won a (majority, plurality) of the 500 votes cast with his total of 208.
18. When they married, they promised to love (each other, one another).
19. The Canon is not that (different from, different than) the Nikon.
20. He had planned the murder very carefully. He obviously had gone (berserk, amuck).
21. Both the union and the company agreed to abide by the decision of the (arbitrator, mediator).
22. The jumbo jet collided with the mountain just after takeoff.
23. Irregardless of the consequences, the president decided to make the recomendation.
24. The Hebrew people speak Jewish.
25. He (persuaded, convinced) them to follow him.

CLARITY

Clarify this story either by editing or rewriting it.

Charles Jones, 18, blind since birth, son of Mr. and Mrs. Frank Jones, 1207 5th St., was being driven by frind, Ted Hanson, 20, 307 Washington St., past pond on Fairview Road near intersection of Laurel Drive. The two heard cries for help coming from the pond in woods west of Fairview. Frank Smithe, 10, son of Mr. Mrs. James Smi Smithe, 107Laurle Dr., had been playing on a raft in the pond and had fallen in. Ted can't swim. Charles, a stron swimmer, plunged into the pond despite the cold and guided by Ted's shouts instructions from shore found the boy. He had to dive to bring him up, and pulled him ashore. Ted helped pull him out adn gave him artificial respiration He had revived by the time fire department with respiration equipment arrived.

Young Smithe was in Mercy Hospital in good condition this morning.

"I thought I was a goner until I felt him grab me under the water," Ted said. He is an only child.

Ted's father said, "We are eternally grateful to him. It was a corageous thing to do."

CLARITY: TRANSITIONS

The following story has a number of problems, particularly with clarity of the language and transitions. Edit the story to reduce these problems and make sure the story conforms to AP style.

A young Bull's Gap man who in 1980 pleaded guilty to breaking into an automobile and drew a 10-year prison sentence has filed a petition acting as his own attorney charing a judge with improper conduct that allegedly deprived him of a fiar trial.

Jerry Gene McBay was 19 in November of 1980 when he was charged with a felony count of breaking and entering an automobile. He and a friend were accused of cutting a car's radiator hose late at night in the parking lot of the Double Portion Church of Christ on Old Sawmill Road.

A chase by witnesses ensued and the two were soon arrested, records showed.

McBay was sented to ten years' imprisonment by Judge A.S. Snider for the crime after being denied youth ful offendor status and probation by the judge. Charges against the other youth were dropped. Records showed that McBay had one previous conviction, for disorderly conduct, although he has had other criminal charged placed against him.

In his 13-page hand-written petition, McBay claims that Snider was "close to" the victim in the case through membership in the same church, that Watson acted improperly in rejected a prosecutor's recommendation for a lesser sentence after plea bargaining in the case, that the judge mishandled the attempted admission of evidence relating to the severity of McBay's sentence and that Snider has a family connection with the school arson case that he said was brought against him for political reasons.

"When my recommendations are refused, I prepare to go to trial because I assume that is all I can do," said Assistant District Attorney Tim Stoner, who brought the petition to the court after it was mailed to him by McBay from aprison in Starkville where he is serving his sentence.

Stoner explained the he was the prosecutor in the case and that he had recommended McBay be sentenced to a year and a day in prison for the offense, but that his recommendation was rejected by Snider.

BREVITY AND CLARITY

The following story needs to be tightened and made clearer for the reader. Make sure it conforms to AP style.

A private economic research organization has announced the findings of its latest study which shows that the biggest growth in new jobs and population over the next 20 years will take place in Texas, California and Florida.

The Wyatt Insitute of Environmental Studies has announced that its study is based on numerous federal and state government figures and statistics, as well as those from many of the major private industries operating in this country.

The study results indicate that a total of 20 per cent of the American workforce will be employed in those three states by the year 2000.

The three states will account for 8.4 million of the 30 million new jobs to be created in the next two decades, the association said, and for about 30 percent of the projected population increase during that period.

The association estimates that the recorded 226.5 million in 1980 population of the United States, will grow by 40 million by the year 2000. Texas will gain the most in terms of population, by adding to it population 5.5 million people, it added.

The smallest increase in jobs — a total of 130,000 over the next 20 years — will occur in the District of Columbia, Delaware and Vermont, said the association.

The biggest growth in jobs in the next two decades will take place in services, trade, communications and finance, it said.

BREVITY

The following story is too wordy. Edit the copy in order to tighten the writing. Be sure to check for style and other errors.

The Trenton School District will attempt to develop a special training program under the federal manpower development act.

The board approved the program Wednesday night on the request of Charles Orson, director of vocational education. Orson explained that the program, which could accomodate up to 250 adults, would be designed to help them increase their working skill level.

Orson said the new program would receive funds from federal sources for the purchase of the equipment. the trainess would recive money to encourage their affiliation with a long-term training plan.

The school district instituted the special program to retrain workers displaced from jobs in the closing of the former Grant Industries plant.

BREVITY

The following story is too wordy. Edit the copy in order to tighten the writing. Be sure to check for style and other errors.

Lester Wilkerson, fire marshal for Taylor County, says that the majority of field fires in the county are the result of direct carelessness.

The Hamilton Fire Co. has received a total of 50 field fire calls since last Saturday.

The fire marshal siad people are aware of the dry nature of brush but act foolishly with open fires. A stiff wind and unattended trash fires caused a number of the field fires. Others started when someone tried to burn off dry grass areas and high winds whipped the fires out of control.

7

WIRE COPY

In addition to the copy available to the newspaper through the work of the local reporting staff, the editor must deal with copy from other sources. Among the most important of these sources are the news services. Two types of news services provide copy: the wire services and the syndicated news services.

THE WIRE SERVICES

Wire copy can be a unique asset to the newspaper. It provides national and international news that most newspapers could ill afford to obtain in any other way. It provides information that is timely, generally reliable, well written, and informed.

In addition, the wire services provide supplemental services designed to aid a variety of news organizations. For example, the major wire services provide photo news services, including black and white and full four-color separations of photographs. They also provide radio news feeds and broadcast services for television clients. They provide a number of specialized wire feeds dealing with sports, finance, features, and regional news coverage.

In the United States, three types of wire services exist. One, the Associated Press (AP), is a cooperative news service. News organizations that buy the AP's service become members of the cooperative. Whatever one member of the cooperative publishes may be picked up by the AP and distributed to the rest of the members of the cooperative. In this way, the AP maintains a powerful method of collecting information in the United States which it can then provide to other members of the cooperative.

In addition to this means of gathering information, the AP hires its own correspondents and maintains bureaus throughout the United States and the world that add to the stories developed through local publications and provide information not found in the columns of local newspapers.

The second domestic wire service in the United States, United Press International (UPI), sells its news services to customers without a cooperative arrangement. UPI has no special privilege to redistribute information being published by the news organizations buying its services. It may pick up information in the public domain but must buy other information from local correspondents.

Like the Associated Press, UPI maintains an extensive worldwide network of bureaus and of reporters and editors assigned to those bureaus. But without cooperative memberships, it has a smaller organization upon which to draw in the United States. This difference does not hold true outside the United States, however.

The result of the differences in these two wire services is a healthy rivalry that has produced benefits for newspapers and broadcast news organizations in the United States.

The third type of wire service in the United States is exemplified by the New York Times News Service. It is a service based upon the news gathering capabilities of the New York Times organization with its worldwide network of respected correspondents. It distributes news in a manner similar to that of the AP and UPI and is a service-providing organization, not a cooperative. The New York Times News Service is only one example of this type of service. Others are maintained by the Los Angeles Times-Washington Post News Service and several newspaper groups.

In addition to the domestic wire services, several foreign wire services are available in the United States. Two of the most popular are Reuters News Service, based in Great Britain, and Agence France Presse, based in France.

HOW WIRE SERVICES WORK

A wire service is a network of news-gathering agents tied together through a system of communication that permits them to distribute information quickly throughout the world. Typically, the headquarters of the organization are tied to regional centers, which are in turn tied to local bureaus, which are tied to local customers. Information is distributed instantaneously by a central computer to the regional and local bureaus and thus to customers. Information collected by the agents of the organization is sent forward from the local bureaus to the headquarters by means of a bureau wire which is not available to customers.

This system permits editing to be done by the local bureau and again by the national headquarters. The result is that copy distributed to local news customers is generally well written and edited.

The wire services generally work on two shifts, an A.M. cycle and a P.M. cycle. It is important for the local editor to keep this distinction in mind, for each cycle will begin by sending versions of news stories that may have moved on the previous cycle. Local editors must always note whether different takes of stories being compiled are from the same cycle. Stories from different cycles generally are not compiled into a single story and if they are, such compiling must be done with special care.

SPECIAL PROBLEMS OF EDITING WIRE COPY

Even though wire copy is generally well written, local copy editors should remember that it is written and edited in the same way as copy produced by local reporters. It is subject to the same kinds of errors. Many students and young editors have a tendency to stand in awe of wire service copy. Some even doubt that they should change obvious mistakes which they find in wire service stories. Wire service copy should not be treated in this way. It needs the same hard-nosed examination the editor would give local copy.

In fact, several factors make wire copy subject to special kinds of errors for which the local editor should be particularly careful to check.

For one thing, wire copy is written quickly and under pressure. The local editor should exercise even more caution than might be required with local copy. While wire copy generally is edited several times before it appears on the local video display terminal (VDT) or hard copy printer, the medium is uniquely subject to errors produced when that process is abbreviated by the force of deadline pressure.

Another problem is that wire copy is filed (or written) in short takes and pieced together by local editors and by wire service editors. This piecing together can result in redundancies, omissions of important detail, and contradictions in what appears in the copy.

THE SLUG LINE

One of the most important tasks the copy editor must face in dealing with wire copy is the problem of compiling the bits and pieces of a single wire copy story into a unified whole. The wire services try to keep their customers current by sending information as they get it. Since breaking stories rarely break all at once, this means that the wire services are constantly updating, adding to, and correcting stories that have been sent. The key to the successful completion of this task is the slug line and its accompanying explanatory lines.

In order to use the slug line correctly, it is important to understand some basic terms used to describe bits and pieces of copy and to examine how these bits and pieces are assembled into a unified story.

Here, for example, is a typical slug line.

B005di *AM-Focus-Andropov, Bjt,2 Takes,450-860* 000022781

First is the number appearing at the beginning of the story: B005di. The wire services refer to this number as the "code" for the story. The code will indicate which wire the story is sent on, its priority, and its basic news category. Each story will be assigned a number according to the sequence in which it is sent by each shift of wire service editors.

The letter "B" refers to the fact that this is an advance on a news story. The number "005" means that this was the fifth story sent on this cycle. The letter "d" refers to the priority of the story (in this case a deferred priority). The letter "i" refers to the category of news in which the story falls (in this case an international story).

Second, each story is identified by a word called the "keyword slug line" appearing at the top of the story. The slug line will be the same on all versions of all the bits and pieces of the story. In our example, the keyword slug line is "AM-Focus-Andropov 450-860." All the bits of the story may be assembled by collecting all the takes having the same slug regardless of code number. In this example, the letters "AM" refer to the fact that this story was sent on the A.M. cycle for publication in morning newspapers. "Focus-Andropov" is the name given to the story. The numbers "450-860" represent the estimated numbers of words in the first take of the story (450) and in the total story, including all takes (860).

Third, the slug line will be followed by a "version section" specifying whether the story was budgeted, how many takes of the story are expected to run, and the approximate word count expected for the story. These version lines include "adds," or additional takes of the story; "leads," or new lead paragraphs, which should be substituted for existing lead paragraphs; "inserts," or material inserted into the middle of existing stories; "substitutions," or material to be substituted for existing words, sentences, or paragraphs of a story; "corrections," or material to be substituted for incorrect material in an existing story; and "write-thru," or a rewrite of an entire story which is supposed to include all updating material sent during the cycle up to that time so that the write-thru serves as a complete new story.

The version section may also include advisories, or messages to editors sent to keep them informed of developments in a breaking story, KILLs, or instructions not to use a story; WITHHOLDs, or instructions to use only part of a story; and ELIMINATIONs, or instructions to eliminate certain parts of a story.

The version section in our example is "Bjt,2 Takes." The letters "Bjt" refer to the fact that the story was "budgeted," or listed on the news digest and planned for the day's news coverage. The "2 Takes" means that the story will appear on the wire in two parts.

Each of these bits may be further broken down by specifying whether they are first, second, third, etc., versions of whatever instruction is being sent. For instance, one may have a first, second, or third, lead or a first, second, or third, etc., insert to a first, second, or third lead, and so forth.

The important thing for the copy editor to do is to keep straight which take, which lead, and so forth he or she is dealing with. Then the editor must keep the story up to date while compiling. The editor must also be careful to monitor the wire in order to make sure the wire service editor does not become confused and send a take that is mislabeled.

The slug line may also be followed by (1) a "reference number" section, which refers the editor to earlier versions of the story by citing the numbers of earlier versions of the story; (2) a "datarecap" section on the high-speed transmission wire, which puts together the pieces of an item for easier handling; and (3) a "format identifier" section, which specifies a story intended for agate and/or tabular material.

Once all the bits of the story have been collected, the process of assembling them into a unified whole may begin.

ASSEMBLING THE STORY

In compiling the bits and pieces of a complex, breaking story into a unified whole, the editor should begin with the most recent complete version of the story. This may be either the original story or the most recent write-thru.

The editor should next assemble all the other pieces of the story that follow that benchmark. On electronic editing devices this may be done by assembling a menu or index of the stories labeled with the appropriate slug. In our example, the slug line menu for the Andropov story might look like this:

```
i005d     1 int     0227 Focus-Andropov1 15.9
i006d     1 int     0227 Focus-Andropov1 14.0
```

In hard copy editing, this must be done by assembling the typed versions of the story.

Once the relevant versions have been assembled, the construction of the story begins.

The editor should begin to update the benchmark story by placing each new version of the story onto the original in the order in which they were sent, following the instructions on the copy itself.

Thus, when a new lead is sent, the editor should note which paragraph of the benchmark story provides the pickup for the new lead and should replace the original lead with the new one, eliminating all the paragraphs of the original story preceding the pickup.

Each of the other versions — adds, inserts, subs, corrections, etc. — will likewise specify which paragraphs are to be eliminated and where the pickups are to be made. The editor should follow the order in which the stories are sent, at least until he or she has a thorough knowledge of how the copy flow proceeds. If the order is not followed, the story may not fit together properly, because the number of the paragraphs to be eliminated or picked up will be specified according to the most recent version of the story.

THE SYNDICATED NEWS SERVICES

Some twenty-five syndicated services offer a variety of news and features to local newspapers throughout the United States. These services send their material by the U.S. mail, and thus it is not as timely as the news offered by the wire services.

Syndicated services provide comics, graphics, photos, features, columns, editorials, news, and virtually every other content type published by daily newspapers.

As with wire services, the content of these materials is usually well written and well edited. In fact, with the additional time available to syndicated services to prepare the material for distribution, there is somewhat less danger of error due to deadline pressure.

However, the syndicated news and feature services are subject to the kinds of errors to which all copy is subject and some other errors as well.

Particularly critical for local editors is the danger that syndicated copy may be out of date. This is particularly distributed relevant to material distributed by syndicated services. While this copy usually is written so as to minimize this danger, it is up to the local copy editor to make sure that nothing has transpired between the time the copy was written and the time it is edited to change the thrust of the content of the copy.

Besides the issue of currency, it is up to the local copy editor to develop relevance to the day's events when handling syndicated copy.

LOCALIZING NEWS SERVICE COPY

Wire copy and syndicated copy share one type of problem that only the perceptive copy editor can solve. This is the problem of making copy written at a distant location relevant to a local reader.

The good local copy editor should be constantly on the lookout for ways to localize wire copy and syndicated copy in order to establish relevance to a local community. This may sometimes mean referring copy to the local news desk for the addition of local information that may demonstrate the impact of a national story on a local community. More often it requires that a knowledgeable copy editor simply add a few sentences or paragraphs reminding readers of local events. Sometimes it requires a couple of telephone calls to provide local facts demonstrating what a national story can mean in a local community.

CONCLUSION

News services provide a dimension to the local newspaper that most modern readers would be unwilling to forgo and that most editors find provides a well-balanced package for their readers.

However, the news services also must be viewed by the editor as another source of information contributing to the overall newspaper. This information, like any other, must be edited to fit the editorial objectives of the newspaper. The editor cannot forget that the editorial policies of the newspaper must control how wire copy is edited and handled to fit local needs.

EXERCISES

EDITING WIRE COPY

Edit the wire story below. Make sure that it conforms to AP style.

B115unPM-Gun Law,180 000080481

Council Bans 'Garden Variety' Gunfire In City

AUBURN (AP) — The Auburn City Council has voted to ban certain gunfire in the citylimits, even if its of the "garden variety."

The council, on a five to two vote Tuesday night, struck down a local law that allowed residents to get a permitt to fire guns in the city. The old law was supported largly by gardeners who fired at pesky squirels and other varments raiding their vegetable patches.

More than a dozen of the gardeners, mostly retirees who have watch-dogged their gardens for years, urged the council not to change the law. They said no one has ever been hurt and that they use proper caution when firing at animals.

But others said the practice is a potential hazard. One Resident, Ed Williamson, said a bullet once whizzed past his head.

Councilman Joe Tremaine said he didn't want to wait until some one was hurt to find a reason to change the law.

The action makes it illegal to discharge a weapon except in self-defense. Law enforcement officials also will continue to have sanction to fire weapons in the scope of their duties.

ap-ax-08-04-82 1041edt

EDITING WIRE COPY

Edit the wire story below. Make sure that it conforms to AP style.

B076raPM-Snipers, Bjt,300 000062481

Three Family Members Killed, One Injured In Sniper Attack Laserphotos NS1,2

COLUMBIA, Tenn. (AP) — Two men were charged today with killing 3 members of a family and wounding a 4th in a sniper attack as the victims fished from a sandbar on the Duck River, authorities said.

William Carroll Kelley, 21, and Phillip wayne Kelley, 19, both of Columbia, were charged with three counts each of first-degree murder and one count each of asault with intent to committmurder in the Wednesday evening shootings, deputies said.

Both Kelley's, who told police they were not related, were being held in the Maury County Jail pending a plea hearing today in Maury County General Sessions Court, about 40 miles south of Nashville.

Judge Jimmy Matthews refused bond on the murder counts and set a one hundred thousand dollar bond for each on the assault charge.

J.T. Estes, 56, a truck driver, was shot in the chest and right arm and reported in satisfacory condition today at Maury County Hospital, officials said.

Estes' wife, Hazel, described as in her late 50s, her son Gary and his wife Diane, both said to be in their late 20s, both were shot to death as they scrambled up a steep, wooded hillside at Vaughn's Landing where the family had been fishing, authorities said.

Sheriff William Voss said as many as four other people believed to be related to the family were also fishing but escaped the gun fire and called police from a nearby convenience store.

Voss said William Kelley was a run-away as a juvenile "and the kind of boy who liked to camp out. He said he didn't know Phillip Kelley.

A purse belonging to one of the women was found 200 yards up river near a campsite, leading investigators to include robbery as a possible motive, Voss said.

"We found spent ammunition from behind two trees high above the river," he said. Two .22-calibre rifles were found hidden in the bushes near the scene, said Chief Deputy Wade Matheny.

ap-ax-06-24-82 0653edt

WIRE STORY, LOCAL INFORMATION

The wire story below has been transmitted to your newspaper. In addition to the story, one of the paper's reporters calls in the information below the story from his police beat phone. Compile the two sets of information into a single story.

B090unPM-Escapes,110 000062481
State Prisoner Disappears From Work Release Center

ALEXANDER CITY (AP) — After apparently playing possum, a state prisoner disappeared early today from the work release center here.

A state prison spokesman, Ron Tate, said Garry L. Thompson, 26, "was last seen at 1:30 a.m. in his bunk, supposedly asleep but apparently playing possum. Half an hour later he was unavailable for the head count."

Dogs from Draper Prison were brought in to help state and local officers hunt for Thompson.

The escapee was serving a total of 29 years on convictions of forgery, robbery and possession of burglary tools. The sentences were handed down in last December.

ap-ax-06-24-82 0806edt

Reporter's information: Thompson is a local man; convicted by jury in local circuit court. Thompson's attorney, J. Randolph Murphy, says appeals of some of Thompson's convictions have been pending before the state court; said Thompson has been a model prisoner but had become frustrated with the time it has taken for the appeals to be complete. "He's basically a good man, just misguided. I hope for his sake he will be apprehended soon and that things won't go to hard on him."

County Sheriff Bledsoe Shots says his department is helping state officials in the search. "We think there's a good chance he might try to come back here. His mother is still living here, and he may try to get in touch with her." The sheriff wouldn't say just what his department is doing to help in the search. "We don't really consider him dangerous, but we're being real careful."

COMPILING A STORY

Compile the takes below into a single story by following the instructions at the beginning and end of each take. Note the time each take was transmitted.

B069riPM-Israeli Invasion, Bjt, 2 takes,450-750 000062481
URGENT Laserphoto NY5 By MICHAEL GOLDSMITH Associated Press Writer

BEIRUT, Lebanon (AP) — Israeli and Syrian tanks and artillery battled in the mountains overlooking Beirut today in a struggle for control of the key Beirut-Damascus highway, as Israeli jets blasted Palestinian positions around Beirut airport.

The Israelis and their Syrian and Palestinian foes accused each other for the third day running of breaking a U.S.-sponsored cease-fire that has virtually ceased to exist.

The Israeli armored forces in the mountains appeared to be trying to consolidate their grip on a 20-mile stretch of the highway linking the Lebanese and Syrian capitals in an effort to bar the Syrians from bringing up supplies and reinforcements for a possible battle for Beirut.

The Christian Phalangist-run Voice of Lebanon radio station said the artillery battle resumed soon after dawn along the Bhamdoun-Mdeirej sector of the highway east of Beirut.

The Syrians fired Katyusha rockets into Israeli lines and the Israelis replied with an air strike, destroying the rocket launchers, the radio said.

In Tel Aviv, the Israeli military command gave a similar account, saying its forces were replying to a Syrian rocket and artillery bombardment begun just after dawn.

A Palestinian communique said an "intense battle" was raging between Mansouriyeh and Bhamdoun, east of the capital. It claimed the Israelis lost 80 soldiers killed and 17 tanks and one armored personnel carrier destroyed in the past 24 hours. There were no accounts of Palestinian or Syrian casualties.

Israel reported seven soldiers killed and 95 wounded in fighting in Lebanon Tuesday and Wednesday.

Today's clashes came one day after a car-bomb killed 50 people in predominantly Moslem west Beirut, where the U.S. Embassy closed and urged Americans to flee.

In Jerusalem, Israel's Cabinet was reportedly anguishing over whether to order an invasion of west Beirut, where 8,000 guerrillas loyal to Palestine Liberation Organization chief Yasser Arafat are entrenched in bunkers, buildings and refugee slums, vowing a bloodbath if Israeli troops invade.

Hundreds of Israeli women demonstrated outside the Parliament in Jerusalem Wednesday demanding an end to Israel's 19-day-old Lebanon invasion, claiming it would only bring sorrow and disaster to the Jewish state.

Fighting Wednesday also spread to the Syrian-dominated Bekaa Valley, in eastern Lebanon, where Israeli forces beat back a Syrian drive to retake Israeli-held territory around Lake Qaaroun, 25 miles east of Beirut, the Tel Aviv command said.

MORE
ap-ax-06-24-82 0612edt
B070riPM-Israeli Invasion, 1st add,300 000062481
BEIRUT: command said.

The clashes shattered a cease-fire arranged earlier this week by U.S. special envoy Philip C. Habib, who has been in Lebanon meeting with the nation's Council of National Salvation. The council, composed of feuding factional leaders, is attempting to get Israeli, Syrian and PLO forces to disengage.

Habib was to fly to Israel later today to confer with Prime Minister Menachem Begin.

The car-bomb Wednesday night blew up a six-story apartment block in west Beirut and detonated a Palestinian ammunition dump inside, Lebanese television said. Police said the primary and secondary explosions killed 50 people, wounded many more and spread a raging fire through the neighborhood.

No one claimed responsibility for the blast.

While Israeli warplanes screamed overhead, Americans lined up with other foreign nationals Wednesday in the Christian-held coastal town of Jounieh, 10 miles north of Beirut, to await passage to safety today. A vessel from the U.S. 6th Fleet and a British transport planned to take evacuees to Cyprus, 100 miles west in the Mediterranean Sea.

U.S. officials said Wednesday they were closing the U.S. Embassy building in west Beirut because of increased risks of destruction. About 300 U.S. passport holders were still believed to be in the embattled sector.

Israel invaded Lebanon June 6 in an operation it said was aimed at halting PLO guerrilla raids into Israel. The victorious forces later expanded the operation to drive the

Syrians out of Lebanon. About 30,000 Syrian troops have been stationed in Lebanon to enforce a truce following Lebanon's 1975-76 Moslem-Christian civil war.

The PLO and the Red Cross have said that at least 10,000 people, mostly civilians, have been killed since Israel invaded, and 600,000 made homeless. The Israelis have sharply disputed those figures, calling them exaggerations and lies to discredit the Jewish state.

ap-ax-06-24-82 0618edt

B079riPM-Israeli Invasion, 1st Ld,200 000062481
URGENT Laserphoto NY5 By MICHAEL GOLDSMITH Associated Press Writer

BEIRUT, Lebanon (AP) — Israel said its warplanes shot down two Syrian MiGs over Lebanon today as Israeli and Syrian tanks and artillery battled for control of the Beirut-Damascus highway and Israeli jets blasted Palestinian positions around Beirut airport.

The fighting escalated as Americans gathered at a Christian-held port north of the embattled Lebanese capital to await today's scheduled evacuation from this nation trapped in the gunsights of three armies.

In Tel Aviv, the military command said its jets shot down the MiGs when they tried to intercept Israeli planes that were attacking Syrian ground targets in central Lebanon during an artillery battle. There was no immediate Syrian comment on the claim.

The dogfight, the first reported by Israel since a short-lived cease-fire two weeks ago, appeared to intensify the Israeli-Syrian ground fighting that flared two days ago.

Today's kills raised to 87 the number of Syrian warplanes Israel claims to have downed since it invaded Lebanon June 6. Despite Syrian claims to the contrary, Israel says it has lost no planes in air combat, but has acknowledged losing only one jet to Palestinian groundfire.

The Israelis, 2nd grafu
ap-ax-06-24-82 0717edt

B092riPM-Israeli Invasion, 2nd Ld,110 000062481
URGENT Eds: Jets pound Beirut slums. By MICHAEL GOLDSMITH Associated Press Writer

BEIRUT, Lebanon (AP) — Israeli jets downed two Syrian MiGs over central Lebanon today and pounded Palestinian strongholds in the slums near Beirut airport as Americans prepared to evacuate the war-torn country.

Intense Israeli-Syrian tank and artillery battles blazed along the Beirut-Damascus highway and Israeli warplanes hit Syrian and Palestinian positions in the mountains southeast of the capital.

The Tel Aviv command said its jets downed the Syrian planes when the MiGs tried to intercept Israeli planes attacking Syrian targets during an artillery battle. Lebanon's state radio also reported the downing of the MiGs.
The dogfight:4th graf
ap-ax-06-24-82 0811edt

8

HEADLINES

Writing good headlines is a demanding task. Some headlines are a sort of poetry:

Nolan Ryan's fastball hums
while all the Angels sing

But most good headlines just tell the story clearly, simply and specifically.

Good headlines are within the grasp of any editor. These heads are accurate and specific and do not mislead the reader; they capture the essence of the story and offer an item of interest to the reader. Most people, given time and practice, can write this kind of headline consistently.

Great headlines — those that sum up a story in a clever and interesting way, that compel readers to read a story all the way through and that fit into the assigned space — are much harder to attain. Few people have the gift of writing this kind of headline consistently. They are the people a publication should value, protect and encourage.

Headlines are one of the most important parts of any publication. They serve a number of interrelated functions which cannot be performed by any other element of the publication. The following are some of those functions.

Identifying and separating stories in the paper. This function is one of the most basic for any headline. Unlike newspaper readers of the eighteenth and nineteenth centuries, when few headlines appeared in any newspaper, twentieth century readers do not have the time to read through a lot of body copy for the items which interest them, nor are they willing, like many readers of those earlier days, to read every item in the paper. Readers need a way of seeing how the publication is organized and a way of finding the items which they want to read. Headlines help them do this.

Giving the publication an attractive appearance. Beyond the basic function of separating the different items in a publication, headlines can be used to make the appearance of the newspaper more attractive. By varying the size and placement of headlines, an editor can create a pleasing appearance for the page and can draw attention to particular stories or other items. How this is done is discussed more fully in Chapter 10.

Creating reader interest in stories or other items. As mentioned before, many newspaper readers scan the pages to see what stories they are interested in reading. The headline may be their only contact with the story. If the headline does not grab and pull them into a story, nothing else will. Few readers are attracted by body type, and many do not associate pictures with stories.

Contributing to the overall quality of the publication. Few elements in the publication can have the impact on the reader's attitude toward a publication that a headline can have. If headlines are dull, lifeless, confusing, or inaccurate, that's how the reader will view the publication. If headlines are bright, lively, specific, and informative, the reader will come away with a more favorable impression of the publication. Headlines alone will not make or break a publication in the eyes of the reader, but they do make a great contribution to how the reader feels about the publication.

In order to make headlines perform these various functions, headline writers should adhere to rules governing space fit, splits, verbs, total count, and proportion. Headlines must be as specific as possible. Above all, they must be accurate and informative. The following section will discuss some of the ways to achieve these goals.

PRINCIPLES OF HEADLINE WRITING

Headline writers must learn to catch the most important and interesting details of news stories as they edit them. They must discover what the reporter is trying to say about the topic and detect those angles and elements of the story which lie at its heart.

Style is important. A copy editor and headline writer must have a complete knowledge of style and an ability to apply that knowledge.

But for the good copy editor, style is only part of the process. Far more important is shaping the story so that excess baggage is cut out and the remaining words clearly create those images and thoughts important to the story. This process of shaping the story and detecting its central elements leads directly to good headlines.

Words must be used precisely. Headlines are abbreviated news stories. Headline writers must create vivid impressions with only a few words. They must be vocabulary experts.

The headline must serve the dual function of informing and interesting the reader. Every word must create understanding. But every word must also create interest. This dual task requires that each word be carefully selected for its maximum impact on the reader.

Good headline writers must be knowledgeable about as many subjects as possible. They must quickly grasp relationships between pieces of information. They must be able to see what reporters are driving at in their copy or even perhaps to see things the reporter may have missed. This requires that headline writers read their own and other newspapers and tune in to as many radio and television broadcasts as possible. The following are some general principles which headline writers must follow.

Accuracy. Above all else, a headline must be accurate. Headlines which contain inaccurate information or leave false impressions are doing a disservice to the reader and to the publication. As in every other activity of the reporter or editor, accuracy is the main goal in writing headlines.

Sometimes inaccuracies are obvious and are the result of laziness on the part of the headline writer. For example, in the headline and story below, the headline writer simply read one thing and thought another.

Arson cause
of school fire

Investigators are searching through the rubble of Joy School today trying to find the cause of the fire which destroyed the 50-year-old building on Friday.

Fire Marshall Benny Freeman said no concrete clues have been found but did not rule out arson as a possible cause of the blaze.

The headline makes a definite statement about the cause of the fire, but the story does far less than that. The writer of this headline simply did not read the story carefully enough and did not understand what it said.

Another example of this kind of inaccuracy is misinterpretation of the story. If the story says one thing, the headline should not say something else, as it does in the following example.

Peacekeeping easy for marines

WASHINGTON (AP) — If the president decides to commit American troops to an international peacekeeping force, it will not be the first time the U.S. marines have been sent abroad in a noncombat role.

While it has happened infrequently, the few times U.S. forces have been employed in peacekeeping efforts have been judged largely successful. . . .

The story says nothing about peacekeeping being "easy" for marines; it simply says that their efforts have been successful. Such a headline creates a serious misimpression for the reader which could have consequences on that person's attitude toward this subject. Headline writers should make sure that their heads are supported by the facts within the story; they should not go beyond these facts.

Logic. Headlines should not only be accurate, they should make sense. Many headline writers assume that readers are going to read the story for which the head is being written. Consequently, they write headlines which can be understood *only* if the story is read. For example,

Senator wants Labor Secretary on leave

was the headline on a story about a senator who called for the Secretary of Labor to take a leave of absence while being investigated. Readers who only read the headline would be confused; they might be able to figure it out, especially if they were to read the story, but the reader is not obligated to figure anything out.

The problem of logic in headlines occurs, as in the example above, when a headline tries to include several disparate ideas. If these ideas are not in logical order, the headline can be confusing. The following two examples demonstrate this kind of confusion.

Judge denies policy on Haitians biased

'Serious case of vandalism,' as train derails, kills one

A headline should stand on its own; it should not depend on the text to make it make sense. Readers often will read nothing about a story except the headline. An editor must make certain that the reader receives some understandable information from just that brief reading.

Another problem with logic in headlines is the attribution of feelings, characteristics, or actions to things which are not capable of such feelings, characteristics, or actions. In literature, we might call this "personification" or a "pathetic fallacy." In headlines, it sometimes doesn't make much sense. For instance,

Martial law rules Bolivia

When you read it closely, the headline doesn't really make much sense. Martial law can't rule anything; people rule, and they may use martial law to rule. Keep in mind what people or things in your headlines can and cannot do.

Specificity. A headline should be as specific as possible in presenting information to the reader. Many beginning headline writers fall into the trap of writing very general headlines, or using words with very general meanings, and their headlines don't really say very much. The reader ought to be able to get a good idea about what is going on in the story from the headline. If this is not the case, the headline needs to be rewritten. Examples of this lack of specificity can be found in the following headlines.

Sex and drugs cause
for combined efforts

Governor waits to announce plan

Nuclear report cloudy

Another problem related to lack of specificity in headlines is that of attribution. Headline writers should not express their opinions in headlines; nor should they express the opinion of others without proper attribution. Remember that headlines are statements of fact, not opinion. To state an opinion as fact is to mislead the reader, as in the following headlines.

Chances for budget passage good

Marine training builds character

The above statements need some form of attribution. Sometimes headline writers can get around this problem by putting the expressions of opinion in quotes (single quotes are usually used in heads). Quotes indicate that the words used come from someone in the story, not from the headline writer. However, when quotes are used, the headline writer should make sure that the words within the quote appear within quotes inside the story. For example, in the headlines above, if we were to put quotation marks around the words "good" and "builds character," we would need to make sure that the stories quoted someone saying these things.

Word precision. Using words precisely is a must for the headline writer. Since headlines appear in larger type than body copy, they are more likely to be read and carry more authority than the smaller type. That's one reason why it is imperative that the words in the head are used for their exact and most common meanings. For example, in the following headline,

Lover's quarrel named
cause of murder-suicide

the word "named" is misused. People might say that a lover's quarrel caused the murder-suicide, but a cause of this sort of thing is usually not "named."

Double meanings. Double meanings, or double entendres, crop up in headlines all the time, and editors should keep a constant watch for them. They can be embarrassing for the newspaper and for the people involved in a story. Double meanings can range from the hilarious to the scatalogical:

Father of 10 shot;
mistaken for rabbit

Three states
hit by blizzard;
one missing

Mother of twelve
kills husband
in self-defense

Churchman urges
more lay activity

Editors should read headlines literally and try to discern every possible meaning that the words in the head could carry.

PRESCRIPTIONS

Headlines must conform to certain rules. These rules may vary according to the publication, but the following guidelines will help you in producing consistent, informative heads.

1. Headlines should be based on the main idea of the story, and that idea should be found in the lead or in the first two or three paragraphs of the story.

2. Use no facts in the headline that are not in the story.

3. Avoid repetition. Don't repeat keywords in the same headline; don't repeat the exact wording of the story in the headline.

4. Avoid ambiguity, insinuations, and double meanings.

5. If a story qualifies a statement, the headline also should.

6. Use the present tense; for the future tense, use the infinitive form of the verb.

7. Linking verbs should be avoided.

8. Alliteration, if used, should be deliberate and should not go against the general tone of the story.

9. Do not use articles -- "a," "an," and "the."

10. Do not use the conjunction "and." Use a comma instead.

11. Avoid using unclear or little-known names, phrases, and abbreviations in headlines.

12. Use punctuation sparingly.

13. No headline may start with a verb.

14. Headlines should be complete sentences or should imply complete sentences.

15. Do not pile up modifiers in a headline.

16. Headlines should come within at least 90 percent of the maximum count.

17. Avoid headlinese — that is, words such as hit, flay, rap, hike, nix, nab, slate, etc. Use words for their precise meaning.

18. Do not use pronouns alone and unidentified.

19. Don't split headlines (don't split parts of a verb between lines of a headline); don't place a preposition at the end of a line; don't split modifiers and words they modify between lines.

20. With a multiline head, try to put the verb in the top line.

21. Be accurate and specific.

PROCEDURE

Headlines are expected to fit into a certain space prescribed by a layout editor. To make headlines fit into those spaces, a writer must count the letters in the head. The following are the basic rules for counting a headline.

Each lowercase letter counts 1. **Exceptions:** m and w count 1 ½; f, l, i, t count ½.
Capital letters count 1 ½. **Exceptions:** M and W count 2; I counts 1.
Numerals count 1 ½. **Exception:** 1 counts 1.
Punctuation marks count ½. **Exceptions:** --, ?, $, % count 1. Space counts 1.

The person who edits the story, having the most thorough knowledge of the story, should be the one who writes the headline. Assuming that is the case, here are some tips on how to produce a headline.

1. Make sure you understand what the story is about.

2. Find the action verb. What is happening in the story? What are the people in the story doing?

3. Sum up the story with keywords; build this summary around the verb you have chosen.

4. Break the head into logical line units.

5. Count the heads.

6. Begin **substitution**. Here a knowledge of vocabulary is most important; don't be afraid to use a thesaurus. Remember the logical substitutions, such as a name for a title and vice versa, such as "Reagan" and "President"; remember nicknames, too, such as "Say-hey Kid" for Willie Mays.

7. If all else fails, begin again.

CONCLUSION

As we mentioned at the beginning of this chapter, headlines are a kind of poetry in the sense that they are abbreviated statements packed with meaning and conveying information about a story to which they are attached. There are probably more specific rules governing the writing of newspaper headlines than any other editing process. One reason for this number of rules is the fact that headlines are such an important part of the publication. They are often the only contact the reader has with the information presented in a particular story. They must be accurate both in terms of the information in their related stories and in terms of the words and phrases that are used.

Students often find headline writing the most difficult of all editing skills to master. They are not used to thinking and writing in such an abbreviated way and working under such a confining set of rules. The only way out of this difficulty is practice. Headline writing does get easier the more that it is done, and writing a good headline — one which tells a story in an interesting way and fits into the assigned space — can be a satisfying and rewarding exercise.

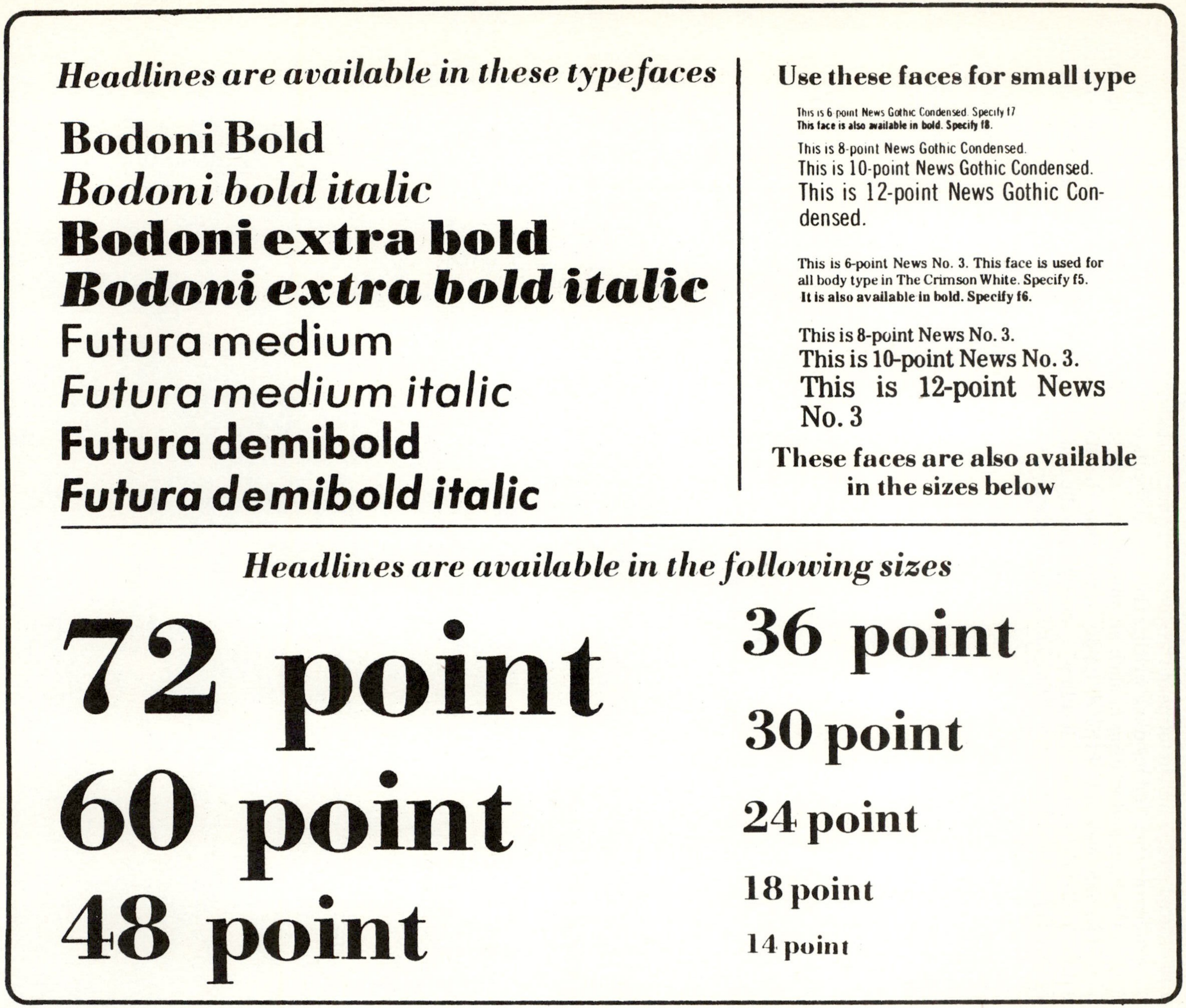

Headlines are available in these typefaces

Bodoni Bold
Bodoni bold italic
Bodoni extra bold
Bodoni extra bold italic

Futura medium
Futura medium italic
Futura demibold
Futura demibold italic

Headlines are available in the following sizes

72 point
60 point
48 point
36 point
30 point
24 point
18 point
14 point

Use these faces for small type

This is 6 point News Gothic Condensed. Specify f7
This face is also available in bold. Specify f8.

This is 8-point News Gothic Condensed.
This is 10-point News Gothic Condensed.
This is 12-point News Gothic Condensed.

This is 6-point News No. 3. This face is used for all body type in The Crimson White. Specify f5. It is also available in bold. Specify f6.

This is 8-point News No. 3.
This is 10-point News No. 3.
This is 12-point News No. 3

These faces are also available in the sizes below

Figure 8-1   HEADLINE FACES AND SIZES

This chart shows the various type faces and sizes which may be available to a newspaper. Bodoni and futura are only two of a great many varieties of type, but they are two which are commonly used in headlines on many papers.

EXERCISES

COUNTING HEADLINES

Count the following headlines.

Stars here for AHSAA games

Daniel takes 1-stroke advantage
as women chase U.S. golf crown

Parents of slain children
ask for renewal of probe

Animated film's 'secret' is its strength

Cocaine smuggler released from French prison

'E.T.' generates market

Third-place beauty irked

Can Trudeau be 'bribed' to quit?

TVA proposes 4.4% increase

Corona: Half-brother
may have been killer

PROBLEM HEADLINES

Identify the problems in the following headlines.

College course discusses ghosts

City probe asked

Argentina's head ousted

Haig rips Soviets over arms

Egypt metes death to 5

Explosion-fire damages tire
company and injures owner

Folsom in race for
second term on PSC

Wilson looks for a double

School survey shows
82 pct. smoke pot

Senate rules part of Lee's blood

Camera draws her to God

12 die in crash

Ford nixes plans for trip

FBI probes attorney's death
by hanging in Dodge jail

Weddings told

PROBLEM HEADLINES

Identify the problems in the following headlines.

Slay victim found

Tree, fishing accidents contribute to state toll

Pair who found statistics
on bias against Jews held

Do enemies of upholstery, home
furnishings lurk in your house?

21-year drinking age urged to stem traffic deaths

Arlington has exhibit
of 1750 to 1910 chairs

Gulf war enters
a volatile phase

Small school players get new experience

Marchers
ask jailing
of police

Bonnett entered in quarter-miler,
then aims for big one at Talladega

HEADLINE WRITING

Write headlines for the following stories using assignments given to you by your instructor.

BLOUNTSTOWN, Fla. (AP) — A babysitter was arrested and charged with murder in the deaths of two of five children who died while in her care, Calhoun County Sheriff W.G. Smith said today.

Strangulation was the cause of death in both cases, State Attorney Jim Appleman said at a news conference today.

Christine Falling was charged with two counts of first-degree murder, Smith said.

The victims, both of Blountstown, were 2-month-old Travis Coleman, who died July 3, and Cassidy "Muffy" Johnson, who died in February 1980, Appleman said.

VATICAN CITY — Pope John Paul II reiterated his stand against artificial birth control today at a meeting with leaders of the Worldwide Council on Women.

The pope met with seven leaders of the council for more than 45 minutes at the Vatican. The meeting was called to discuss problems women face and what the Catholic Church could do to help.

The leadership group reportedly asked the pope to reconsider the church's stand on artificial birth control, but if such a request was made, it was not heeded.

"The church remains opposed to forms of birth control which inhibit the natural processes," the pope said through a spokesman.

KINGFISHER, Okla. (AP) — Four window-shopping goats jailed in this central Oklahoma town are waiting for someone to fork over their bail.

The Kingfisher County sheriff's office is trying to find out who owns two mother goats and two kids captured as they tried to butt their reflections in storefront windows in downtown Kingfisher early Monday.

The animals were held in an antique jail cell in a city park Monday and later were taken to the animal shelter, where they are to be kept until claimed.

NEW YORK (AP) — A construction crane atop a 43-story mid-Manhattan skyscraper collapsed Wednesday, raining rock, metal and glass on pedestrians and buildings below. One man was killed and nine people suffered minor injuries.

A two-ton, 30-foot piece of the crane was left dangling over East 53rd Street by a single metal tube, forcing the evacuation of nearby buildings and the closing of some of New York's busiest streets.

Fire officials noted that the toll could have been much worse. The crane gave way just before 11 a.m., an hour before thousands of workers poured into the streets for the lunch hour.

Eyewitnesses told of pieces of masonry flying though office windows; of a pool of blood where one police officer said the dead man, Warren Levenberg, a circus employee, "got his head crushed in" by a falling chunk; and, mostly, of an awesome noise.

HEADLINE WRITING

Write headlines for the following stories using assignments given to you by your instructor.

COLUMBUS, Ga. (AP) — An Alabama man already sentenced in Georgia to life in prison in the slaying of his wife was handed five years for attempted extortion here and still faces a murder-during-kidnapping charge in his home state.

Roger Martinesqu, 30, pleaded guilty Tuesday in Muscogee Superior Court to writing a letter to Jeffrey Smith of Columbus and threatening to implicate him in a crime if he didn't drop robbery charges against Martinesqu's brother and pay him $1,000.

Judge Will Latis ordered three years of the five-year sentence be served consecutive to Martinesqu's life sentence.

The Alabama charges stem from the Feb. 1 slaying of Connie Winslow Martinesqu, 21, whose body was found in a car off a rural road in Topes County.

One man was killed and two people seriously injured when a truck jumped a median on Interstate 63 last night and struck a motorcycle and two cars.

Paul Sargant, 24, was died instantly when he was thrown from his motorcycle. His address was not immediately known but police investigating the accident said the motorcycle had an Illinois tag.

Also injured in the accident were Mary Ellen Lanice, Rt. 4, Maryville and Conrad Huxley of Brownsville, Texas, the drivers of the two cars involved in the collision. Both were listed in serious but stable condition at City General Hospital this morning.

The driver of the truck, Lesley Speight of Sawmill, Ark., suffered only minor cuts and bruises. He has been charged with vehicular homicide and wreckless driving and is being held at the county sheriff's office pending arraignment and bail.

House prices in the metro area soared to a median $65,000 last year and "cast a pall over the universal dream of homeownership," local savings and loan officials said today.

The $65,000 price tag meant average down payments of $14,050 and monthly housing payments of $722, including taxes and insurance, according to statistics released in a new study prepared by the local Board of Realtors.

First-time buyers typically paid $54,900 for a house and agreed to monthly housing expenses of $688 after making a $8,600 downpayment.

After hearing repeated complaints by parents, the State Board of Education banned the use of five social studies textbooks in the state's public school classrooms.

Board members discussed the books in a meeting with Governor Frank Dentene at the Governor's mansion on Monday night. Dentene, who is chairman of the Board of Education, told the members that he too was upset with some of the books on the list.

The books were removed today from a list recommended by the State Textbook Committee for use this fall. None of the books are currently in use, said board officials.

HEADLINE WRITING

Write headlines for the following stories using assignments given to you by your instructor.

Nolan Ryan and two relievers held Chicago in check and Houston took advantage of Allen Ripley's wildness to beat the Cubs.

Ryan, 10-9, pitched five shutout innings, allowing three hits before leaving the game because of a sore hip. Mike LaCoss allowed four hits in 2 ⅓ innings, including Chicago's only run on Leon Durham's homer, and Frank LaCorte earned his second save of the season with 1 ⅓ innings of hitless relief.

Houston scored in the first inning on a triple by Dickie Thon and a wild pitch by Ripley, 3-2. In the sixth, another wild pitch allowed Danny Heep to go from second to third base, and he scored on Art Howe's single.

MOBILE, Ala. (AP) — Police used tracking dogs and captured three Mississippi men charged in a drugstore robbery Wednesday.

The three were identified as Dana Allen Watson, 24, Patrick Anthony Sullivan, 28, and Joseph Sullivan, 27, all of Biloxi, Miss.

Drugs taken in the armed robbery of Skyland Discount Drugs were recovered. No one was injured.

Police cornered the suspects in a wooded area and captured two of them. Dogs tracked Watson to a hospital where he was arrested.

ROME (AP) — Police said Wednesday that they have seized hundreds of files on judges, politicians, anti-terrorist policemen and high-ranking military officers from a hideout used by the Red Brigades terrorist gang.

Police raided the apartment in May shortly after the arrest of Annunziata Francola, a suspected member of the leftist gang's Rome column, but news of the discovery of the files was withheld.

Miss Francola has been charged with subversive association and homicide in connection with the killing of a policeman.

ISLAMABAD, Pakistan (AP) — An Afghan peasant who arrived in Pakistan Wednesday said 1,100 people were killed in a Soviet shelling operation in Logar province, along the Afghan-Pakistan border, earlier this month.

Mohib Ali said he lost four family members in the attack, which started July 12.

"Afterward, they conducted house-to-house searches and shot everybody in sight," Ali told the Afghan Information and Documentation Center, a private organization based in Peshawar, Pakistan that attempts to insure accurate reporting of the situation in Afghanistan.

His report could not be independently confirmed, but a team of French doctors who recently returned from the area said they had been told that about 200 guerrillas were killed in the attack.

9

PICTURES AND CUTLINES

Pictures are one of the most important parts of a newspaper. Pictures help editors and reporters tell the stories they must tell. They inform and illustrate. They give the reader, who lives in a visual world and who expects visual messages from the print media as well as from the broadcast media, something to see as well as read.

Many news editors believe pictures to be the most important design element with which they have to work (see Chapter 10). On a printed page full of type, the picture stands out. Of all the elements, it is the one most likely to catch the reader's eye first and hold his attention the longest. A good picture can focus the reader's eye on the page and direct his attention to other parts of the page.

Because of these qualities, pictures can make a vital contribution to the overall quality and credibility of a newspaper. Pictures should not be treated as an afterthought or merely as matter to go along with the stories and break up the type. Editors should treat pictures as they treat any other of the paper's elements, using them to help achieve the newspaper's goal of accuracy in the telling of the day's events.

The person who selects and directs pictures for publication is the picture editor. Only a few of the larger newspapers hire people solely for this purpose. More often, the picture editor's position may be combined with that of news editor, city editor, or chief photographer. A picture editor does not necessarily have to be a photographer. The skills required to be a good picture editor are quite different from those required to take a good photograph. The picture editor must be an expert in the three basic processes of putting photographs into a publication: selection, cropping, and scaling. Beyond that, however, the picture editor must demand high quality photographs from his photographers, and he must know how to reward their creativity and enterprise. Proper handling and display of good pictures can inspire photographers to increase the quality of their work.

The picture editor has a variety of types of pictures to work with, including the following:

News photos. These are pictures which are most likely used to illustrate a news story (although occasionally news photos may be included without reference to stories). These pictures are used to illustrate the action, drama and humor of the day's events and to draw the reader's attention to a particular story.

Feature pictures. These, too, may go with stories the paper prints, or rhey may stand by themselves. Those that go with stories are specifically tied to feature stories and may include staged or posed shots as well as action photos. Some feature pictures may stand alone; that is, they may not illustrate a story but may be used because of their subject or photographic qualities to brighten the page and catch the attention of the reader.

Head or "mug" shots. These pictures are usually one, and sometimes two columns wide, and they show only the face or head of the subject. These photos may be used because they contain an unusual facial expression or because an editor needs them to break up some body or headline type on a page.

Community art. These pictures (used especially by smaller newspapers) show groups of people either handing checks, awards, or papers to one another; looking at something in front of them; shaking hands; or staring at the camera. One of the pejorative terms for this kind of picture is "the grip 'n' grin shot." Community art also includes many "society" page pictures, such as engagement and wedding pictures and photos of club parties and teas.

Illustrations, graphs, and drawings. These are not pictures as such, but are often treated exactly like pictures. Wire services will usually send graphs and other illustrations through their photo machines when stories call for such items. Some newspapers have an artist on staff who can generate these kinds of items for local stories.

A picture editor must go through three distinct editorial processes before a picture makes it into print: selection, cropping and scaling. Each process takes particular skills an editor should master.

SELECTION

What makes a good photograph? Why is a particular photograph selected for publication and another not selected? What are the technical and aesthetic qualities editors look for in selecting photographs for a newspaper? There are many answers to such questions. A great many divergent factors go into an editor's decision to use a photograph, and there are no definitive guidelines governing the selection of photographs. The three major purposes of publishing photographs are to capture the attention of the reader, to illustrate and supplement the editorial content, and to make pages look more presentable.

In the process of selection, an editor will be concerned with all three of these purposes, but at the beginning of the process of selection the first purpose (capturing the attention of the reader) will most likely be the major consideration. What kinds of photos do people look at? The following are some photographic elements editors consider in the selection process.

Drama. It is the pictures that tell a story that are most likely to be chosen by an editor for publication. Pictures that have high dramatic quality are those in which readers can clearly tell what is happening; in fact, there may be several things happening, as in an accident scene with someone standing nearby with an anguished expression.

Emotion. Like dramatic pictures, those with emotional qualities often tell a story. Yet they may also be the type that do not contain highly dramatic or story-telling qualities but rather evoke some emotion in the mind of the viewer. An old journalistic proverb says that readers will always look at pictures of children and animals. These are the kinds of pictures that make the readers feel something.

Action. Editors, and readers, are most likely to be drawn to pictures with some action or movement in them. Pictures suggesting movement will be seen and studied by readers more readily than still-life pictures. Even though a photograph by itself cannot move, if its content indicates movement, it can be an extremely good attention-capturing device for the editor to use.

Artistic or technical quality. Here we are talking about the good photograph, the one that has sharp, clear focus, and good framing or that presents a subject in an unusual or pleasing manner. This kind of picture often appears in newspapers, especially with the change of seasons. Nature lends itself particularly well to this kind of photograph.

Bizarre or unusual subjects. A picture of something unusual, something not likely to be seen by readers in their everyday lives, makes a good candidate for publication. Unusual subjects may stem from the day's news events, such as a fire or wreck, or they may be simply something a photographer has happened upon or heard about, such as a twelve-pound tomato or an old man's wizened expression.

Prominence. Like the news value of the same name, prominence is a quality editors often consider in selecting pictures. Pictures of famous people are always likely candidates for publication, even when they do not contain any of the qualities mentioned above. Readers will look at pictures of famous people, and editors will use such pictures for precisely that reason.

These elements are not a checklist of criteria for the selection of photographs; they are rather a list of things an editor may consider in deciding which pictures to publish. A good picture editor must have a "feel" for spotting the good photograph, one that will capture the attention of the reader, illustrate the editorial content, and enhance the overall quality of the publication.

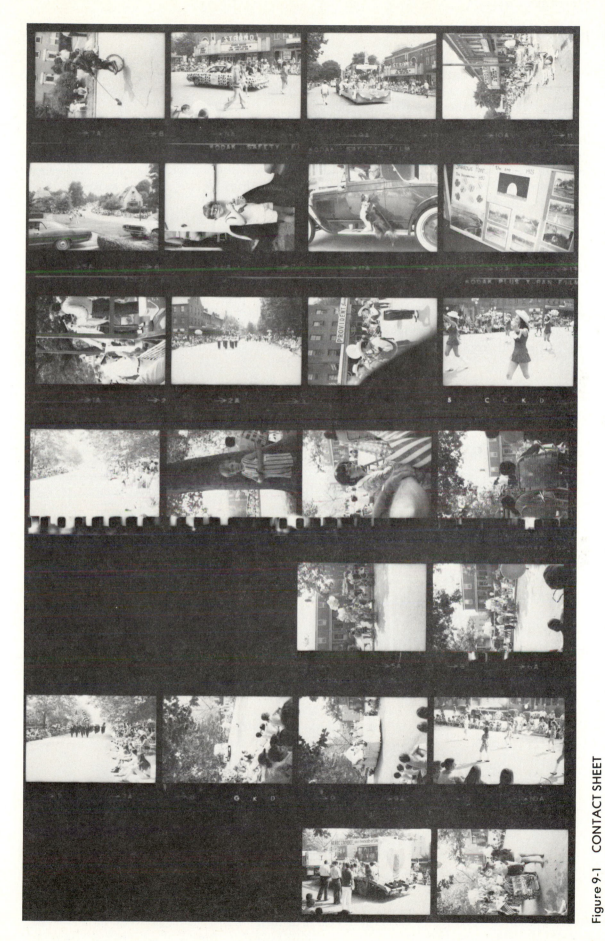

Figure 9-1 CONTACT SHEET

Editors often select pictures from contact sheets. These sheets are produced directly from the photographer's negatives and allow editors to see quickly the pictures which are available.

CROPPING

After the selection process has taken place, or along with it, comes the process of cropping. Cropping means taking out parts of a picture. It has two purposes: eliminating unnecessary parts of a picture and emphasizing or enhancing parts of a picture.

Eliminating unnecessary parts of a picture. Some parts of a picture may simply be unnecessary to the subject and purpose of the photograph, and they should be eliminated. Often these parts are not only wasteful but also distracting. An editor must use the space in the paper efficiently, and proper cropping of a photograph is one way to do this. Good, tight cropping of pictures is just as important as editing to eliminate unnecessary parts of a story.

Emphasizing or enhancing parts of a picture. One photograph may contain many pictures within it. A good picture editor must have an eye for these pictures within pictures and must be able to see and choose the picture that best fits the intended purpose. Cropping is a way of bringing out the particular picture the editor wants to use, of emphasizing the part of the picture that readers should notice. A picture that seems ordinary at first glance may be made dramatic by good cropping.

Pictures published in newspapers are generally rectangular, and cropping must be done with straight lines along each side. Occasionally, pictures are not rectangular but follow the lines of the subject. These are called drop-outs or cut-outs and may be used for good dramatic effect.

PHOTO TAG	
Slug	DEMONSTRATION
Page	1
Date	3/30/83
Reproduction width	5 1/16 inches
Reproduction depth	3 13/16 inches
Percentage	100
Ordered by	SMITH

Figure 9-2   CROPPING

Editors crop pictures to exlude unnecessary material. Crop marks are made on the margins of the pictures, such as in the illustration above. A photo tag is usually attached to a picture telling the backshop crew how the picture should be handled.

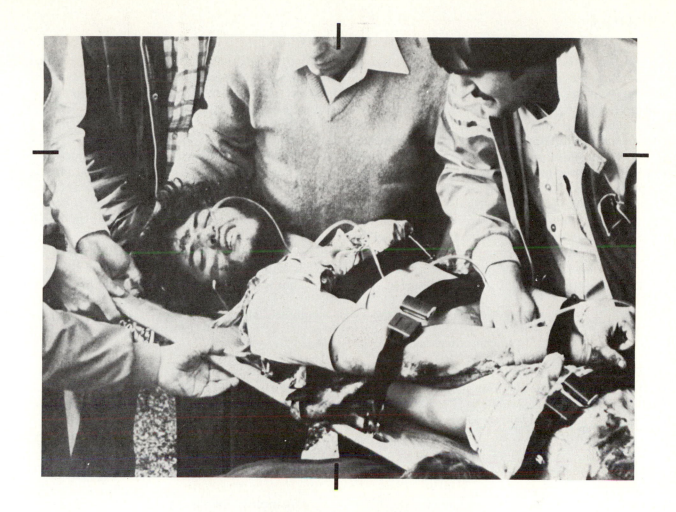

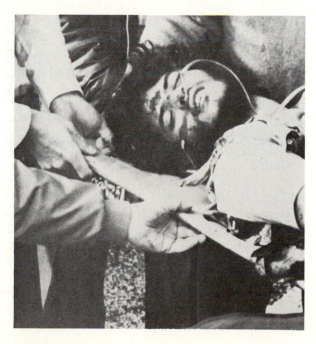

Figure 9-3   CROPPING FOR EMPHASIS

Cropping is sometimes done to emphasize certain parts of a picture as in the illustration above. Notice how the emphasis of this picture has been changed by the cropping.

SCALING

Scaling is the process of changing the size of a picture area by enlarging or reducing it while keeping the proportions of the original. Once an editor has selected and cropped a photograoh for use in a publication, chances are the picture will not be the exact size needed. Enlargement or reduction will probably be needed to make the picture fit the standard column widths of the publication. When that reduction or enlargement is made, the editor will have to find out how deep the reproduction of the picture will be. Scaling is the process of finding that dimension.

The concept of proportionality must be understood by those who work with the scaling process. For our purposes, proportionality means that the width and depth of a picture must stay in the same proportion to each other whether the picture is enlarged or reduced. Let's say a cropped picture is two inches wide and four inches deep -- that the depth is twice the width. Given these dimensions, it does not matter how much the picture is enlarged or reduced; the depth will always be twice the width. The proportion must remain the same. The only way it can be changed is to re-crop the picture.

Two of the most common ways to scale a print are through use of arithmetic and through use of a mechanical device, such as a picture wheel or a slide rule. The arithmetic method involves some simple multiplication and division, with substitution of the dimensions being used into the following formula.

$$\frac{\text{Original width}}{\text{Reproduction width}} = \frac{\text{Original depth}}{\text{Reproduction depth}}$$

Let's say an editor has a cropped picture which is 4 inches wide by 6 inches deep and wants that photo to run as a three column picture, which means it should be about 6 inches wide. The editor will then have to find out how deep it is by using the formula above. By substituting these dimensions into the formula, the editor will come up with the following.

$$\frac{4}{6} = \frac{6}{X}$$

The editor will then have to solve for the missing value by multiplying diagonally: 6 x 6 = 36 and 4 x X = 4X, then 4X = 36. X would then equal 9. The reproduction depth of the picture is 9 inches.

The problem with this method of scaling is that frequently it is necessary to work with odd dimensions, such as 6 5-16 inches or 7 3-4 inches. Cross multiplying these dimensions requires elaborate multiplication and allows more chance of error. One way of getting around this problem is to measure the picture in picas rather than in inches. By doing this, an editor is more likely to have whole numbers to work with than fractions.

The most popular method of scaling is by using some mechanical device, and by far the most popular of these devices is the picture wheel. The picture wheel is made up of two circular pieces of cardboard braided together to allow the two pieces to turn independently. The inside portions of the picture wheel represent the original (or cropped) dimensions of the photograph, and the outside wheel represents the reproduction dimensions.

Figure 9-4 shows how we can take the problem described above and solve it with a picture wheel. An editor would start by finding the four-inch mark on the outside wheel. Holding the two wheels together at this point, the editor would then look around on the inside wheel that mark is lined up with. As you can see in the illustration, that number is nine.

You should note one additional thing about the picture wheel. On the inside portion of the original wheel is a window which gives the "percentage of the original size." For this problem the percentage is 150. This percentage is important because it is the only figure needed by the operator of the copy camera which will enlarge or reduce this print. The operator is never concerned with the original dimensions of the picture, and editors should always make a note of the desired percentage on the back of the photograph.

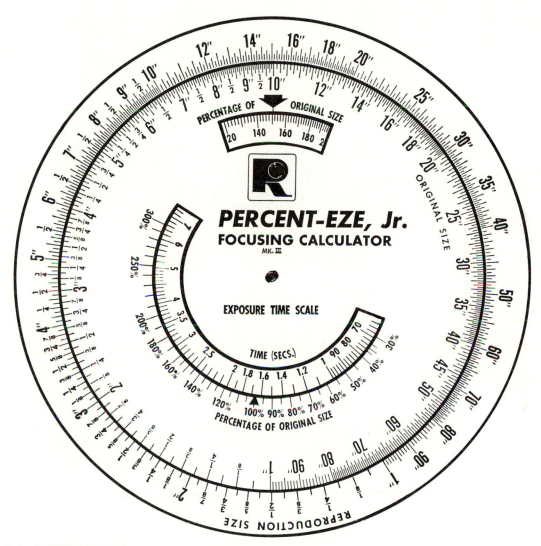

Figure 9-4   PICTURE WHEEL

The picture wheel is one of the editor's most useful devices. With it the editor can quickly calculate the reproduction size of a picture.

Figure 9-5   REDUCING AND ENLARGING A PICTURE

The three pictures in this illustration are exactly the same but produced at different sizes. The first has been reduced to 67 percent of the original; the second is the original, or 100 percent; the third has been enlarged to 100 percent of the original. Notice that all three have the same proportions.

PRINTING THE PICTURE

When an editor finishes selecting, cropping, and sizing a photo, it is sent to the backshop so that the picture can be prepared for printing according to the editor's instructions. The process of getting a photograph into print is one with which most editors have little to do, but they need to know how that process works. There are many variations in this process, but the following is a description of the most basic and commonly used techniques.

Photographs may be enlarged or reduced, according to the instructions an editor gives. If the person doing the enlarging or reducing has a negative to work with, this process can be done with a normal darkroom enlarger and can be done while the print is being made. If the print of the photograph already exists, it may be enlarged or reduced by using a copy camera.

The important part of this process is screening the picture or making the picture into a halftone. Pictures themselves cannot be used in the printing process, because printing presses cannot reproduce the gray tones of a picture with varying amounts of ink. Only a specified quantity of ink can go on paper during a press run, and this quantity has to be uniform. Consequently, a photograph must be transformed so that the gray tones do not exist. This process is called screening.

If you look closely at any printed photgraph, you will see that it is made up of a series of dots. Where there are more and larger dots in an area of the picture, more ink will accumulate and thus the darker tones of the picture will be created. Where there are fewer and smaller dots, less ink will accumulate and lighter tones will be created. In order to transform a photograph into a series of dots, a glass or plastic screen is laid over the picture or negative when the photograph is being made or being processed for print (See Figure 9-6.) The result is a PMT (which stands for photo mechanical transfer).

Screening is not the only way of getting a picture into print, but it is the method most commonly used, particularly with offset printing. While editors may not have to understand the intricacies of this process, they should know what screening is and why it is so important.

More publications are using more color photographs these days, and here too editors should be aware of the basic process for reproducing color. There are two kinds of color in a publication: spot color and full color. Spot color is simple enough. A separate plate is made for the press consisting only of parts of a page which are to be in color. Only one color at a time can be used on a plate. Spot color is used in advertisements and for boxes and headlines or graphic illustrations that need only one or two colors.

Reproducing a full color photograph is more complicated. Four color separations must be made from the original. To do this, the original print or color slide is rephotographed through red, green,

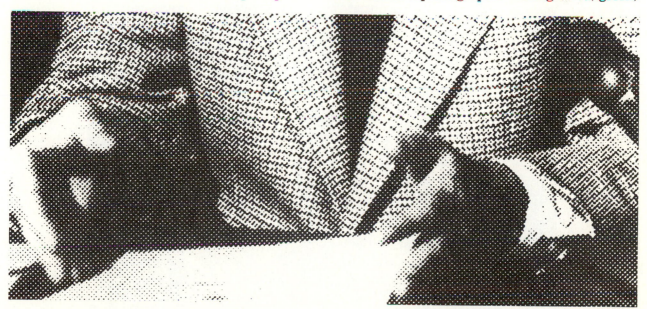

Figure 9-6   HALFTONES

A halftone is a set of dots which appear to be a picture. This enlarged illustration shows how the halftone process works.

and blue filters. The positive made from the red-filtered photograph is called the cyan printer and includes all of the areas of the photograph that do not contain red or variations of red. The positive made from the green-filtered photograph is called the magenta printer and will cut out all the green areas of the photograph. The postive from the blue-filtered photograph is the yellow printer and will cut out all the blue areas of the photograph.

Plates are made from these three positives, but together they will not produce a true reproduction of the photograph. A fourth positive made from the original, known as the black printer, must be made so that the gray and darker areas of the photograph can be neutralized. Doing this makes for a more faithful reproduction of the photograph.

Wire services are unable to send color photographs through the wire photo machines located in newspaper offices. What they can do, however, is to send the positive separations so that the newspapers can make the separate plates from them. Figure 9-7 provides an example of these separations.

Figure 9-7   COLOR SEPARATIONS

When a publication wants to produce a color photo, it must have at least three color "separations," as desribed in the text. These separations allow the different color inks to mix together properly.

(DTW109)DETROIT, JULY 17--CYAN PRINTER--Republican presidential candidate Ronald Reagan and running mate George Bush are joined on the podium of Joe Louis Arena in Detroit Thursday night as the 32nd edition of the Republican Convention draws to a close by former President Gerald Ford.(AP COLORPHOTO)(wt60045stf)1980

Cyan Printer

AP Color Separation

(DTW111)DETROIT,JULY 17--YELLOW PRINTER--Republican presidential candidate Ronald Reagan and running mate George Bush are joined on the podium by former President Gerald Ford in Detroit Thursday evening as the Republican Convention draws to a close. (AP COLORPHOTO)(wt6005stf)1980

Yellow Printer

AP Color Separation

OTHER ILLUSTRATIONS

Newspapers carry a variety of illustration material other than pictures. Some examples of this kind of material can be seen in Figure 9-8. Much of this material is handled by the editor as if it were a picture. It may be cropped and reduced or enlarged within certain limits. Most of this material is in the form of line drawings and will not have to be screened, but otherwise it must go through the same process pictures do. The following is a list of some of the illustration material that a newspaper editor will want to have available.

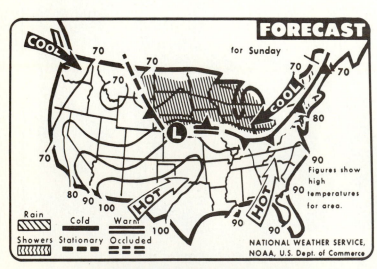

Jordan Shooting Scene

(NY17-May 30)--JORDAN SHOOTING SCENE--This map, based on an illustration by the Fort Wayne Journal-Gazette, shows the area in Fort Wayne, Ind., where National Urban League President Vernon E. Jordan Jr. was shot early Thursday. Crosses locate alleged site where gunman stood and spot where Jordan was shot outside his motel. (AP Laserphoto)(See AP AAA Wire Story) (bg61015ar) 1980

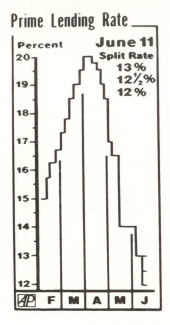

Prime Lending Rate

(NY43-JUNE 11)-PRIME LENDING RATE CHART- Chart illustrates the fluctuation of the prime lending rate over the past five months from February to mid-June 1980.The First National Bank of Boston lowered its prime lending rate Wednesday by one percentage point to 12 percent,undercutting the higher rates being charged by the nation's larger banks.(AP LASER-PHOTO)(SEE AP AAA WIRE STORY)(sav41500ar) 1980

FORECAST

(NY23-June 14)FORECAST--Rain is fore-cast Sunday across the northern tier of states from Montana and Wyoming to Michigan and Ohio, according to the National Weather Service.(AP Laser-photo)(mks71115ar)1980

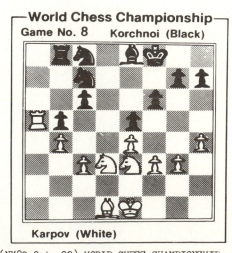

World Chess Championship

Game No. 8   Korchnoi (Black)

Karpov (White)

(NY89-Oct. 22) WORLD CHESS CHAMPIONSHIP-- These are the positions shown on the wall board at the World Chess Championship in Merano, Italy Thursday when the eighth game of the tournament was adjourned. U.S. Grandmaster Robert Byrne said Karpov has a slight advantage, but expects the match will end in a draw. Karpov leads challenger Viktor Korchnoi 3-1. First man to win 6 games is the winner.(AP Laserphoto)(rjk 52010ar)1981 slug: CHESS

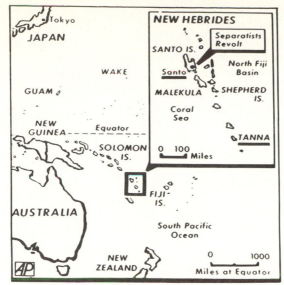

(NY16-May 31)--REVOLT IN NEW HEBRIDES--
Map locates Santo, the second largest
town in the New Hebrides island chain
of the South Pacific, where armed
separatists supported by American
businessmen and French planters took
control Friday, according to Austral-
ian government sources. New Hebridian
police had retaken control of Tanna,
another island in the group, after an
exchange of gunfire, the sources also
said. (AP Laserphoto)(See AP AAA Wire
Story)(bg61120ar) 1980

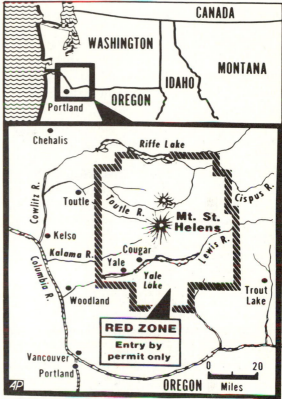

(NY13-June 7)RED ZONE OPENED--The red zone
around Mount St. Helens, a 20-mile radius
which covers approximately 1,500 square
miles, is indicated on this map by the
heavy broken line. Loggers, reporters and
residents are now allowed, by special permit only, into this area. Until Friday it
was off limits to all but rescue workers.
(AP Laserphoto)(See AP AAA Wire Story)(mks
71140ar)1980

(FOR USE WITH CONSUMER SCORECARD)
(NY15-May 30)--RACE WITH INFLATION--This cartoon
by AP artist Joe Yeninas is transmitted for use
as desired with Louise Cook's Consumer Scorecard
column on keeping pace with inflation.
(AP Laserphoto)(See AP AAA Wire Story)
(bg60935ar) 1980

Figure 9-8   ILLUSTRATIONS

Newspapers, especially those that subscribe to wire services, have a variety of non-picture illustrations which editors may use.
The above examples are just a few of the illustrations produced by the Associated Press for its members.

Maps. The provision of maps pinpointing the locations of news events is one of the most useful services of a newspaper. Maps help the editor tell a more complete story and set an event in its context. Many papers reserve the use of maps for describing international events, but maps should also be used for national and local events. Besides their informational assets, maps provide a pleasant break in the gray type on a page and enhance the look of a page.

Maps are available from a variety of sources. A newspaper that subscribes to one of the major wire services will have a collection of maps at its disposal. AP and UPI provide their subscribers with many maps keyed to news events. Editors may obtain maps from their staff artists for local stories or they may get them from mail syndicates to which the paper subscribes. (Maps should not be copied from atlases or other printed sources unless permission has been obtained to use them.)

Graphs. Graphs are another good set of illustrative material, although they are somewhat harder to come by than maps. Again, the wire services provide editors with a variety of graphs keyed to stories, and the newspaper with a good staff artist can obtain graphs for local stories. Editors, however, should be careful in making sure that a graph is not confusing and that it adds to a reader's knowledge and understanding. Artists often try to put too much into a graph or to get too fancy with it. Clarity in graphs is an absolute requirement, and an editor should not hesitate to reject a graph that will confound the readers.

Drawings. Wire services are also a good source of drawings that illustrate stories they have sent, and newspaper staff artists have turned out some exceptional drawings for their readers. As with all illustrative material, editors must take care in handling drawings. The point of a drawing should be readily apparent, and its appearance on the page should add to the reader's ease, information, and enjoyment.

ETHICS AND TASTE

A local man who is nationally prominent dies. Many prominent people from all parts of the country attend his funeral. The family has opened the funeral to the public, but it has said that no cameras should be used in the church or at the gravesite. Thousands of people attend the funeral and burial. Your photographer comes back to the office with some dramatic photographs of the family leaving the gravesite along with some highly prominent people....

A woman is held hostage by a crazed killer for most of a day. She is made to take off all her clothes to prevent her from escaping. Somehow she manages to get away from the killer and out the front door of her house. Your photographer is there with other newsmen and shoots pictures of her escape. The pictures the photographer shows you do not reveal any of the woman's private parts, but it is clear that she does not have any clothes on....

The president dozes off while listening to a visiting head of state speak to the White House press corps. The wire services send several photos of the president with his head down and eyes closed sitting behind the speaker....

A movie star is decapitated in a car crash. The wire services send several pictures of the accident scene, including one of the actress' head placed on the car....

Pictures present editors with special problems of taste and ethics. These problems do not occur every day, fortunately, but they happen often enough that eventually every editor must make some decision for which he will be criticized. Some newspapers have tried to produce guidelines for handling certain kinds of pictures, but these guidlines do not cover all situations and sometimes do not provide the editor with sufficient guidance in making a decision. The following is not a set of guidelines but a list of things an editor should consider in deciding whether to run a photograph. None of these considerations is primary in every case; they should all be part of an editor's decision-making.

Editors should remember that their business is to cover the news and inform their readers. A newspaper is supposed to give a full and accurate account of the day's news. Sometimes it takes a photograph to accomplish this mission. Generally, editors should avoid making agreements prior to covering an event that would restrict the coverage of an event.

Editors should be sensitive to their readers. There are a number of subjects that will offend readers or that parents will want to keep from their children. An editor should be aware of these subjects and the sensibilities of the readers. He or she should try to avoid publishing pictures that are unnecessarily offensive.

Editors should be aware of the feelings of the people in the pictures. Even people who are photographed a great deal and who are in the news a lot have feelings that need consideration. Pictures can put people in a bad light or in embarrassing situations even when editors print those pictures with the most innocent of motives. One example may serve to illustrate this point. A newspaper in a medium-size town decided to publish a special section on home furnishings. In putting this section together, the editors looked in their files and found a picture of one of the town's prominent women in her living room. The picture was about a year old but fit perfectly with the theme of the section. The editors were all set to run the photo until they learned that in the year since the picture had been taken she had lost nearly one hundred pounds. The editors decided not to run the picture.

Editors must remember that some photographs can get them into legal trouble. Even though a picture is taken in public and constitutes coverage of a newsworthy event, it may constitute libel or an invasion of privacy. When there is any question about a photograph, editors should be extremely careful. The wrong decision in this regard could cost them and their newspapers thousands of dollars.

Decisions about pictures are often among the most difficult decisions an editor must make. Pictures are dramatic and powerful. They have an impact on readers, on their subjects, and on the newspaper itself. The watchwords for an editor in handling pictures are caution, sensitivity, and courage.

CUTLINES

Cutlines are explanatory and descriptive copy that accompanies pictures. They range widely in style and length, from the one-line identifier called the "skel line" to the full "story" line. Cutlines are necessary to practically all pictures because of the functions they serve: identification, description, explanation, and elaboration.

A well-written cutline answers all of a reader's questions about a picture. What is this picture about? What is its relationship to the story it accompanies? Who are the people in it? Where are the events taking place and when? What does the picture mean? The cutline should answer these and other questions in such a manner that material found in any accompanying story is not repeated verbatim but is reinforced, amplified, or highlighted.

Every newspaper has its own particular standards for cutline writing and display. For example, a newspaper may use one typeface for "story cutlines" (cutlines for pictures without accompanying stories) and another for cutlines on news pictures. What is important is that each publication be consistent in its use of cutlines. An established style should exist for each particular type of cutline so that the reader will know what to expect from the publication and so that cutline writers experience a minimum of difficulty in deciding how to present information.

Cutlines are one of the most neglected parts of the newspaper. They are often written as an afterthought when all other parts of a story are finished. Sometimes reporters are assigned to write cutlines; other times it is the job of copy editors; and sometimes the photographers themselves have to write the cutlines. Whoever does the writing should remember that cutlines are as important as any other part of the paper and should be treated with care. The following are some general guidelines for writing cutlines.

Use the present tense to describe what is in the picture.

Always double check identifications in a cutline. This rule cannot be stressed too much. Many newspapers have gotten themselves into deep trouble through misidentification of people in a cutline, so cutline writers should take great care.

Be as specific as possible in cutlines. Add to the reader's knowledge, and go beyond what the reader can see in the picture. A cutline is useless if it simply tells the reader what can be seen already.

Try to avoid cutline clichés. "Looking on," "is pictured" and other such expressions are trite and usually avoidable.

Because cutlines are different from other kinds of information the newspaper has to present, they should be displayed differently. The following are some commonly used guidelines which many newspapers use in displaying cutlines.

Cutlines should contrast with the publication's body type to make for easier reading. Using boldface or type one step larger than body type can accomplish this.

Cutlines should be set at different widths than most body type. For instance, if a column is three or four columns wide, a cutline should be set in two stacks of type under the picture. Cutlines should also take up all or most of the space allotted to them.

Catchlines (headlines above the cutlines) look best in eighteen or twenty-four point type and are generally centered above the cutline.

Two general principles should govern an editor's use of cutlines. One is that every picture should have some kind of a cutline. The words used in the cutline may be few, but they can add enormously to the reader's understanding of the picture and the story the editor is trying to tell. The second principle is that everyone in a picture should be identified. Nameless people are not very interesting, and their presence indicates a lack of interest on the part of the editor in doing a thorough job.

Cutlines are important because of the information they contain and because of the way they enhance the appearance of the paper. Cutlines should be simply and clearly written and displayed, and they should be given the same attention by the editors which other parts of the paper receive.

Figure 9-9   CUTLINE STYLES

Newspapers may have a variety of cutline styles, as seen from the examples in this illustration.

Jake Butcher

Uplifting

Helen Zechmeister is lifting weights when others in her age group are finding comfortable rocking chairs. The 78-year-old woman is shown here lifting from a dead start position as part of her training regimen. From Los Altos Hills, Calif., she recently lifted 214.75 pounds to take first place in her age group.

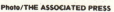

Photo/THE ASSOCIATED PRESS

Fred Neikirk, foreground, and Bob Dean enjoyed the unseasonable temperatures as they fished at Jacobson Lake in Lexington yesterday. As it turned out, however, they had better luck with the weather than they did with the fish.

'This program operates so loosely that it offers maximum opportunity for politics.'

State Rep. Herb Morgan

Associated Press

Massacre survivors gather in makeshift refugee camp.

EXERCISES

PICTURE EXERCISE

Follow your instructor's directions in dealing with this picture.

Cutline information: Funeral service for General Omar Bradley; general during World War II; lead U.S. Army in Europe; shown here is caisson bearing his body, honor guard and riderless horse crossing Memorial Bridge into Arlington National Cemetery, Washington, D.C.

PICTURE EXERCISE

Follow your instructor's directions in dealing with this picture.

Cutline information: Fourth of July parade; crowd gathers along Main Street to watch for beginning of parade, sponsored by City Fire and Police Departments and City Civitan Club; parade including marching bands from local university and three surrounding counties; parade's grand marshal was Alvin Picket, former mayor.

PICTURE EXERCISE

Follow your instructor's directions in dealing with this picture.

Cutline information: Fourth of July parade; Elm Street; clown on unicycle is Vinton Johnson, son of Mrs. Thelma Johnson, 123 State Avenue; he attends Lincoln Middle School.

PICTURE EXERCISE

Follow your instructor's directions in dealing with this picture.

Cutline information: Fourth of July parade; vendor Artie Sams; girl's name not known; Artie's 50th Fourth of July parade selling souvenirs from his wagon. Artie is also a part-time volunteer fireman.

PICTURE EXERCISE

Follow your instructor's directions in dealing with this picture.

Cutline information: Ian Evans, labor leader from Scotland; spoke at AFL-CIO rally yesterday; photographer unidentified; 400 people attended rally; Evans said, "Equal opportunity is a bureaucratic falsehood; organization is the only hope of the masses." Rally part of AFL-CIO local May Day celebration.

PICTURE EXERCISE

Follow your instructor's directions in dealing with this picture.

Cutline information: Polish refugees in Vienna, Austria; members of the banned Solidarity movement; contingent of 20 ready to take part in Workers' Day parade in Vienna; leader said the marched to show support for their compatriots who are still in Poland.

10

DESIGN AND LAYOUT

Newspaper design refers to the overall appearance of a newspaper. Layout is the day-to-day creation of a newspaper design. Design takes in not only the way the stories are laid out on any one page but also how different sections relate to each other, the kind of body type and headline faces that are used, the way pictures are cropped, the positioning of advertisements, and the types of designs and shapes used in standing heads and logos.

Editors must make many decisions in developing a design for their publications. These decisions provide the general rules or guidelines for the layout of the publication.

Newspaper design has three basic and interrelated purposes:

1. It should make the paper easy to read. A newspaper has a set design for the same reason it has a set style: consistency. A reader will be confused if he or she finds several spellings in the paper of the same word; so too will the reader be confused if there are numerous styles of body type and headline faces, odd shapes and sizes, and various locations for the daily features of the paper. A good newspaper design sets the rules for reading the paper; these rules should be consistent and functional and should be changed only for specific purposes.

2. Newspaper design (the overall objective) and layout (the day-to-day execution) send messages to the reader. The layout of a newspaper is not content-free; that is, with the design and layout, an editor tells the reader what stories are the most important, what elements (pictures, headlines and story) should be tied together, and which groups of stories are related. A good newspaper design sets the rules for the editor (and the reader) but also allows for some flexibility in day-to-day work.

3. Design and layout establish a newspaper's "graphic personality." It is important for a newspaper to establish a particular appearance for the reader and to be consistent in that appearance. Many newspapers, such as the **New York Times**, the **Louisville Courier-Journal**, and the **Wall Street Journal**, have done just that. On appearance alone, there is no mistaking these newspapers. It is true that bad newspapers may be clothed in good design, but it is also true that good newspapers with bad or inconsistent designs put added strain on the loyalty of the readers. There is no reason for a newspaper to sacrifice form for function— the best papers have both. A newspaper with a pleasing and consistent design — a "graphic personality" — builds faith and credibility with the reader.

Another important reason for a newspaper to have a clean, consistent graphic personality is that it shows craftmanship and professionalism on the part of the editors and builds pride among the staff. Staff writers who know that their stories will be well displayed, easy to find, and easy to read will probably work harder to make sure the facts are straight and the stories are well written.

TYPES OF NEWSPAPER DESIGN

Since the advent of headlines, pictures, and other typographical devices, three types of newspaper design have evolved into general use: vertical, horizontal, and modular. Most other designs are variations on these general models, and the student of layout and design should be familiar with the characteristics of each.

Canada's Export

Harlequins: the Romance of Escapism

By STANLEY MEISLER
Times Staff Writer

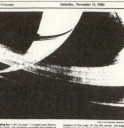

Passing by— As Voyager 1 cruised past Saturn and its rings, the cameras recorded this image of Saturn can be seen clearly through the rings. The picture was made at a distance of about 930,000 miles. (Story in Part I, Page 30.)

Reputed Mafia Figures Convicted on 11 Counts

5 Defendants in Long Trial Found Not Guilty on 9 Other Charges, Including Murder of Informant

By GENE BLAKE, Times Legal Affairs Writer

Meese, Baker Get White House Posts

To Be Counselor and Chief of Staff to New President

By WILLIAM J. EATON
Times Staff Writer

Ed Meese

James A. Baker

Fed Increases Discount Rate for Banks to 12%

By ROBERT A. ROSENBLATT
Times Staff Writer

William French Smith May Be Attorney General Choice

By ROBERT SHOGAN, Times Political Writer

Manhattan Not Peking

Koch Back-Pedals on N.Y. Bike Lanes, Rips Them Up

By JOHN J. GOLDMAN, Times Staff Writer

East, West OK Accord to Save Madrid Talks

By DON COOK
Times Staff Writer

Union, City Officials Hope for Weekend Strike Accord

By JUDITH MICHAELSON and BILL BELLITTER, Times Staff Writers

INDEX	

U.S. Industry Production Increases, Fed Reports

The Salt Lake Tribune

Vol. 221, No. 22   Salt Lake City, Utah—Saturday November 15, 1980—Mail Edition   Price Twenty-Five Cents

Ends Two-Month Harangue

U.S.-Soviet Compromise Saves Madrid Confab

By James M. Markham
New York Times Writer

Reagan Taps Meese, James Baker as White House Aides

By Robert Furlow
Associated Press Writer

Schoolchildren Freed From Terror Group

Inside The Tribune

Voyager Sees Saturn Moons As Huge Orbs Of Rock, Ice

Pope Arrives in W. Germany Today; 5-Day Visit Controversial, 'Delicate'

By John Tagliabue
New York Times Writer

Iran's Supreme Council Meets; War Intensifies

BAGHDAD, Iraq (UPI) —

Coming Sunday In The Tribune

Utah's New Catholic Bishop

A Father's Fight To Ban Handguns

Kenny Rogers Fetes the Steelers

No Hurdle Too High

A Couple Of Routs

Reagan Picks Mr. Inside, Mr. Outside

LOS ANGELES (AP) —

JAMES A. BAKER III
Chief Of Staff

EDWIN MEESE III
Special Counselor

Pope Talks About Sex In Germany

COLOGNE, West Germany (AP) —

Iran Considers U.N. Transfer For Hostages

KUWAIT (AP) — Iranian revolutionary leader Ayatollah Ruhollah Khomeini is considering a proposal to turn over the 52 American hostages to U.N. Secretary General Kurt Waldheim, the independent Kuwaiti newspaper Al-Watan reported today.

FOREST FIRES ARE MONITORED IN MILTON OFFICE OF FORESTER JERRY WIMER
Radio Dispatcher Kyra Johnson, Left, Takes Reports From Hose Controllers

Rain, Reinforcements Fight Fires

By BILL BYRD
Of The Daily Mail Staff

40 Years In One Room

Countess' Lockup Raises Questions

ROME (AP) —

American MP Slain In Turkey

ANKARA, Turkey (AP) —

Top Of The Evening

CHARLEY WEST SAYS

Do You Have The Midas Touch?

10-1 VERTICAL, HORIZONTAL AND MODULAR DESIGN

These front pages typify the modern varieties of vertical, horizontal and modular design. On the *Los Angeles Times* page, all of the headlines are one- or two-column, and eye movement on the page is up and down. The *Salt Lake Tribune* page features large pictures and multicolumn heads. Eye flow is across the page rather than up and down. On the *Charleston Daily Mail* page, every story package forms a rectangle, the major characteristic of modular design. Each story package is a self-contained unit, yet units are placed on the page in a way that achieves balance and unity.

Vertical. Vertical design demands an up and down movement of the reader's eye on the page. Pages using this design have a long, narrow look to them. They feature one- or two-column headlines with long strips of body type dropping down from them. The most prominent example of vertical design is the **Wall Street Journal**.

Horizontal. In horizontal design, the elements on a page typically lie along horizontal rather than vertical lines. This effect is created by larger pictures, multicolumn headlines, wider columns of body type than normally found in vertical design and generous but carefully controlled white space. The theory behind horizontal design is that natural eye movement is across a page rather than up and down. Horizontal design developed as modern printing methods were developed which allowed editors to break column rules (the lines between columns of type) or eliminate them altogether, include larger pictures and headlines and set copy in differing widths. Many newspapers have now adopted this design.

Modular. Modular design requires that story packages — headlines, photographs or illustrations and body type — be shaped into rectangles on the page. These boxes create a unified and unmistakable space for all related items on a page. Such pages are laid out with these boxes in mind rather than the individual elements within each module. Modular design is an outgrowth of editors' tendency toward horizontal design and away from vertical design.

LAYOUT I: PRINCIPLES

Once a consistent design, or graphic personality, has been developed, editors must attend to the daily production of the paper. Someone must lay out each page according to the rules the publication has set. In doing this, editors must give consideration to the five major aspects of newspaper layout: proportion, balance, focus, dynamics, and unity.

Proportion. Proportion is concerned with two interrelated items: the shape of the elements on the page and the relationship of these elements to one another. The most pleasing shapes are those of the 3 x 4, 5 x 7, and 10 x 8 variety, such as those below. Shapes in which the sides are wildly out of proportion to one another are distracting, confusing, or even boring (such as the square).

A newspaper should work to create pleasing shapes of proper proportions for its readers. Such shapes are simple, familiar, and easy on the eye, and they give the appearance of a neat, well-planned page. In other words, they make things easy on the readers.

This is not to say that every shape in the newspaper should be rectangular or modular. There is certainly room for variation. However, editors should avoid the jagged or ragged shapes caused by inattention to the bottom portions of a story unit or multiline headlines that do not fill out their assigned space.

Proportion also refers to the relative size of the elements on the page. It means that the headline space should have the proper relationship with the body of the story and with other headlines on the page, that the pictures should be large enough to show the subject adequately, and that large blocks of type unbroken by other elements should not dominate the page. In fact, no typographical element should have accidental dominance over the page.

Balance. Balance refers to the relationship of all the elements on the page and the impression this relationship has on the reader. Pages with a lot of pictures or heavy typographical elements in any one particular part of the page are referred to as being heavy (top-heavy, for example), and editors, except in rare occasions, should try to avoid heaviness. Instead, the page should have a good distribution of pictures and headlines.

The page should also have a mixture of headline styles — that is, there should be a mix of one-, two- and three-column heads, as well as some single-line and multi-line heads. A paper may also use devices such as kickers and hammerheads to create white space in the middle of the page and to offset the areas of heavy graphics. Inside pages can be balanced in part by placing pictures away from ads or other unrelated pictures.

Focus. It is natural that the reader's eye should be drawn to some typographical element on the page. The editors should control what that element is, and they should take care that other lines, shapes, and elements on the page do not distract from that focusing element.

A page should be built around a major element, usually a picture. Pictures should not be buried next to ads, nor should pictures or other elements be in competition with each other. The reason editors should pay close attention to the focus of their pages lies in another of the major considerations of newspaper layout: dynamics.

Dynamics. Readers generally read a page in a Z-like fashion, beginning with the upper left and moving down the page. It is important for an editor to select a focus at the top of the page to control the reader's beginning. If the upper left portion of the page is a jumble of heads, pictures and other typographical elements, readers will be confused and easily distracted from what may be really important. Not knowing where to go on the page, they may miss something or may turn to another part of the paper entirely.

Another way of understanding dynamics is through the concept of rhythm. Rhythm refers to the logical flow of elements that readers are trained to expect when they see a newspaper. A page which has headlines or pictures bunched together may disrupt a reader's rhythm. Readers may then be unconsciously thrown off balance and not know what to expect or where to go in the paper to find the items they really want.

Unity. Newspaper pages should be thought of as a unit rather than a set of typographical elements. These elements should relate well to one another on the page, just as the elements of a story package (story, headline, picture, cutline) should form a cohesive unit. The concept of unity takes into account all of the factors discussed above. A page should look as if it were planned on one editor's desk, not on the desks of several people with differing ideas of how the final product should look.

NEWS JUDGMENT

On many newspapers the person who lays out the news pages is called the news editor. This person does not carry the title of layout editor because it would not be fully descriptive of the job. The news editor has a more important function than drawing the dummies (scaled layout sheets) for the different pages. This function is one of selection and placement of stories, pictures, and other elements in the story.

To do the job correctly, a news editor must not only have a sense of what will look good on a page and how a page will fit together but must also have a keen sense of news judgment. News judgment is the ability to choose and position the stories, pictures, and other material that are important to the readers and are expected from the paper.

The news editor's first job is to select the news of the day. In doing this, it is essential that the editor keep up with the day's events and be able to understand their relative importance. The editor must first read the paper in order to know what stories have been printed and what needs continuous coverage. A newspaper cannot afford to be episodic in its coverage of important, breaking news events. The news editor must also be aware of the content of other media, not only other newspapers but also radio and television. Many newspapers provide their newsrooms with television sets so that editors ant reporters can watch the local news to make sure they have not missed any major items; they may also watch the national news to get an idea of what other journalists have deemed important for that day.

The news editor must also make sure that the paper carries the standard items the readers have come to expect from the paper, such as weather reports, advice columns, and news briefs. Compiling and placing such items are tedious jobs, but they are necessary for providing continuity to the paper.

Not only must news editors select items for inclusion in the paper, they must also decide where to place them. (It should be noted that on many newspapers these decisions are made at a daily meeting of editors, but often these decisions provide only guidelines for the news editor.) These decisions about placement are often difficult and sometimes delicate. A story may be "played up" or "played down," according to where it goes in the paper and what kind of headline the news editor assigns to it. To make these decisions, a news editor must have a definite idea of what kind of publication the editors and publishers want the newspaper to be and what the expectations of the readers are.

The Philadelphia Inquirer

Crime in the suburban sanctuary: Stealing the sacred

Soviets open to changes in SALT II

U.S. group holds talks in Moscow

For reform, they seize school bus

Big business said to rule solar power

For $130, he hints they'll see Reagan

Unlocked
Countess freed after 40 years

Reagan's early choices make New Right edgy

The Washington Post

Reagan Picks 2 Top Staff Aides

Tax Cut Crunch: Keeping Promises

Moscow Compromises On Continuation of Madrid Conference

Senate Figures, Once Powerful, Ponder Future

Iran's Hostage Panel Sets Talks Today

Prince George's Surpasses D.C. In Population

Proposal to Admit Women Is Agitating Cosmos Club

Md. Sniper: Angry Victim Of Vietnam

The Oregonian

Northwest power bill showdown nears

Iranian jets raid six Iraqi cities

Iran offers no response on hostages

Reagan picks two for White House staff

Panel raises defense bill $6.4 billion

HOSTAGES — Children held hostage Friday wait aboard hijacked bus in the parking lot of the Belgian state radio and television building in Brussels.

Police grab three, end school bus hijacking

10-2 NEWS JUDGEMENT

These front pages were published on the same day. Note the different ways the editors played the same stories, and note the variety of stories used. You may also make the same comparison of the pages in Figure 10-1.

Figure 10-3   FIRST AND FINAL EDITIONS

Many newspapers print several editions every day. These editions require news editors to change or "make over" pages to get later stories in the paper. These pages are from the first and final editions of the *Miami Herald*. The sports pages must go through this same process, too.

Sports News

Wednesday, Jan. 19, 1983   The Miami Herald   Section C

The unknown force: Dolphins' Dwight

By LARRY DORMAN

X-rays reveal fracture, cloud von Schamann's status

Arroyo's learning the ropes

Youngster gets a top rating

By MARK NEWMAN

Long and short of it

Lions' White may sign today with USFL club

S. Rosenbloom suffers skull fracture in fall

'Spring Fever' leaves its audience cool

Jim Martz
Tennis

Sports News

Wednesday, Jan. 19, 1983   The Miami Herald   Section C

Dwight's might making Dolphins right

By LARRY DORMAN

Dwight Stephenson: 'I've done some things well.'

Fracture is found in Uwe's back

X-rays reveal hairline crack in low vertebra

By GEORGE STEIN

HAIRLINE FRACTURE OF THE TRANSVERSE PROCESS

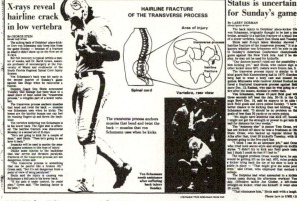

Status is uncertain for Sunday's game

By LARRY DORMAN

USFL's Blitz to raid NFL, sign Lions' linebacker White

'Spring Fever' earns wintry reception

Jim Martz
Tennis

The news editor plays a critical role in the life of a newspaper. On a daily basis, this editor's decisions have more to do with the kind of publication that is presented to the reader than do the decisions of any other editor. (It should be noted that different departments within the news and editorial division often have separate editors who function as news editors. For example, the sports, living, entertainment, national, and foreign desks may each have such an editor.)

TOOLS AND ELEMENTS

A news editor has various tools and elements with which to work. His tools include a picture wheel (see Chapter 9), a pica pole or some other measuring device and straight edge, pencils and dummy sheets. This last tool is particularly helpful. A dummy sheet is a scaled sheet of paper which is sectioned off in columns according to the number of columns on the page. Numbers on each side of a dummy sheet correspond to inches on a newspaper page. This sheet allows a news editor to draw a picture of how the page should look when it is completed.

The elements of layout are also fairly obvious. They include body type, headlines, pictures and various other typographical elements. These major components are discussed below.

Body type. Body type is the typeset version of the story itself. A news editor must be able to choose the width of the body type for any story and, after the width has been chosen, to determine the length, which is measured in column inches. A column inch is one inch of type set in any width. Widths are usually measured in picas, an old printer's measure. There are about 6 picas to an inch; a pica is divided into 12 points.

Body type for a newspaper is usually set in 8- or 9-point type, although type for editorials is usually somewhat larger. The standard column width for an eight-column format is 9 or 9 ½ picas, or 9 picas and 6 points; the standard column width for a six-column newspaper is 12 ½ or 13 picas. Because of the versatility of most typesetters, however, body copy may be set at just about any width a news editor desires. All editors should remember that type which is too narrow or too wide is unattractive and difficult to read.

Most electronic editing systems give the editor easy access to a variety of type sizes and column widths. Editors must understand how to operate their systems to obtain this variety as needed. The commands used to gain this variety are generally called parameters. Parameters allow an editor to change a number of things about the way copy is set. For instance, the following set of parameters might appear on a VDT system:

ss sm1300 sz08 sf1090 ft1 ss

A   B   C   D   E   F

A and F. This is a supershift command. A supershift tells the automatic typesetter that the following information is a typesetting instruction and is not to be set in typeitself. Many typesetters require that supershift commands (or a similar command convention) surround the typesetting instructions, as they do in the one above.

B. The "sm" means "set measure" and refers to the width of the column. In this particular command, the column width desired is 13 picas; the last two zeros are for points, if necessary. If the column width the editor wanted is 9 ½ picas, the designation for this set of parameters would be "0906."

C. The editor must designate the size of the type desired. In this case, the editor wants 8 point type.

D. The editor must also designate how much space the typesetter should leave between the lines of type, or the leading. In the days of hot type, when a printer wanted to make a story a little longer, he would "lead it out," or put some metal slugs in between the slugs of metal type. Today, most newspapers do not use metal type, but the term is still with us. Leading is usually measured in points, and in this case, the editor has asked for 9-point leading (the size of the type plus the white space). (The designation for 9 ½-point leading would be "096.")

E. The editor must finally tell the typesettter what font the copy should be set in. A typesetter may have a variety of fonts available, and these will usually be numbered according to a system the newspaper has established. Many times in a font series, 1 will mean roman or straight or regular; 2 will mean italic; 3 will mean boldface; and 4 will mean extra-bold.

(Please note that the example above gives a set of parameters for one system only. Every typesetting system has a different means of designating parameters; editors should learn how to do that as quickly as possible. The main thing for now is to know the elements generally required in typesetting parameters.)

The parameters in the example above will produce a block of type like that pictured in Figure 10-4. (On this typesetter, font-1 designation is News No. 3 type). Figures 10-5, 10-6, 10-7 and 10-8 show how the appearance of the type will change if any one item in the parameters is altered. Changing column widths, typefaces and leading is a relatively simple matter on most editing systems. Editors should be fully aware of the kinds of type their typesetters can produce.

Headlines. Much of what has been said about body type may also be said for headlines. A newspaper will probably use only one or two typefaces for its headlines (see Chapter 8). The editor will have to select the point size and width for the headline on any particular story. The editor needs to have a good idea of what sizes are proper and how much room headlines will take up on a page. If the newspaper allows a mix of roman and italic headlines, the editor must try to maintain a variety of each on all pages containing numerous headlines.

GUATEMALA CITY (AP) — A man and woman from Colorado, imprisoned for 28 days here on charges of participating in guerrilla attacks, celebrated their freedom by dining on steak and champagne, relatives said.

A special court Tuesday ordered the release of Michael Ernest, 27, of Golden, Colo., and Maria Molenaar, a native of Spain's Canary Islands who has been living in Golden.

They said they planned to fly to Denver today by way of Mexico City and Los Angeles.

10-4   PARAMETERS

The column of type shown in this figure was set according to the example of the parameters described in the text. The editor has had to make a separate decision about each part of the parameter command.

GUATEMALA CITY (AP) — A man and woman from Colorado, imprisoned for 28 days here on charges of participating in guerrilla attacks, celebrated their freedom by dining on steak and champagne, relatives said.

A special court Tuesday ordered the release of Michael Ernest, 27, of Golden, Colo., and Maria Molenaar, a native of Spain's Canary Islands who has been living in Golden.

They said they planned to fly to Denver today by way of Mexico City and Los Angeles.

10-5   COLUMN WIDTHS

This column of type is the same as the one in the previous figure except for the width of the column, which has been changed to 18 picas.

GUATEMALA CITY (AP) — A man and woman from Colorado, imprisoned for 28 days here on charges of participating in guerrilla attacks, celebrated their freedom by dining on steak and champagne, relatives said.

A special court Tuesday ordered the release of Michael Ernest, 27, of Golden, Colo., and Maria Molenaar, a native of Spain's Canary Islands who has been living in Golden.

They said they planned to fly to Denver today by way of Mexico City and Los Angeles.

10-6   TYPE SIZE AND LEADING

This column of type is the same as the one in Figure 10-4 except for the type size and leading. The type size has been changed to 10 point and the leading to 12 point.

GUATEMALA CITY (AP) — A man and woman from Colorado, imprisoned for 28 days here on charges of participating in guerrilla attacks, celebrated their freedom by dining on steak and champagne, relatives said.

A special court Tuesday ordered the release of Michael Ernest, 27, of Golden, Colo., and Maria Molenaar, a native of Spain's Canary Islands who has been living in Golden.

They said they planned to fly to Denver today by way of Mexico City and Los Angeles.

10-7   LEADING

This column of type is the same as the one in Figure 10-4 except for the leading which has been changed from 9 point to 10 point.

GUATEMALA CITY (AP) — A man and woman from Colorado, imprisoned for 28 days here on charges of participating in guerrilla attacks, celebrated their freedom by dining on steak and champagne, relatives said.

A special court Tuesday ordered the release of Michael Ernest, 27, of Golden, Colo., and Maria Molenaar, a native of Spain's Canary Islands who has been living in Golden.

They said they planned to fly to Denver today by way of Mexico City and Los Angeles.

10-8   FONT

This column of type is the same as that in Figure 10-4 except for the font designation, which has been changed to boldface.

Pictures. Pictures are often the most important typographical element a news editor has. Readers are more likely to see pictures on a page than anything else, and modern design calls for the use of more and larger pictures. News editors should have a variety of pictures with which to work. If the newspaper subscribes to a wire photo service, the editor will have more pictures than can be used in any one day. In addition, there will be pictures taken by the newspaper's own photographers, those which the newspaper has on file in its library (such as head shots of prominent people), and pictures submitted by non-staff members. Editors must then select, crop, and scale the pictures they want to use (see Chapter 9). Editors must also remember to leave room for catchlines and cutlines. These are as much a part of the photograph as the picture itself.

Other typographical elements. A news editor has a variety of other typographical elements with which to work, such as standing heads and logos, lines, drawings, and graphs. An editor may be able to use spot or full color on a page, depending on the capacity of the press. Individual papers are likely to have established rules and customs governing the use of these elements.

PROCEDURE

When a news editor has assembled the elements with which he will work on any given day, the complex procedure of putting the pages together begins. The procedure is a complex one because numerous decisions have to be made at once, and almost every single decision that is made has some effect on all other layout decisions. For instance, while deciding what to put at the top of a page, the news editor must also be considering what will go at the bottom of the page in order to create the proper balance and contrast.

Because the procedure is so complex and because it will change each day due to the different elements to be used, there is no step-by-step guide on how to lay out a page. There are, however, some general guidelines or considerations that can be suggested to beginning students who are faced with various typographical elements and a blank dummy sheet.

1. Begin at the top. If the flag is stationary (that is, always located at the top of the page) draw it on the dummy first. If the flag floats (can be moved to another position on the page), make some decision about where it should go on the page.

2. Order the stories and pictures, or make some preliminary decisions about where they will be placed on the page. Readers generally will begin looking at a page at the upper left (which is called the primary optical area, or POA). The editor should therefore select for this area the most important item or the one which will capture the attention of the reader. When a decision about the primary optical area has been made, the next logical decision is usually about what will go in the upper right corner of the page.

3. Decide what will be in the lower-right corner of the page. This decision needs to be made next, because the upper-left element will need some balancing element in the lower right. As with the top of the page, making this decision may also help the news editor decide what should be placed in the lower-left corner of the page.

4. When the corners of the page have been filled, the editor should go back to the top of the page and fill in toward the center. Here, of course, the decisions that have already been made on the page will determine what the editor can or cannot do with the rest of the page. Working from the corners to the center of the page is preferable to starting from the top and working down because by working from the corners the editor is less likely to leave small or odd holes at the bottom of the page. The center of the page offers the news editor more flexibility than the borders.

While front pages come in infinite varieties and therefore cannot be laid out by any formula, inside pages — especially those carrying advertisements — are a little more standard. The following are some guidelines and suggestions for handling inside pages.

1. Each page should carry a dominant headline.

2. Each should have a good attention-getter, a focus around which the other elements on the page revolve.

3. Each should have a good picture, especially at the top of the page and set away from the ads. This could be the attention-getter referred to above.

4. If a page is tight (that is, if there isn't much room for editorial matter on the page) one long story is preferable to several shorter ones.

5. If a page is open (that is, at least one-third is left for news), try to fill in a story to align with the highest ad, thus squaring off the rest of the page for editorial matter. Doing this can increase the flexibility of the editor and help produce a more interesting layout.

Another thing editors who deal with both front and inside pages must be concerned with is "jumps." A story beginning on one page and continuing onto another is known as a "jumped story." The part of the story continued on the second page is called the "jump" and the headline over that part of the story is called the "jump head." "Jump lines" are those lines at the end of the first part of the story ("Continued on Page 2") and at the beginning of the jump ("Continued from Page 1").

A newspaper should have a consistent style in handling jumped stories, jump lines, and jump heads. Some newspapers, such as Gannett's new national daily, **USA Today**, try to avoid jumps almost entirely, but most papers find that this policy is not feasible. The best jump lines try to inform the reader of the jump head and the page number of the jump, such as "See PRESIDENT, Page 2." Jump heads may be just one word or rewrites of the first page headline, or they may refer to an element in the jumped portion.

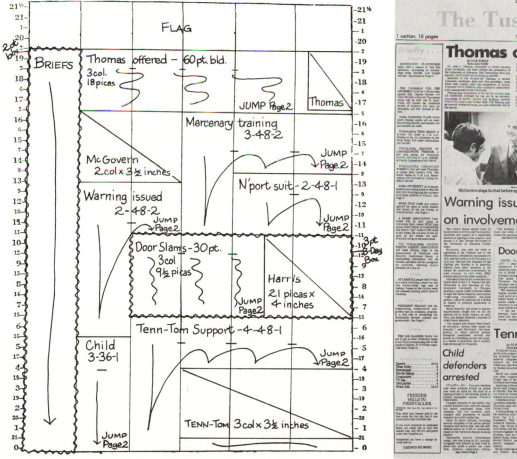

Figure 10-9   FRONT PAGE DUMMY

This figure shows a layout dummy used to build the accompanying front page. Note the information about stories and headlines that appear on the dummy.

Figure 10-10 INSIDE PAGE DUMMY

Inside pages are dummied in much the same way as front pages. Ads are placed on them first by the newspaper's advertising department, and then they are given to the news department. In this example, note how the editors squared the page off at the top of the ads. The large picture at the upper left balances the large ad in the lower right. Also note the variety of column widths used on the page.

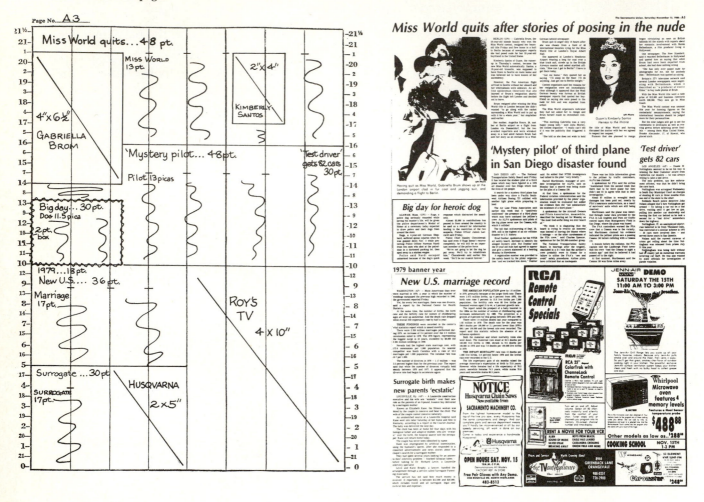

TWELVE RULES

The following are some basic rules governing layout of newspaper pages. Not every newspaper follows every rule all the time, and there are cases when these rules can legitimately be broken. Most of the time, however, these rules should be observed as closely as possible.

1. Avoid "tombstoning" headlines. Tombstoning means running different headlines together on the page. When headlines are run together, they can be confusing to the reader and create an unattractive and cluttered appearance for the page. News editors should try to isolate major elements on a newspaper page. Headlines are more easily seen and break up gray areas better when they stand alone.

2. Avoid placing one headline directly under part of another without copy between (it's called "armpitting"). Again, the idea is to isolate the headline to help it be seen. If headlines run directly under one another, they lose isolation and create confusion.

3. Avoid splitting the page. A split occurs when an alley is not crossed by a headline or a picture somewhere in the lower three-quarters of the page. Modern design calls for a unified page. If a gutter runs the length of the page, it splits the page in two, destroying both the unity of the page and the reader's eye flow.

4. Avoid heavy blocks of body type. Masses of gray type discourage even the most interested reader from becoming involved in the story. Make sure there is a good variety of body, headlines, pictures, and other typographical devices on every part of the page.

5. Place major stories on the primary focal point of the page, usually the upper left-hand corner. This should be the strongest part of the page — the one where the editor places the strongest typographical elements.

6. Use contrasting but not conflicting headline typefaces. The faces should complement each other and be consistent. Mixing serif and sanserif faces violates this principle. Simplicity of design and uniformity of page development are the objectives.

7. Use few typefaces and vary size and tone (roman and italic). This is again designed to isolate headlines and make them distinctive. Simplicity is also an abiding consideration. A reader should not have to wade through a variety of typefaces but should have a page which presents enough variety to be interesting.

8. Follow the "step-down" rule. The step-down rule requires that larger headlines appear at the top of the page, with gradually smaller headlines appearing below them. This rule may be violated to maintain balance, but these violations should only occur to accomplish specific objectives.

9. Let pictures seem to stand on or hang from something. Photos are major attention-getters. They should always draw the eye to some other major element on the page that can lead the reader through the page.

10. Never wrap a story out from under its headline. Headlines should provide a kind of umbrella for the story. Running copy out from under that umbrella leads to confusion, especially if that copy moves below another headline.

11. Try to avoid wraps that create odd shapes. The more regularly shaped a wrap is (rectanglular, square, etc.), the easier it is for a reader to isolate it visually.

12. Make sure the tops of story packages are level. Story packages include the headline, body type, pictures, and any other material related to the story grouped together on a page. The tops of these groups should form a straight line on the page. Avoid, for instance, a three-column headline with a four-column related headline under it.

EXERCISES

LAYOUT EXERCISE

Lay out a front page and an inside page for a local newspaper with the following stories and photos.

National and International Stories:

PRESS CONF — At a press conference today, the president asks Congress to set aside three million more acres of wilderness land in the Western U.S. and Alaska for mineral and resource development. The president says preliminary studies have shown large amounts of oil and coal in the lands and that the nation's energy future depends on Congressional action. 21 inches

REACTION — General reaction to president's request for development of wilderness in Western U.S. Environmentalists say the president is committing too much land to the project; energy developers say it isn't enough; and Congressional leaders remain noncommital. 15 inches

GUNMAN — A man with a gun continues into a second day holding three members of a San Mateo, Cal. family hostage in their home. The man's motives are unclear. Police have the house surrounded and are attempting to negotiate with the man. 17 inches

IRAN — Government officials announce they will be seeking a smaller increase (8 percent) than expected at the next meeting of OPEC. The unofficial explanation for the increase is that Iran is having serious problems with inflation and that a higher increase would fuel an already overheated economy. 12 inches

UNEMPLOYMENT — The Labor Department announces that unemployment for the previous month was 5.4 percent, down a half percentage point from the previous month reported. According to department officials, this is the largest drop in monthly unemployment in five years and indicates a resurgence of the economy as a whole and several industries in particular, such as auto and steel manufacturing and construction. 20 inches

ARTHRITIS — Medical researchers at Michigan State say they may have discovered a substitute for aspirin which will give more relief to arthritis sufferers. Many of the nation's 2.5 million arthritis sufferers get upset stomachs by taking aspirin, and this new drug, admirol, is said to be much easier on the stomach than aspirin. 10 inches

NBC SHAKEUP — National Broadcasting Company Chairman Charles Fitch announces a new shakeup in the upper levels of NBC, which for the fourth straight year is third in the overall network ratings. The president and head of programming for the network have resigned, and the head of network news, Banks Warhead, will now be president of the network. A search for a new programming head is underway. 16 inches

BOMB — A bomb blast in a crowded pub in Northern Ireland kills five and injures 21. The Irish Republican Army has taken responsibility for the blast, and the British government has promised a tough crackdown on terrorists. 12 inches

State and Local Stories:

LEGISLATURE — The State Senate psses a bill increasing the sales tax on gasoline by five cents on the gallon. The vote was 15-14. The House passed the same measure last week so the bill will now be sent to the governor for his signature. 14 inches

SENTENCE UPHELD — The State Supreme Court upholds the death sentence of a local man, Robert Smith, convicted last year of raping and murdering two night nurses at a local hospital. A date for the execution will be set next week. 9 inches

SHERIFF — The sheriff of a county in the southern part of the state is on trial for bribery and extortion. Today he takes the witness stand and denies all charges against him. The case is expected to go to the jury tomorrow. One of your local reporters is coverning the trial. 20 inches

GROUNDBREAKING — Groundbreaking ceremonies are held at the University for the new $3.5 million music building. University officials say they expect the building to be completed in six months. 13 inches

COMMISSION — The City Council passes an ordinance increasing fine for owners of dogs picked up by the Humane Department. Fines go up from $35 to $75 for the first offense. 10 inches

CLEANUP — County residents and businessmen are cleaning up after last week's flooding. Official estimates of flood damage are now up to $4 million. 12 inches

Photos:

PRESIDENT SPEAKS — The president speaks to newsmen during his news conference in Washington. (Proportions are 5 inches wide by 7 inches deep.)

POLICE SEIGE — San Mateo, Cal. police surround a house where a gunman holds three hostages. (8 inches by 10 inches)

LABOR GRAPH — A graph produced by the Department of Labor showing the downward trend of unemployment during the last year and the large decrease during the previous month. (4 inches by 4 inches)

BLAST VICTIMS — Rescue workers remove some of the bodies of the five people killed in a bomb blast in a pub in Belfast, Northern Ireland. (8 inches by 10 inches)

MUSIC BLDG — Standup shot of five officials, including the governor and president of the University, at groundbreaking ceremonies for the University's new music building. (5 inches by 7 inches)

CLEANUP — A county furniture store owner inspects the water and mud damage to his merchandise from last week flooding. (8 inches by 10 inches)

LAYOUT EXERCISE

Lay out a front page and an inside page for a local newspaper with the following stories and photos.

National and International Stories:

PRISON RIOT — A group of 20 prisoners in the state penitentiary in Nashville, Tenn. continue into the second day holding three guards and three prison officials hostage. They are demanding removal of certain guards and improved conditions in the prison. 15 inches

DISSIDENTS — In a surprise move, the Soviet Union has allowed three top Jewish dissidents to fly to Israel. The families of the dissidents, all of whom had spent many years in Soviet labor camps, will follow them to Israel sometime next week. 12 inches

BUDGET — The president has sent to Congress his budget proposals for the coming fiscal year. The budget calls for an across-the-board cut in income taxes of 5 percent for this year and a more selective cut of 10 percent for low and middle income families next year. 20 inches

TERRORISTS — A group of five terrorists have attacked the headquarters of the ruling Christian Democratic Party in Rome, Italy. The attack killed three lower party officials and wounded six office workers. The attack was apparently led by a woman calling herself Maria Red. 17 inches

ELECTIONS — After 12 years of military rule, Brazil has a new civilian president after yesterday's elections. He is Juan De Portas, and he has promised an end to martial law and a restoration of many civil rights including an end to censorship of the press. 13 inches

COFFEE PRICES — After two years of steadily falling coffee prices, two of the nation's largest coffee producers have announced an increase in retail prices. General Foods and National Products say they will be charging about five percent more for ground coffee and three percent more for instant. The price rise is blamed on the decreased production of several major country producers. 14 inches

WEATHER — The Northeast was covered by a huge snowstorm which ground traffic and some businesses to a halt. Buffalo, N.Y. had as much as 30 inches of snow on the ground, and more snow is expected today for most of the areas affected. 15 inches

State and Local Stories:

GARBAGE STRIKE — City sanitation workers continue their strike for the third day. Workers say they are still dissatisfied with pay increases offered during the current contract negotiations. City officials say they are offering the workers all the city can afford. 16 inches

STRIKE REACTION — City residents and businessmen react to the current garbage strike. Most say they are sympathetic with the workers' demands but admit the strike is beginning to cause some inconvenience. Health officials fear an increase in the rat population due to the garbage piling up. 14 inches

DEATHS — Two city residents were killed and another seriously injured when the car in which they were riding was struck by a train at a crossing on the east side last night. One of those killed was John Scott, a former mayor of city. 14 inches

LEGISLATURE — The State House Education Committee has authorized the allocation of $10 million in initial outlays for the building of a new community college in the southern area. The bill must now be voted by the full House where it is expected to meet stiff opposition, especially from legislators representing the northern and central parts of the state. 16 inches

Photos:

PICKETS — Striking sanitation workers picket City Hall demanding higher wages. (Proportions are 8 inches wide by 10 inches deep.)
GARBAGE — While the workers strike, garbage is being piled up along University Blvd. (8 inches by 10 inches)
WRECK — The wreckage of the car in which former Mayor John Scott and another person were killed when it was hit by a train is dragged away from the crossing. (8 inches by 10 inches)
ITALY — Officials of Italy's leading Christian Democratic Party look over the ruin of their party headquarters after it was hit by a terrorist attack. (5 inches by 7 inches)
SUNSET — Feature pix of the sun setting over Lake Smith. (3 inches by 4 inches)

LAYOUT EXERCISE

Lay out a front page and an inside page for a local newspaper with the following stories and photos.

National and International Stories:

FLOOD — Torrential rains in India have produced the worst flooding in decades in some areas. The death toll has reached 2,000 and is expected to total three times that number. More rain is predicted for many low-lying areas tomorrow. The Indian government has declared a state of national emergency and is petitioning the UN for aid. 20 inches

ART FAIR — The governments of Argentina, Venezuela and Brazil have jointly prepared a touring exhibition of South American folk arts and are offering to take it to major cities throughout the world. However, some nations, including Mexico and Panama, say they don't want the exhibition because they fear political terrorism might result. 15 inches

PRESIDENT — At a press conference today, the president publicly denied rumors that he is undergoing treatment for lung cancer. The frequent visits of a noted Washington cancer specialist which spawned speculation about the president's health are merely for consultation on a variety of scientific and medical matters, he said. 10 inches

DOCTOR — An interview with Dr. Evan Topias, Washington cancer specialist and unofficial presidential adviser, confirms the president's statements about the purpose of Topias's frequent visits to the White House. Topias says that the president has never consulted him on a personal basis, and that he does not even know the president's personal physician. 12 inches

INTEREST — Major U.S. banks lowered their prime interest rates by 2 percent yesterday. This is the largest one-day drop in interest rates in more than three years. 10 inches

HARRIS — A new Harris Poll has found that most Americans believe the economy is healthier today than one year ago.   Fifty-four percent say they believe general economic conditions are better than a year ago, 44 percent say things are about the same, and six percent said they thought general economic conditions were worse. 10 inches

FOUND — Four-year-old Mandy Wilton, missing from her parents' home in San Fransisco for more than two years, was found by police yesterday in San Diego. She was living with two single women who claimed to have "rescued her from the middle class" by kidnapping her from her home. The girl was identified after the two women were arrested in a drug bust. 16 inches

State and Local Stories:

LINCOLN — You are working on Saturday's paper, and Sunday is Abraham Lincoln's birthday. One of the services you subscribe to has sent you a copy of an essay about Lincoln written in 1910 by Carl Sandburg. You want to use this essay on Page 1, accompanied by line art from your art department. 15 inches

FIRE — The state Capitol was damaged yesterday when fire broke out in a storage room near the governor's office. No one was injured, but several thousand dollars' worth of supplies were destroyed, and there was smoke and water damage to the entire first floor of the building. Arson is suspected. 20 inches

WRECK — A 12-year-old local boy was killed last night when the pickup truck he and his father were in collided with another truck. The driver of the other truck, a 21-year-old college student, has been arrested and charged with murder in the case. Police say the man was "much more than legally drunk" when the accident occurred. 13 inches

INSURANCE — Local FBI officials and other law enforcement personnel are warning people about an insurance scam they have uncovered. Several men have been selling life insurance policies with a non-existent company to local residents, particularly elderly people. 14 inches

Photos:

FLOOD — Rescue workers dig victims of the Indian floods from the collapsed ruins of their homes. (Proportions are 5 inches by 7 inches.)

PRESIDENT — At a press conference, the president denies he is being treated for cancer. (4 inches by 6 inches.)

TOPIAS — Head shot of Dr. Evan Topias, the Washington physician who acts as "informal adviser" to the president. (3 inches by 5 inches.)

LINCOLN — Line art of Abraham Lincoln produced by your art department (8 inches by 10 inches.)

CAPITOL — Government employees watch as firemen work to control the blaze that destroyed a supply room in the state Capitol yesterday. (5 inches by 7 inches.)

LAYOUT EXERCISE

Lay out a front page and an inside page for a local newspaper with the following stories and photos.

National and International Stories:

TOXIC — Clean-up has begun on a toxic waste dump near Albany, N.Y., where sealed barrels of the banned insecticide DDT have been leaking into the local water supply for 10 months. EPA officials estimate the clean-up will take six to eight months and cost more than $2 million. 20 inches

SHOOTING — Five sanitation workers in Detroit were killed yesterday when an unemployed auto worker went on a shooting rampage in a downtown area where the five were collecting trash. The mayor calls the deaths "a great tragedy of our economic problems." The gunman, identified as Everett Mick, 36, was arrested and charged with five counts of murder. 15 inches

TALKS — Representatives of all NATO countries are meeting in Bonn, West Germany to discuss the international implications of the development of nuclear armaments in third-world nations. American diplomats say the potential for limited nuclear war in undeveloped countries is becoming a greater threat to world peace than the struggles between the superpowers. The NATO group hopes to come up with policies for dealing with threats of war coming from the third world. 12 inches

CAT — Elverton, the 3 year-old cat who recently began portraying the finicky feline in a new series of television commercials for cat food, was found dead by his owner last night. The cat had been poisoned, California toxicologists revealed. 10 inches

CONGRESS — The U.S. House of Representatives turned down a chance to give themselves a raise yesterday. The House voted 300-221 against a bill which would have raised congressional salaries 15 percent. The bill also included provisions for renovations of congressional offices. 14 inches

FRENCH — French Socialist Party leaders are predicting victory for most of their candidates in the upcoming national elections. The Socialists have been strong in French politics for a number of years, but this is their first chance in the last several elections to completely dominate the government. 12 inches

COMPUTER THEFT — Japanese government officials say they are "shocked" by the arrest of Yukio Asada, a customs officer in Tokyo who has been charged with the theft of more than $4 million worth of new IBM computer parts headed for Japanese universities. Asada has confessed to the theft and also admitted to being a KGB contact. Soviet officials have refused to comment. 20 inches

AFGHANS — The suicide rate in Afghanistan is the highest in the world, according to a new report issued by Kabul University Research Center. More than six percent of the Afghan population attempts suicide each year; half of those are successful. Sociologist Yuri Retrof of Kabul University attributes the high rate of suicide to political and social upheavals in the country. 13 inches

State and Local Stories:

ESCAPE — A convicted rapist and murderer has escaped from a maximum security prison in the northeastern part of the state. The man is believed to be hiding out in a state park near the prison. Police have the park cordoned off and are searching the 200,000 acre area with the help of National Guardsmen. 15 inches

PARENTS — Angry parents are converging on the state capital today to protest the adoption of controversial history textbooks by the State Textbook Commission. The group, led by Rev. Tommy Esbrook, believes the books present too favorable a picture of socialist and communist governments. They plan to picket the capitol building until the Commission reverses its recommendations. 14 inches

HOME RENOVATION — The publisher of your paper is particularly interested in antiques and the renovation of old homes in your town. His sister-in-law and her husband have recently completed the renovation of one of the city's oldest homes, at a cost of some $590,000. He wants a front page story - and picture - on their project. 25 inches

SALARIES — The mayor and City Council have announced that salaries for all municipal workers will be frozen indefinitely at current levels due to reduced tax revenues. An eight percent across-the-board raise had been scheduled to go into effect next week. 15 inches

Photos:

TOXIC — Workers begin removal of barrels leaking DDT into the water supply near Albany, N.Y. (Proportions are 6 inches wide by 8 inches deep.)

CAT — Elverton in happier days. (8 inches by 10 inches.)

PARENTS — Parents begin picketing the state capitol in protest of state Textbook Commission recommendations. (5 inches by 7 inches.)

RENOVATION — Owners of one of the city's oldest homes show various aspects of their $590,000 renovation of the building. Three photos (one 5 inches by 7 inches, two 8 inches by 10 inches.)

SHOOTING — Police arrest Everett Micks, a 36 year-old unemployed auto worker from Detroit who shot five city sanitation workers in that city. (5 inches by 7 inches.)

11

THE EDITOR AND THE LAW*

Editors today live in a world of litigation. America has become a society which places increasing reliance on the judicial system. Our law schools are graduating more lawyers than many legal experts feel is necessary to service the system. Congress, the federal bureaucracy, state legislatures, and city and county governments continue to fill volumes of statute books with new laws and regulations. Citizens are more frequently turning to the courts for redress of grievances. Editors find themselves more and more the focal point of legal disputes, so it has become incumbent upon editors to know the law and to know how to use it to their advantage.

The thrust of most of today's court battles, laws, and regulations is to keep editors from getting and publishing information or to punish them for having already published information. Many forces are allied in these battles against editors, from those who seek to protect their reputations to those who want to hide their actions from public scrutiny. Editors should remember that their primary responsibility is to publish accurate information, and they should do so in a way which can best serve their readers and which will help them avoid as many legal hassles as possible.

The best weapon that editors have on their side is the First Amendment to the United States Constitution:

> Congress shall make no law respecting an establishment of religion, or prohibiting the free exercise thereof; or abridging the freedom of speech, or of the press; or the right of the people peaceably to assemble, and to petition the government for a redress of grievances.

Interpretation of the First Amendment continues to be a controversial exercise. Yet as it stands, the First Amendment is a powerful statement for the right to speak and to publish and for the tradition of America as an open society. Editors should work diligently for a liberal and expansive interpretation of the First Amendment and should be unwilling to compromise on its basic meaning. The First Amendment offers basic protections for all citizens, not just editors, but editors are often required to fight a lonely battle in its defense.

LIBEL

Libel is the most dangerous problem facing an editor. Libel laws are extensive and in many areas are being strengthened. The threat of a libel suit often causes reporters and editors to withhold information which the public should have. Large libel judgments have a devastating financial impact on a publication and increase the chances that other libel suits will follow.

In the 1960s, courts, beginning with the Supreme Court's **New York Times v. Sullivan** decision in 1964, built a substantial wall protecting publications from the devastating effects of libel suits. The Supreme Court realized that libel judgments were being used as a means of punishing and repressing publications which fell into disfavor with particular individuals or groups. The court felt that for the First Amendment to work in the way in which it was intended, it would be necessary that libel not be an oppressive burden for editors.

That protection was reduced in the 1970s, and in the 1980s, libel has once again become an instrument of punishment and even repression. More and more suits are being filed, and the cost of

*By Marian Huttenstine and Jim Stovall

233

defending them is enormous. Juries today are more inclined to interpret libel laws liberally and to award massive judgments against media organizations. One recent study has found that media defendants lose about 80 percent of the libel cases which go to trial and lose an even greater percentage of those which are decided by a jury. Many of these judgments are reversed on appeal, but by then the media organization has gone to considerable expense and trouble to defend itself. Courts may fashion a 1960s-like protection for the media at some point in the future, but until then, editors should be extremely well versed in libel law and in the ways to avoid and to defend themselves in libel suits.

Libel is injury to reputation that exposes a person or group to hatred, ridicule, shame, contempt, or disgrace. Libelous material may also be considered to be that which lowers a person in the eyes of a part of the community or which prevents a person from making a living in his chosen line of work. The law requires proof of four things before a libel action can be sustained: defamation, indentification, publication and fault.

Defamation. The words which a libel plaintiff complains of must be defamatory, either in and of themselves or within their context.

Identification. The libel plaintiff must be identified as the object of the defamating words. The plaintiff cannot get by with simply saying, "I know the article was about me even though I wasn't named;" rather, plaintiffs not named specifically must establish concretely that they were the subjects of defamatory words. The idea of identification can become a prickly one when a libelous statement is made about a group of people. Courts have said that if the group is small enough for each individual to be identified, then each member of the group may have a valid libel case. If the group is a large one, such as an entire race of people, individuals cannot establish identification.

Publication. A libelous statement must be transmitted to a third party. It does not necessarily have to be printed or broadcasted in the mass media. A letter which is mailed to a person who is not the object of the libel or a statement made to a small group of people may constitute publication.

Fault. In those situations in which the topic is of genuine public concern or in which the person named is a public official, it will be necessary for the person to establish that the media acted with fault. That is, it must be proved that the offending material was published either with knowledge of its falsity, with reckless disregard of its truth or falsity, or with deliberate intent to harm.

BASIC LEGAL DEFENSES AGAINST LIBEL

When a libel suit is filed by a person who is a private figure, editors have a number of defenses available.

Truth. A number of states have written into their libel laws that truth is an absolute defense for libel — that is, if the truth of a libelous statement can be proven, the plaintiff has no case. That sounds good, but an editor should not fall into the trap of feeling safe because what he or she has printed is "true." Truth, in reality, is a very weak defense, because a statement must be **provably true**. The editor must present evidence in court that a statement is true, and such evidence is very rare.

Privilege. Privilege is a good defense when a libel suit revolves around coverage of public or government meetings and actions. Courts have tried to protect reporters and editors from libel actions resulting from journalists having to report libelous statements which are made by public officials or during public events. Although two kinds of privilege are recognized by the courts, in general it is the lesser or weaker which applies to journalists. Qualified or conditional privilege usually applies to that coverage which is about public issues or events. Such reports must be fair and accurate; they must also not be made with either traditional or actual malice. Absolute privilege was originally accorded only members of congress, judges, etc. in the performance of their official duty. More recently the courts have used this term in referring to reporting about that which occurs in open court or that which occurs on the floor of the legislature (either state or federal). The courts seem to assume that such coverage will be full, fair, and accurate.

Fair comment. The fair comment defense applies more to statements of opinion than to statements of facts. Many courts, including the Supreme Court, have recognized that the holding of opinions should not be penalized even though at times those opinions may be libelous. Although we have a long legal tradition which declares that there is no such thing as a false idea, courts are now less protective of this notion. Fair comment is a reasonable defense, but today it is not an especially strong one. When applied to editorial and arts criticism it is reasonably effective, unless there is an intent to harm.

CONSTITUTIONAL DEFENSES

Although the traditional defenses for libel are good ones, in times of social tension they may not be sufficient. During the civil rights movement of the 1960s a new legal approach to libel was created. In **New York Times v. Sullivan** the United States Supreme Court decided that a constitutional defense against libel should be created that would encourage the press to report more aggressively information about public officials and public issues. To accomplish this the Supreme Court established "actual malice." Defined as knowledge of falsity or reckless disregard of whether the material is true or false, actual malice as a fault standard was designed to make it more difficult for the media to lose libel cases. Gradually this standard came to be applied to libel actions brought by others in the public eye, people who typically are not public officials, but who are nonetheless involved in important issues, typically by their own voluntary actions. For a brief period even those involuntarily caught up in public events were considered "public" and had to prove acutal malice to be successful in litigation against the media. By 1974 the definition of "public figure" had become so all-inclusive that the Supreme Court began to restrict it. This process of redefinition is still occurring.

The "public" question is almost always the most important fact in libel cases involving the media. Because the court has never been explicit in defining who is a public figure, this decision is reached on a case-by-case basis. Courts have also been narrowing the definition of a "public official." Few such persons are now public in all aspects of their lives. The **New York Times** malice standard works best in those situations where the material is clearly about the public role of the official. Most courts now seriously examine the relationship of the content to the role. Thus, the term public official is more limited that we in media would like to think.

The following guidelines for avoiding libel suits may prove helpful to you. Although there is no way to guarantee that a libel action will not follow stories which do harm to a reputation, following these guidelines lessens that possibility. At the same time, should a defense prove necessary, adherence to these guides will make it easier to put forth a strong case in court.

1. Advanced planning is the best way to prevent a suit entirely or to defend against it. When beginning a highly sensitive investigative story, make sure that safe parameters and procedures have been developed. A preliminary discussion with your paper's attorney and your editors can be most helpful. Should a suit be filed later, you have established a strong "due care " or "prudent publisher" defense.

2. If you have deep feelings about a subject or are personally involved with a subject or the topic of an article, do not do the story yourself. Strongly suggest to the assignment editor that someone else do it. If you are an editor, do not assign a reporter to a potentially libelous story if you think the reporter has strong feelings about the subject. To do otherwise creates a problem with "malice" should a libel suit develop.

3. If, in the course of working on a story, doubts develop as to the accuracy of the information or the honesty of a source, resolve those doubts or drop the story. In the end it will often be your personal conviction as to the accuracy of your information which will prove the key to a defense.

4. Do not use the "camera rolling" or hidden mike technique. Although well-known news programs sometimes use this technique, well-known news programs have a lot more money to spend on legal fees. You are attempting to report news, not make it.

5. Do not break the law — that is, don't attempt to interview members of a grand jury, impersonate a police officer, trespass, steal evidence, etc. Any such activity makes a defense which would otherwise stand vulnerable to attack. In addition, such activity does not favorably impress a jury.

6. Do not, either inside the newsroom or outside, make disparaging remarks about story subjects. Such comments make it easy for the opponent to establish "intent to harm." Comments of this type also destroy many usually effective defenses. Make sure your discussions of the story, your sources, your intent, etc. are fit to be taped.

7. Use the following rule of thumb to determine whether you have a potentially libelous story: (a) Is the information accurate? (b) Is the story fair? (c) If the story were about you, what would your reaction be?

8. Before providing assurances of apology, retraction, or correction, discuss the matter with your editor and an attorney. Many times, in the process of "correcting" the problem, you can make it.

9. If at all possible, get a comment from the subject of a story who is being cast in a bad light. Make certain that the subject talks for the record and include this comment in the story. (So doing makes it difficult for the subject to later claim malice.)

10. Bankruptcy has become a problem. When reporting about this, especially regarding private companies, use public records. If you add material from your files or from sources other than public records, make certain that the content is specifically related to the bankruptcy pending.

11. Use extreme caution when making evaluative or competency statements about professionals, such as lawyers and doctors. Damages are so easy to establish by professionals that liability tends to be most expensive. Check, double-check, and use public records and sources when possible.

12. Use "on-the-record" sources and be prepared to defend yourself on the basis of accuracy. Remember that even an accurate quote simply means that you have company in the possible suit. Because a source usually speaks to a single person — you — and you in turn speak or write to many, yours is the greater contribution to any resulting harm to the subject. In such situations, it is best to use double and triple sources, use documents and use public records. An accurate quote does not grant you absolute protection.

13. Do not use confidential sources in those situations where an accusation is made. Should your source insist upon making an accusation, insist that it then be on the record.

14. Double check pictures of criminals and indicted persons to make sure that they are of the correct person and that use will not endanger that person's chances of receiving a fair trial. In broadcasting, use an audio identification and, when possible, a visual identification as well.

15. Get releases from minors or institutions giving you permission to use their pictures. A written consent form should do nicely. Because news photos frequently survive as feature photos, it is a good idea to get releases when possible. Always get releases for non-news photos!

16. Headlines may of themselves provide the basis for a libel suit. Make certain that the headline matches the content of the story.

17. Avoid guilt by association. If you have an accurate story about Smith being a crook, do not mention his prominent friends unless there is evidence that they were aware of or party to his illegal activities. Although it makes interesting reading to include associates, the legal cost can be high.

18. Play lawyer yourself while writing or producing the story. Think through the potential problems. Use other reporters, editors, lawyers, and others to do the same. Anticipated problems can often be eliminated by redraft or modification. Others can successfully be defended because of record-

keeping or procedural change. Note: confidentiality is not compromised by providing editors with the name and backgrounds of confidential sources. Caution: Some courts will be prejudiced against a journalist who grants confidentiality. Provide confidentially only after considerable thought.

19. If you are sued for libel, always use a communication attorney; general practitioners just aren't sufficiently knowledgeable in the field to adequately (or successfully and efficiently) defend you. In addition, when in doubt about whether a story is libelous, consult an attorney. As a reporter, keep in mind that you will be named personally in any charge filed against your story or clip; you thus have a special need to have such counsel.

PRIVACY

Compared to libel, privacy is a fairly recent legal concept. Libel has been around for centuries. Privacy is a twentieth-century phenomenon. The right of privacy has achieved some constitutional standing in the federal courts and has been accorded either constitutional or common law status in most states. Some states have specific privacy laws. Consequently, legal privacy may mean one thing in some places and something else in others.

Most of us think of privacy as the right to be left alone. Legal privacy takes in more than that, however. There are four major areas of privacy: appropriation, intrusion, publication of private facts and false light.

Appropriation. Appropriation, or the right of publicity, is the right to use one's name and image for one's own benefit. It means that someone else should not take your name, your face or your property and make money with it without your consent. For instance, an advertisement which uses your face or name in endorsing a product is illegal unless you have given your consent.

Newspapers make money in part by printing the names and pictures of people who are in the news. Generally, appropriation does not apply to news organizations, however. Courts have ruled that people who are in the public eye and who make news do not have the right of appropriation when it comes to their newsworthy activities. If a person makes a speech which is open to the public, he or she may be photographed with specific consent and those pictures may be run as part of the coverage of a news event. This is true only so long as the coverage is demonstrably newsworthy. If the news organization used the photograph in some other way, however, the question of appropriation might arise.

Intrusion. Newspersons may not come on to private property to gather information or to take pictures without the specific or implied consent of the owner. Nor may photographers use long-range lenses to take pictures of people in private places. Journalists are also barred from going into places where police or firefighters are investigating incidents unless there is a general policy allowing access or unless they have been specifically invited by the investigating officials.

If journalists take pictures of or describe the activities of people in public places — places which can be viewed by the general public — such pictures or descriptions are not considered intrusion. If a photo or description focuses attention on a person or small group and there is a possibility of embarrassment or harm to someone's reputation, that coverage may be the basis for a privacy action. If journalists illegally enter a place which is barred to the public, or if they misrepresent themselves to gain entry, they may be guilty of intrusion.

Intrusion differs from other parts of privacy law in one important respect. The intrusion occurs when the illegal act occurs, not when something is published about it. Not long ago, intrusion was considered a minor problem for journalists, but recent court cases and the closing of many places to journalists have increased the possibility that a journalist might be accused of intrusion. The increased use of data retrieval systems and data banks to store private information also represents a danger for journalists.

Publication of private facts. The courts have deemed that some information is too private or embarrassing for publication, particularly when it concerns people who are not well known. Courts have been reluctant to define what facts may be too private or embarrassing for publication because of First Amendment considerations, but journalists still need to be careful.

The one area that could mean some trouble for media defendants here is the "passage of time." Publication of private or embarrassing facts may be defended at the time because of their newsworthy nature. Republication at a later date may not have the same defense. Courts have ruled that newsworthy subjects can cease to be newsworthy after the passage of time, but they have not been specific about how much time must pass before this occurs. Editors should take care in these particular situations to make sure that the subjects they are writing about are still newsworthy and of public interest.

False light. Creating a false image of a person or placing that person in an atypical light can put an editor and publication in legal difficulty. For example, a publication may run a story about mob control of gambling casinos and may illustrate the story with pictures of people around a blackjack table. Those people may not be connected with organized crime, but their appearance with the story could place them in a false light. As such, they may have the basis for a successful suit against the publication.

Another area of false light is the making up or fictionalizing of incidents about a real person. Several years ago a man wrote a book about a famous baseball player in which conversations between the player and acquaintances were reported verbatim. It turned out that the writer had made these conversations up, and the baseball player successfully sued the writer for placing him in a false light. The mix of imagination and fact — adding detail, constructing conversations and otherwise augmenting reality — is genuinely dangerous for the journalist. Such activities, of course, are not the standard procedure for responsible journalists, and we would hope that journalists would have little fear of this area of privacy law.

False light is important to journalists, however, because of its connection with libel law. Often, when libel suits are filed, they contain concurrent charges of invasion of privacy-false light violations, and publications must defend themselves against these charges. It is sometimes difficult to defend against both these charges.

DEFENSES AGAINST INVASION-OF-PRIVACY CHARGES

Two defenses are available for journalists charged with invasion of privacy suits: newsworthiness and consent.

Newsworthiness. We have already referred to the newsworthiness of a subject several times in this section. Because of the First Amendment, courts have been reluctant to place limits on the editorial discretion of editors. Judging what is and is not news is the job of journalists not judges. Consequently, newsworthiness, according to modern and accepted definitions of news, is a very strong defense. Journalists are expected to cover events that are important and of interest to society, as long as they do so within the law. Courts have been generally willing to protect them in that activity, but the law may be changing in this regard.

Consent. Consent is a strong defense if it is obtained properly and given by people who can give their consent. Some people, such as children and the mentally handicapped, cannot always give their consent. However, consent to interview or to enter places, when it is given by authorized people, can be extremely valuable to journalists. As a rule, photographers should carry picture release forms with them at all times and should ask their subjects to sign them if there will be any question about invasion of privacy. The same is true for all reporters who are dealing with non-news subjects. Although the granting of an interview is usually viewed as "implied consent," some courts do not always hold to this view.

NEWSGATHERING

Journalists are encountering many difficulties in gaining access to places where news occurs and in getting records necessary for news stories. They are also coming under fire for wanting to keep certain information, such as sources, confidential. Legislatures and courts have had much to say about these controversies recently. While many of these situations initially involve only reporters, it does not take long for editors to be brought into them. Editors should know the law thoroughly in these areas so as to be able to give the proper direction to reporters.

Access to places. One of the few victories which journalists have gained recently in the area of access to places was contained in the U.S. Supreme Court's 1980 **Richmond Newspapers v. Virginia** decision. The court confirmed that journalists have a constitutional right to gather news — something it had never said before — and that they have limited right to gain access to places where news occurs. The full effect of the **Richmond** decision has not been felt yet, but many journalists and communications attorneys are hopeful that this part of the decision will receive an expansive interpretation by other courts.

Despite the **Richmond** decision, journalists are still restricted from many places where news can be obtained. As we mentioned earlier, reporters may not automatically have access to places where police or firefighters are investigating incidents. Access to these places is often controlled by a "custom and usage" rule — that is, what has been done before will be upheld as the rule. Courts have also ruled that access to federal prisons and prisoners may be restricted by officials.

State "open meetings" laws have helped journalists gain access to meetings of many government and quasigovernmental bodies. These laws require that most sessions of city councils, county commissions, school boards, and other regulatory bodies be open to the public, and they usually require that proper notice be given of such a meeting. There are weaknesses in many of these laws, however. Many states allow or require closure of meetings when the "name and character" of a person is being discussed. Because almost any topic may be discussed under this heading, this exemption allows officials a lot of leeway in closing meetings. Journalists should work for narrow interpretations of these exemptions and for changes in the laws to allow greater access to these meetings. Tennessee has one of the nation's strongest open meetings laws, one which allows for very few exceptions, and many groups lobbying for open-meeting legislation have used the Tennessee law as a model.

At the federal level, an open meetings law requires that meetings of the regulatory bodies be open to the public. Consequently, journalists now may attend most meetings of the various regulatory commissions. The flaw in this law is that staff meetings are not included. As a result, journalists who cover the federal agencies have said that the federal open meetings law has not had much effect on their ability to report on the agencies' activities.

Open records. Many states have laws which state that certain city, county and state records must be open to the public. By the same token, there are a number of laws which restrict access to records, particularly medical records of persons housed in state institutions, records of juvenile justice, and records of welfare and child assistance. What journalists should realize is that just because a record or document is in the possession of the government, it is not automatically open to public inspection. But they should also realize that many city, county, and state officials are as unaware of records laws as are most citizens. When officials try to withhold records from journalists, they should always be challenged, and journalists are at a distinct advantage when they know the law thoroughly.

The Freedom of Information Act (FOIA) governs access to records at the federal level. The act was passed originally in 1966 and amended in 1974 and has the purpose of making available to the public as many records and documents as possible. The act contains nine exemptions, definitions of the records which an agency may legally withhold. Each of these exemptions has been the subject of litigation, but not always to the advantage of journalists. In a number of cases, the Supreme Court has refused to expand the definition of a record and has granted agencies the right to refuse releasing records in a number of questionable instances. The Reagan administration, too, has made several proposals to restrict the provisions of the Freedom of Information Act and has even proposed to withdraw a number of agencies, such as the Federal Bureau of Investigation and Central Intelligence Agency, from its scope entirely.

Getting records under the FOIA is a lengthy and sometimes costly procedure. Identifying what records are to be requested is often the most difficult part of the search. Agency public information officers and the **Federal Register** can help in this regard, but the journalist should be as specific as possible. When the identification has taken place, a letter should be written to the appropriate agency requesting the documents under the FOIA.

If a request is denied, an appeal should be made to the agency. This appeal must be enacted soon. If the appeal is denied, a court suit may be initiated. Journalists should remember that the FOIA applies only to agencies of the federal executive branch — not to Congress or the judicial system. They should also remember that requests, and court suits, can be expensive. Although agencies can find many reasons for withholding records, the FOIA needs to be used to the fullest extent and expanded by journalists. Its original intent, to make government more open, is in line with the intent of the First Amendment, and journalists have a responsibility to see that this intent is carried out.

Shield laws. The question of the journalist's privilege, or shield, has also been the subject of much controversy during the last two decades. Journalists have argued that they have the right to keep certain information (such as the names of sources) confidential even from police or courts. This privilege between a journalist and a source, they say, is much like that granted to lawyers and clients or to doctors and patients. Since many journalists use confidential sources in gathering information, such a privilege is necessary if they are to remain effective and credible.

More than half of the states have recognized this need and have enacted shield laws which give journalists some protection from having to reveal the names of sources during criminal investigations or court proceedings. Shield laws come with a variety of inherent problems, however. Some shield laws define journalists in a narrow way so that not everyone who considers himself a journalist is protected by the laws. Other shield laws provide so many exceptions that they become meaningless. Because shield laws are state laws, the protection they provide varies from state to state. Finally, courts have interpreted shield laws very narrowly. There have been several instances in which journalists have gone to jail for failing to reveal information even in states which have "strong" shield laws. In general, shield laws today offer journalists little in the way of protection if a judge is determined to get the information a journalist has. Editors and reporters should not place too much reliance on state shield laws.

No federal shield law exists even though Congress has talked from time to time about passing one. Current Justice Department guidelines prevent federal prosecutors from forcing a journalist to reveal a confidential source unless that information goes to the heart of a case and all other avenues of obtaining that information have been explored. In the federal courts, a qualified privilege based on the First Amendment has been recognized in some instances, but that privilege is not yet a strong one and is certainly nothing that journalists can rely on.

The whole question of the use of confidential sources is an ethical one as well as a legal one, and editors would do well to come to some understanding with their reporters about it. Reporters should have a clear understanding of the editors' attitude toward the use of confidential sources and their willingness to support a reporter's claim of confidentiality. Confidential sources should be used with care and caution, and shield laws notwithstanding, reporters should be prepared to go to jail if a promise of confidentiality is given.

Newsroom searches. The press scored one victory for confidentiality in 1980 when Congress passed the Privacy Protection Act, which in most instances prevents law enforcement officers from obtaining search warrants for newsrooms. This is in response to police use of such warrants rather than subpoenas to obtain information. A search warrant allows police to look at anything in the newsroom, including confidential files. A subpoena requires that certain information be produced but does not allow police to search for it. Journalists had been fearful that police would use search warrants to comb through their files at random, particularly since the Supreme Court had upheld such actions in the 1978 **Zurcher v. Stanford Daily** decision.

The present law requires that federal and state police officers present a subpoena for the information or evidence they are seeking. Journalists may then respond to the subpoena in whatever way they see fit. Police officers may obtain a search warrant for a newsroom only to prevent physical harm to individuals or in cases.

COPYRIGHT

All editors need to know how to register a copyright for their publications. Although they are not required to submit all issues for filing, editors should individually submit those issues which have special reuse or informational value.

LIBELOUS WORDS

Libel actions usually develop out of lack of thought or temporary mental lapses on the part of the communicator. No list of problem words and phrases is ever quite complete; but this is a beginning. Use these words and phrases with caution.

adulteration of products	defaulter	intemperate	rogue
adultery	disorderly house	intimate	
altered records	divorced	intolerance	scandal monger
ambulance chaser	doublecrosser		scoundrel
atheist	drug addict	Jekyll-Hyde personality	seducer
attempted suicide	drunkard	John, Jane	sharp dealing
			short in accounts
bad moral character	exconvict	kept woman	shyster
bankrupt		killer	skunk
bastard child	false accounts	Ku Klux Klan	slacker
bigamist	false weights used		smooth and tricky
blackguard	fascist	liar	sneak
blacklisted	fawning sycophant		sold his influence
blackmail	fool	mental disease	sold out to a rival
blockhead	fraud	moral delinquency	spy
boozehound		murderer	stool pigeon
bribery	gambling house	mutilator	stuffed the ballot box
brothel	gangster		suicide
buys votes	gouged money	Nazi	swindle
	grafter		
cheats	groveling office seeker	paramour	unethical
collusion		peeping Tom	unmarried mother
communist (or red)	humbug	perjurer	unprofessional
confidence man	hypocrite	plagiarist	unsound mind
coward		pockets public funds	unworthy of character
crook	illegitimate	price cutter	unworthy of credit
	illicit relations	profiteering	
deadbeat	incompetent	prostitute	vice den
deadhead	infidelity		villain
deceiver	informer	rascal	whore

Editors should also exercise due caution when dealing with staff members who freelance for other publications. Under the law, the employer of a professional is the "author of record" for each and every piece created by that staff member. Any variance from this standard should be separately negotiated.

In the same vein, editors are responsible for the use made by reprinters of other copyrighted stories or sources. Although ideas may not be protected, the expression of an idea may be. Therefore, although ideas, sources, and concepts may be freely used, the expression of data may not be. This is a special concern with material gained for limited circulation sources. Any such use now must fit within the "fair use" standard. Thus, the editor must examine impact on the marketability, the proportion of the total work used, and the purpose or function of the use. Violation of such standards creates both creator and user concerns.

Appendix A

ENGLISH DIAGNOSTIC TEST

Explanation: This test contains items in three categories: grammar, spelling, and punctuation. Some items are easy; others are hard. Do your best to answer all items within the one-hour time limit.

PART I. GRAMMATICAL USAGE

Directions: Read each sentence and decide whether there is an error in usage in any part of the sentence. If you find an error, note the letter printed immediately after the wrong word or phrase, and write the letter on your answer sheet. If you do not find an error, write the letter "E." No sentence has more than one error. Some sentences do not have any errors.

SAMPLE:

Roger, Jane (A) and Henry is (B) coming to (C) the party at (D) our house.

In this sentence, "is," is wrong. Place the letter "B" on your answer sheet.

SAMPLE:

The (A) Indian (B) flung (C) his tomahawk (D) at the intruder.

In this sentence, there is no error in any of the underlined words or phrases; therefore, an "E" should be written on the answer sheet.

Exercises:

1. Its (A) up to him (B) to complete (C) the job on time, according (D) to the contract.

2. Whatever the consequences, (A) he (B) and her (C) must unfailingly be absolved (D) of all responsibility.

3. The Spanish took the first printing press (A) in North America to Mexico City, where it's (B) first issue (C) was a religious (D) work.

4. Armbruster confessed that, unlike most men, (A) he actually (B) enjoyed the procession (C) of fad's (D) in women's hats.

5. "It's (A) she!" (B) Conrad breathed softly as the spotlight illuminated (C) for a moment (D) a hauntingly beautiful face in the crowd.

6. Having (A) fought in World War II, (B) your Aug. 25 editorial, (C) "Civilian Casualties in Vietnam," (D) is puzzling.

7. Although (A) Drake was not expected to give UCLA much of a battle, everyone (B) got their (C) money's (D) worth when the Uclans finally won in overtime, 85-82.

8. Each one of the Miss Teen-Agers were (A) judged on her (B) talent, her (C) poise and her (D) personality.

9. They invited (A) my wife and I (B) to the party, but neither (C) of us was (D) able to go.

10. If you hope to use the English (A) language correctly, (B) you must be sure each (C) pronoun agrees with their (D) antecedent.

11. Among the countries (A) that fought over feudal (B) claims during (C) the 12th century was (D) France and England.

12. Among the 10,000 persons (A) who sometimes lived at Louis XIV's (B) Palace of Versailles were hundreds of parasites (C) and hangers-on.(D)

13. "Lay (A) down and be quiet for an hour," (B) he ordered. "If you make a sound, I'll (C) skin you alive."(D)

14. The 6-year-old (A) boy was just sitting (B) there in the ruins, (C) trying (D) not to cry.

15. After lunch she laid (A) down for a nap, (B) but the doorbell rang (C) before she could fall (D) asleep.

16. Its (A) one of the fastest-growing (B) and most profitable (C) lines in (D) the entire steel industry.

17. Whom (A) do you think will be eliminated (B) in the semifinals (C) of the golden gloves tournament (D) Saturday?

18. He was tall, dark, and (A) good looking, (B) in the lean-and-hungry (C) tradition (D) of the American West.

19. "I wonder who's (A) bicycle (B) this is," the patrolman (C) mused as he stood at the scene of the mysterious (D) crime.

20. According to my uncle's (A) will, the automobile will be her's (B) and the colonial (C) furniture (D) at the house will be mine.

21. Henry was elected chairman by unanimous (A) vote, and (B) will officiate only at irregular (C) intervals. (D)

22. Neither of the winners were (A) willing to shake hands after the disastrous (B) match at Wimbledon (C) last (D) year.

23. The crow is often thought of as a predator; (A) hence, (B) it's (C) function as a scavenger (D) is sometimes overlooked.

24. There (A) he stands on the bluff, looking (B) moodily (C) across the Mississippi toward (D) the lost lands of his ancestors.

25. She, (A) as well as many others of her sex, do (B) not appreciate (C) the fine art of wrestling. (D)

26. Nobody (A) is more (B) generous (C) than him, (D) not even my own father.

27. Quentin payed (A) his debts in full; (B) then, almost penniless, (C) he began the promotion that was to make him (D) a millionaire, once more.

28. Swinging from the telephone wire, they (A) saw the remnant (B) of a kite's (C) tail and some tattered (D) paper.

29. The Optimists Club and the newer (A) group, the Civic Society (B) for Advancing Commerce and Culture, was (C) helping in the drive. (D)

30. A box of tongue (A) depressors (B) are (C) a useful object (D) to have around the house, according to a report in the "AMA Journal."

31. He (A) and she (B) makes (C) big plans to honor the seven well-known (D) guests.

32. Only (A) one of us are (B) going to town today, although (C) three of us (D) will go tomorrow.

33. The rose smells sweetly, (A) particularly (B) when it blooms in a southern garden bathed (C) in the light of an early August (D) moon.

34. The seven-man (A) team gives (B) it's (C) trophies to its (D) sailing club.

35. The oldest (A) twin was born (B) shortly before midnight (C) on Dec. 31, 1834, in the midst (D) of one of the worst snowstorms of the century.

PART II. SPELLING

Directions: In some of the following groups of words, one word is misspelled. If you find a wrongly spelled word, note the letter printed before it and write the letter on your answer sheet. If you think all four words are correctly spelled, write "E" on the answer sheet.

Exercises:

1. a. boundry
   b. certain
   c. audible
   d. bankruptcy
   e. none wrong

2. a. development
   b. deceitful
   c. allies
   d. cheif
   e. none wrong

3. a. abscess
   b. condemn
   c. accommodate
   d. committee
   e. none wrong

4. a. caulk
   b. drownded
   c. artillery
   d. bananas
   e. none wrong

5. a. equaled
   b. battalion
   c. basically
   d. boisterous
   e. none wrong

6. a. customary
   b. contemptable
   c. buries
   d. chauffeur
   e. none wrong

7. a. unanimous
   b. vaccinate
   c. warrent
   d. yield
   e. none wrong

8. a. varicose
   b. coller .

   c. wherever
   d. zephyr
   e. none wrong

9. a. exorbitant
   b. entrance
   c. fundamental
   d. fragrent
   e. none wrong

10. a. guidance
    b. hopeless
    c. ghost
    d. heroine
    e. none wrong

11. a. itself
    b. judicial
    c. irrevelant
    d. knowledge
    e. none wrong

12. a. ptomaine
    b. rehearsal
    c. rhyme
    d. seperate
    e. none wrong

13. a. utility
    b. verified
    c. wholly
    d. untill
    e. none wrong

14. a. wheather
    b. yourself
    c. visa
    d. zoology
    e. none wrong

15. a. encourage
    b. frivolous
    c. gueusome
    d. hazardous
    e. none wrong

16. a. interfere
    b. loneliness
    c. menu
    d. nullify
    e. none wrong

17. a. annual
    b. accomodate
    c. forty
    d. height
    e. none wrong

18. a. ladies
    b. khaki
    c. illiterite
    d. jealous
    e. none wrong

19. a. alot
    b. bureau
    c. article
    d. biscuit
    e. none wrong

20. a. defendent
    b. chimney
    c. detriment
    d. continually
    e. none wrong

21. a. tariff
    b. sherrif
    c. radiator
    d. quarter
    e. none wrong

22. a. ambiguous
    b. built
    c. chassis
    d. desperate
    e. none wrong

23. a. gnawing
    b. February

    c. handkerchief
    d. economize
    e. none wrong

24. a. recieve
    b. knuckle
    c. immigrate
    d. legislation
    e. none wrong

25. a. kindergarten
    b. lavender
    c. immovable
    d. inaccuracy
    e. none wrong

26. a. magizine
    b. nearby
    c. oblige
    d. pageant
    e. none wrong

27. a. pathos
    b. obscene
    c. necessary
    d. mahagany
    e. none wrong

28. a. nickel
    b. occurence
    c. necessary
    d. paralysis
    e. none wrong

29. a. indetify
    b. pendulum
    c. monstrous
    d. neutral
    e. none wrong

30. a. rarity
    b. quietly
    c. sauerkraut
    d. temprament
    e. none wrong

PART III. PUNCTUATION

Directions: Read each sentence and decide whether there is an error in punctuation at any place in the sentence. If you find an error, note the letter printed immediately after the place where the error occurs and write it on your answer sheet. If you think the sentence is punctuated correctly, write the letter "E" on your answer sheet. No sentence has more than one error. Some sentences do not have errors.

SAMPLE:

The tough, (A) hard-(B) boiled center (C) began to cry, (D) his leg was broken.

In this sentence, the comma after cry is wrong; it should be a semicolon. Thus the letter "D" should be written on your answer sheet.

Exercises:

1. The average person (A) is not financially able to do a great deal of traveling, (B) therefore, (C) he will probably never have the chance to see the places he reads about. (D)

2. The executioner, (A) who inherited his rituals from his father and grandfather (B) reported only the customary, doleful (C) "It is done!" (D) to the commissioner of police.

3. In his long, (A) glowing letters to his son-in-law (B) in the old country, Old Jules, (C) the patriarch of the settlement (D) made the desert seem like an Eden.

4. Knowing nothing, (A) of the terms of the contract, (B) Peterkin hesitated; (C) nevertheless, (D) driven by anxiety, he signed it.

5. Waters said that the network documentary depicting hunger among migrant workers did not startle the American people, (A) it only stirred them momentarily in their (B) "fat," (C) smug complacency. (D)

6. Columbus's (A) luck changed (B) after he made three acquaintances; (C) a shipbuilder, a financier (D) and a friend of the King of Spain.

7. Since air is dissolved by water at the surface (A) the shape of an aquarium is important; (B) too small an opening (C) may cause an oxygen deficiency. (D)

8. The dean, (A) so far as I could tell (B) shared my feelings; (C) but he made little effort to establish responsible student government. (D)

9. The hot (A) days of summer (B) make me feel (C) that I could cheerfully leave Dubuque, Iowa (D) forever.

10. For breakfast (A) I usually have an egg, (B) some toast (C) coffee (D) and a glass of prune juice.

11. "Get (A) off at the next main intersection," the bus driver shouted. (B) The (C) park entrance is two blocks to the right." (D)

12. Last night's (A) paper had been used (B) to wrap garbage (C) but I found one dated two weeks (D) earlier.

13. Mrs. Bones tried not to gasp as she viewed her daughter's garb; (A) pointed black shoes, black tights (B) and skirt, orange lipstick (C) and bleached yellow hair pulled back (D) in an untidy bun.

14. The assistant (A) who ordinarily is highly efficient, (B) was all thumbs (C) in today's (D) experiment.

15. A week later the murder remained unsolved, (A) however, (B) Lt. (C) Holme's squad had discovered (D) some new clues.

16. He wasn't (A) much help on the farm that year, (B) he was always off chasing butterflies and (C) looking for birds' (D) nests.

17. The night manager (A) said that he sought a man who had four qualities (B) in particular: (C) honesty, (D) imagination, inquisitiveness and responsibility.

18. "Usually, (A) he wasn't (B) available (C) Jane, so we had to find another helper," (D) Farley explained to the girl.

19. Harvey soberly told the group that, (A) "there's (B) not a chance" (C) of repairing (D) the heavily damaged bridge.

20. Members of the advisory (A) board were as follows; (B) John Fox, Miami; Joseph Horn, Denver; (C) and Arthur Block, (D) Pittsburgh.

21. "If I'm (A) not allowed to go (and I suspect I won't be), (B) I'll (C) just have to make the best of a dull vacation here," (D) Mary said.

22. The governor's (A) temporary financial adviser, (B) had no time for what he considered (C) stupidity, (D) but was tolerant of laziness.

23. Twenty-five tons (A) of TNT were used in blasting the 300-foot (B) tunnel (C) at the west terminal of King's (D) Highway.

24. The award went (A) to George Kellers, (B) 17, (C) of 2345 Heather Drive, (D) who submitted a group of five poems.

25. "I can't (A) find Liechtenstein on this map," said Lovel, (B) "but (C) my best guess is that its (D) near Switzerland."

26. Finally grasping Twain's (A) purpose (B) in retelling (C) the story (D) the crowd roared.

27. The Clean Government Society, (A) an organization (B) opposed to the present (C) city administration (D) will meet tonight.

28. The Indian ambassador said that Americans shouldn't (A) expect developing (B) nations (C) to copy the United States' (D) economic institutions.

29. "You'll (A) never understand Victorian (B) England, (C) Myrtle (D) unless you grasp the significance of the Industrial Revolution," Miss Prentice lectured her pupil.

30. Jasper W. Whipp, (A) grand kleagle of the Hominee County chapter (B) thundered, "The time has come (C) to return to the robes and the torches!" (D)

31. The busy housewife (A) may walk 20 miles a day (B) and never leave her home, (C) furthermore, a lot of travel (D) may be up and down a flight of stairs.

32. Snow choked the sidewalks, (A) streets and highways and buried the bushes (B) and park benches, (C) it covered windows and does of the ranch-(D) style homes in suburban Elmwood Heights.

33. The social worker found the little house (A) tremendously cluttered with badly worn furniture, books, clothing and babies' (B) toys; but the children were reasonably clean (C) and obviously most happy with their pleasant, (D) if somewhat untidy, mother.

34. They scraped up a hasty, (A) catch-as-catch-can (B) dinner from the assortment of canned foods before beginning the 28 (C) mile hike to the trail (D) camp.

35. In most respects the hotel (A) is admirably situated. (B) It is near the corner of Fifth Avenue and 52nd Street, (C) within walking distance of mid-(D) town points of interest.

Appendix B

CODE OF ETHICS

The following is the code of ethics of the Society of Professional Journalists, Sigma Delta Chi. The code was adopted in 1926 and was revised in 1973.

The Society of Professional Journalists, Sigma Delta Chi, believes the duty of journalists is to serve the truth.

We believe the agencies of mass communication are carriers of public discussion and information, acting on their Constitutional mandate and freedom to learn and report the facts.

We believe in public enlightenment as the forerunner of justice, and in our Constitutional role to seek the truth as part of the public's right to know the truth.

We believe those responsibilities carry obligations that require journalists to perform with intelligence, objectivity, accuracy, and fairness.

To these ends, we declare acceptance of the standards of practice here set forth:

I. RESPONSIBILITY

The public's right to know of events of public importance and interest is the overriding mission of the mass media. The purpose of distributing news and enlightened opinion is to serve the general welfare. Journalists who use their professional status as representatives of the public for selfish or unworthy motives violate a high trust.

II. FREEDOM OF THE PRESS

Freedom of the press is to be guarded as an inalienable right of people in free society. It carries with it the freedom and the responsibility to discuss, question, and challenge actions and utterances of our government and of our public and private institutions. Journalists uphold the right to voice unpopular opinions and the privilege to agree with the majority.

III. ETHICS

Journalists must be free of obligation to any interest other than the public's right to know the truth.

1. Gifts, favors, free travel, special treatment, or privileges can compromise the integrity of journalists and their employers. Nothing of value should be accepted.

2. Secondary employment, political involvement, holding public office, and service in community organizations should be avoided if they compromise the integrity of journalists and their employers. Journalists and their employers should conduct their personal lives in a manner which protects them from conflicts of interest, real or apparent. Their responsibilities to the public are paramount. That is the nature of their profession.

3. So-called news communications from private sources should not be published or broadcast without substantiation of their claims to news value.

4. Journalists will seek news that serves the public interest, despite the obstacles. They will make constant efforts to make sure that the public's business is conducted in public and that public records are open to public inspection.

5. Journalists acknowledge the newsmen's ethic of protecting confidential sources of information.

IV. ACCURACY AND OBJECTIVITY

Good faith with the public is the foundation of all worthy journalism.

1. Truth is our ultimate goal.

2. Objectivity in reporting the news is another goal, serving as the mark of an experienced professional. It is a standard of performance toward which we all strive. We honor those who achieve it.

3. There is no excuse for inaccuracies or lack of thoroughness.

4. Newspaper headlines should be fully warranted by the contents of the article they accompany. Photographs and telecasts should give an accurate picture of an event and not highlight a minor incident out of context.

5. Sound practice makes clear distinction between news reports and expressions of opinion. News reports should be free of opinion or bias and should represent all sides of an issue.

6. Partisanship in editorial comment which knowingly departs from the truth violates the spirit of American journalism.

7. Journalists recognize their responsibility for offering informed analysis, comment, and editorial opinion on public events and issues.

8. Special articles or presentations devoted to advocacy or the writer's own conclusions and interpretations should be labeled as such.

V. FAIR PLAY

Journalists should at all times show respect for the dignity, privacy, rights, and well-being of people encountered in the course of gathering and presenting the news.

1. The news media should not communicate unofficial charges affecting reputation or moral character without giving the accused a chance to reply.

2. The news media must guard against invading a person's right to privacy.

3. The media should not pander to morbid curiosity about details of vice and crime.

4. It is the duty of news media to make prompt and complete corrections of their errors.

5. Journalists should be accountable to the public for their reports, and the public should be encouraged to voice its grievances against the media. Open dialogue with our readers, viewers, and listeners should be fostered.

VI. PLEDGE

Journalists should actively censure and try to prevent violations of these standards, and they should encourage their observance by all newspeople. Adherence to this code of ethics is intended to preserve the bond of mutual trust and respect between American journalists and the American people.

Appendix C

GLOSSARY

Acetate: Transparent sheet placed over art in mechanical color separations.

Ad: Advertisement.

Add: A typewritten page of copy following the first page. "First add" is the second page of typewritten copy.

Agate: Name of a type size usually used in advertising.

Air: White space.

A.M.:   A morning newspaper.

Art: Illustrations used in a publication, including photographs, drawings, charts, graphs and so on.

A wire: Usually the main slow-speed wire of a news agency.

Background: Information that may be attributed to a source by title, but not by name; for example, "a State Department official said."

Backgrounder: Story that explains and updates the news.

Banner: Headline extending all the way across a page.

Barker: Type of headline in which the "kicker" is in larger type than the lines below it. Also called a hammer.

Bastard type: Type that varies from the standard column width.

Ben Day: A pattern of lines or dots giving a shaded effect as background for type or illustrations.

Blanket head: Headline extending over several columns of type or over type and illustration.

Blow-up: Enlarged photo or art.

Body type: Type set for text, usually from five to fourteen points in height.

Boldface: Heavy, black typeface; type that is blacker than the text with which it is used. Abbreviated bf.

Box: Printed rule arranged in rectangular shape, usually to enclose a special feature, photos, etc.

Brace: Type of makeup, usually with a banner headline and the story in the right-hand column. A bracket.

Break: Point at which a story turns from one column to another. An exclusive story.

Break over: Story that jumps from one page to another.

Broken box: Box with lines split in order to accommodate words or pictures. Also called a split box.

Budget: List of the day's important wire service stories.

Bulldog: An early edition, usually the first of a newspaper.

Bulletin: A brief statement about a major, late-breaking story.

Bumper: Two elements placed side-by-side or with one immediately beneath the other. A bumped headline is also called a tombstone.

Business department: The newspaper department that handles billing, accounting and related functions.

Byline: A line identifying the author of a story.

Canopy head: A streamer headline from which two or more readout heads drop.

Caps: Capital letters; same as upper case.

Caps and lower case: Word's initial letters are capitalized as necessary; other letters are small. (See **lower case.**)

Caption: Written description accompanying photo or art. Also called a cutline.

Centered: Placed in the middle of a line.

Center spread: Two facing pages made up as one display in the center of a newspaper section; also called a double truck.

Cheesecake: Slang for photographs emphasizing women's legs. Also called leg art.

Circumlocution: Wordy, roundabout expressions. Also known as redundancy.

Circus makeup: Flamboyant makeup featuring a variety of typefaces and sizes.

City editor: The individual (also known as the metropolitan, or metro, editor) in charge of the city desk, which coordinates local coverage. At some papers the desk also handles regional and state news covered by its own reporters.

Clean copy: Copy with a minimum of typographical or editing corrections. Clean proof is proof that requires few corrections.

Clips: Stories clipped from your own or competing newspapers.

Code of ethics: The accepted practice in journalism as outlined in several documents adopted by such national organizations as The Society of Professional Journalists, Sigma Delta Chi.

Coding: Designation of symbols for the computer.

Cold type: In composition, type set photographically or by pasting up letters and pictures on acetate or paper.

Color separations: Breaking (by use of filters) color art or photos into primary ink colors (yellow, magenta, and cyan) for color reproduction.

Column: The vertical division of the news page. A standard-size newspaper is divided into five to eight columns. Also, a signed article of opinion or strong personal expression, frequently by an authority or expert.

Column inch: Unit of space measurement; one column wide and one inch deep.

Column rule: Printing units that create vertical lines of separation on a page.

Combo: Several pictures of the same subject used as a single unit.

Command: An operator's order to the computer, given through a terminal.

Compose: To set type in a composing room (by a compositor).

Composition: All typesetting.

Controller: The computer that drives a video display terminal or optical character recognition system.

Copy: What reporters write. A story is a piece of copy.

Copy block: A paragraph or two on a photo page, identifying the photos and the theme depicted in them.

Copy cutter: The composing room employee who cuts the news manuscript into lengths or "takes" convenient for setting quickly and who has charge of the distribution of copy among the compositors.

Copy desk: The desk at which final editing of stories is done, headlines are written, and pages are designed.

Copy editor: A person who checks, polishes, and corrects stories written by reporters. Usually copy editors write headlines for those stories, and sometimes they decide how to arrange stories and pictures on a page.

Copy fitting: Estimating the space a given piece of typewritten copy will fill when set in type.

Correction: Errors that reach publication are retracted or corrected if they are serious or someone demands a correction. Libelous matter is always corrected immediately, often in a separate news story rather than in the standard box assigned to corrections.

CQ: Symbol used in editing to indicate that the word or spelling is correct.

Crash: Computer malfunction that renders the machine inoperable.

Credit line: The line that designates, if necessary, the source of a story or cut. "By the Associated Press" preceeding a story, is a credit line.

Crop: To cut or mask any unwanted portions, usually of a photograph.

Crossline: A single-line headline.

CRT: Cathode ray tube, also known as video display terminal, terminal, tube, VDT. Devices on which reporters write their stories directly into computer typesetting systems.

Cub: A beginning reporter.

Cursor: A rectangle of light on a video display terminal that indicates the writer's or editor's position within the text of the story. Changes in text are made through the keyboard and appear on the screen where the cursor is located.

Cut: Printed picture or illustration. Also, to eliminate material from a story.

Cutline: Any descriptive or explanatory material accompanying a piece of art.

Dateline: Name of the city or town and sometimes the date at the beginning of a non-local story.

Day side: That part of the newspaper oganization that functions in the daytime.

Deadline: Time by which a reporter, editor, or desk must have completed scheduled work.

Deck: An element in a headline placed below the main line. Also known as a bank or a drophead.

Delete: Take out. The proofreader uses a symbol to mark deletions.

Desk: A term used by reporters to refer to the city or copy editor's position, as in, "The desk wants this story by noon."

Dingbat: A printing term to indicate either a decorative symbol or typographical devices, such as stars or check marks, used to separate portions of a story or stories.

Directories: Electronic file cabinets or storage units for edited or unedited material.

Dirty copy: Matter for publication that needs extensive correction, usually because the reporter has made unreadable markings on copy.

Display advertisements: Newspaper advertisements designed to promote products by means of headlines, copy blocks, illustrations, and imaginative arrangement.

Display type: Type used for heads and display matter in ads, fourteen points or larger.

Double truck: Ad or feature layout that occupies two adjacent pages.

Down style: Newspaper style using a minimum of capital letters.

Dummy: A sheet of paper on which editors arrange stories and illustrations for a newspaper page. Also called a layout.

Duotone: Printed halftone in two colors (usually black plus another color) which blend to form a third-color effect.

Dutch wrap: Breaking body type from one column to another not covered by the display line. Also called a dutch turn or a raw wrap.

Ear: Boxed material on either side of the nameplate, usually carrying weather or promotional copy.

Edition: One version of a newspaper. Some papers have one edition a day, some several. Not to be confused with the **issue**, which usually refers to all editions under a single date.

Em: A printing measurement; an em is the square of the type size.

Extra: Now rare, a special edition published to carry an important news break.

Face: A particular variety of type, such as Bodoni, Caslon, or Tempo.

Family: As applied to type, all the type in any one design. Usually designated by a trade name.

Fat head: Headline too large for the space allowed for it.

FAX: Short for facsimile or transmission by wire of a picture.

Fix: To correct. A correction.

Flag: Printed title of a newspaper on Page 1. Also called column closers and shorts.

Flash: The first announcement on a news wire of an impending news development of importance.

Flashing: Alternate illumination and darkening of a video display terminal screen, sometimes indicating malfunction or improper keyboarding.

Flat: Composite negative used to make offset printing plate.

Float: Ruled sidebar that may go anywhere in a story. To center an element in a too-large space.

Flop: Illustration reversed in engraving.

Flush: Even with the column margin on either the left or the right side; no indention as for a paragraph. "Flush and indent" or "flush and hang" is a direction to set the first line of a piece of copy without indention and to indent the succeeding lines at the left side. Same as hanging indention.

Font: All the characters of a particular typeface in a particular size.

Formats: Computer codes used to determine type size, column width, and styling. To format is to put proper coding on a terminal story.

Freebies: Gifts such as food and liquor given to reporters and editors to influence their coverage of news.

Galley: Metal tray used to hold hot type.

Galley proof: Print of the assembled type, used in proofreading.

Gobbledygook: Editor's slang for material characterized by jargon and circumlocution. Also spelled goddledegook.

Graf: An abbreviated term for paragraph, as in, "Give me two grafs on that fire."

Gravure: A process of photomechanical printing, also called rotogravure or intalgio, in which printing ink is transferred to paper from areas sunk below the surface.

Gutter: Vertical space separating one page from another on two facing pages. Also, the long unbroken space between two columns of type on a page.

Hairline: Extremely thin printing rule, or a thin stroke in a letter.

Halftone: A reproduction of a photograph, art, or other continuous tone copy that has been converted into a plate composed of dots of various sizes.

Halftone dropout: A halftone in which dots have been removed from the highlight (white) portions. Also called a highlight halftone.

Hammer: See **barker**.

Hanger: Headline that descends from a banner. Also called a readout.

Hanging indent: Headline style in which the top line is set full measure and succeeding lines are indented from the left.

Hard copy: In electronic editing, a computer printout.

Hardware: Equipment; a computer and its associated gear.

Headlinese: Short words which are overused in headline writing, such as cop, nab, nix, set.

Head shot: Photo of person's head or head and shoulders. Also called face shots and mug shots.

Hole: Space on a newspaper layout or page that has not yet been filled by copy or art. Also, the amount of news space in an edition of a newspaper.

Hood: Border over the top and both sides of a headline.

Horseshoe: Copy desk, once shaped like a horseshoe.

Hot start: System of restarting a computer system after a crash or other temporary interruption.

Hot type: Metal type.

HTK, HTC: Abbreviation for "head to come." The designation placed on the first page of a story rushed to the composing room in takes, it indicates that the headline will follow. Used only on hard copy.

Hugger mugger: Newspaper lead crammed with details.

Index: Newspaper's table of contents, usually found on Page 1.

Insert: Material placed between copy in a story. Usually, a paragraph or more to be placed in material already sent to the desk.

Issue: All copies produced by a newspaper in a day.

Italics: A kind of type in which letters and characters slant to the right.

J and H, or H and J: Hyphenation and justification by computer.

Jump: To continue a story on a following page. The continuation is known as the jump or runover.

Jump head: The headline that identifies the continuation of a story.

Junkets: Free trips given to reporters and editors to influence their coverage.

Justify: Spacing out a line of type to fill the column; spacing elements in a form so the form can be locked up.

Kerning: Typographical process in electronic editing of tucking one letter under another, used often for appearance and sometimes to make headlines fit.

Kicker: Overline over a headline. Also called an eyebrow.

Kill: To delete a section from copy or to discard the entire story; also, to spike a story.

Label: A headline that has no life or force, or a mere caption.

Label head: Dull, lifeless headline. Sometimes a standing head such as "News of the World."

Lay out (v.):   The process of preparing drawings of pages to indicate to the composing room where stories and pictures are to be placed in the newspaper.

Layout (n.):   The completed page drawing, or dummy.

Lead: The first paragraph or first several paragraphs of a newspaper story (sometimes spelled "lede"); also, the story given the best display on Page 1; also, a tip.

Lead out: To justify a line of type.

Lead story: The major story displayed at the top of Page 1.

Legend: Information under an illustration. Also, a cutline.

Letterpress: A technique of printing from raised letters in which ink is applied to the letters, paper is placed over the type and pressure is applied to the paper.

Library: Newspaper's collection of books, files, and so on. Also called a morgue.

Line engraving: A photoengraving made up of only solid lines with no intermediate tones.

Line gauge: Pica rule or a rule marked off in pica segments.

Line printer: Device used to print computer output, which is known as "hard copy."

Linotype: A machine that casts lines of type from hot lead; used in letterpress printing.

Logotype: A single piece of type containing two or more letters commonly used together such as AP or UPI. Also, a combination of the nameplate and other matter used to identify a section. Also, an advertising signature. Commonly abbreviated "logo."

Lower case: Small letters, as opposed to capital letters.

LTK: Designation on copy for "lead to come." Usually placed after the slug, it indicates that the written material will be given later.

Makeover: To redo the layout of a page, as for a new edition of the paper.

Makeup: Assembling type, photos, and heads into a page layout by a printer. Sometimes also refers to layout by editors.

Managing editor: The individual with primary responsibility for the day-to-day operation of the news department.

Masthead: Formal statement of a newspaper's name, officers, place of publication, and other descriptive information, usually on the editorial page. Sometimes confused with flag or nameplate.

Mat: A cardboard or papier-maché mold from which type is cast in letterpress printing.

Measure: The length of a line of type.

Menu: VDT display listing the stories recorded in a particular file.

Metropolitan editor: City editor.

Minion: Seven-point type (hot metal).

More: Designation used at the end of a page of copy to indicate there are one or more additional pages.

Morgue: The newspaper library, where clippings, photographs and resource material are stored for reference.

Move: To send a story by wire.

Mug shot: A photo of a person's face.

Must: Indicates that a story must appear in the newspaper.

News editor: The supervisor of the copy desk. At some newspapers this title is used for the person in charge of local news-gathering operations.

Newshole: The amount of nonadvertising space available in a given issue of a newspaper.

Newsprint: The pulp paper on which the newspaper is printed.

Nonpareil: Six-point type. It is also a unit of measurement for type widths, as the agate line is the measurement for depth.

Obit: Short for obituary; a story about a death that usually includes biographical material.

OCR: Optical character recognition. The process in which reporters write their stories on electric typewriters and a device called an optical character reader translates the typed material into electrical impulses for processing.

Offset: Method of printing differing from letterpress. A photograph is taken of an assembled page. Then the negatives are placed over a light-sensitive printing plate and light is exposed through the negative. The result is that the letters are hardened and the nonprinting surface is washed away. The method of printing involves inking the printed plate with water and then with ink. The water resides only on the nonprinting surface, whereas the ink resides on the printing surface. The inked letters are then printed on a rubber blanket, which in turn prints (or offsets) on paper.

On-line: Electronically connected or wired, such as a phototypesetter on-line to a computer.

Op-ed: The page opposite the editorial page.

Overnight: Story usually written late at night for the morning newspapers of the next day. Most often used by the press services. The overnight, or overnighter, usually has little new information in it but is cleverly written so that the reader thinks the story is new. Also known as second-day stories.

Overset: Type for which there was not enough space in the newspaper.

Pad: To expand a story by including nonessential information.

Page down: Moving material down on a VDT screen by the same number of lines shown on the terminal at any one time.

Page up: ''Page down'' in reverse; to move a page up.

Pagination: Full-page layout done electronically on VDTs.

Parameter: Symbol in computer programming indicating a constant.

Password: A word or set of characters that gives a person access to a computer file.

Paste-up: A layout with type affixed in place, ready for the camera.

Pica: A printing measurement, approximately one-sixth of an inch. Used to designate the width of lines of type, photo dimensions, etc.

Pickup: Material in type that is to be used with new material, such as a new lead.

Pix: Short for pictures. The singular may be pic or pix.

Pixel: Small picture element to denote gray or color values for computer storage.

Play: Handling of a news story, as in ''Let's play this one on the front page.''

P.M.: An afternoon or evening newspaper.

Point: A printing measurement usually used to designate the size of type. A 72-point headline is one set in type that is one inch high.

Precede: Story written prior to an event; also, the section of a story preceding the lead, sometimes set in italic.

Proof: Material in type submitted to editors for correction of typographical errors.

Put to bed: Closing the pages for an edition.

Queue: A holding area within a VDT system. It is the electronic equivalent of an in-basket.

Race: A classification of type, such as roman, text, script.

Read in: Secondary head leading in to the main head.

Readout: Secondary head accompanying a main head.

Regional split: Interruption in the wire to permit the transmission of regional news.

Register: Alignment of plates to get true color reproduction.

Replate: To re-do a page for a new edition or to correct an error.

Rewrite: To write for a second time to strengthen a story or to condense it.

Ribbon: Another name for a banner or streamer headline.

Rim: The outside of a U-shaped copy desk. Copy editors sit here to prepare copy for printing and to write headlines.

Rivers: Streaks of white space within typeset columns caused by excessive word or letter spacing.

Roman: Type with serifs based on historic letter forms. Roman type comes in three basic categories: oldstyle, transitional, and modern.

ROP: Run of the paper. Stories or art that do not demand an up-front position. Ads that may appear anywhere in the paper. Color printed in a newspaper without the use of special presses.

Rotogravure: A printing process in which ink is printed onto paper from tiny recessed wells etched in a copper cylinder. Used to print roto sections, such as the Sunday magazine, usually on glossy paper.

Rough: A dummy that gives little or no detail or an uncorrected, unjustified proof.

Roundup: A story that joins two or more events with a common theme, such as traffic accidents, weather, or police reports. When the events occur in different cities and are wrapped up in one story, the story is known as as an "undated roundup."

Rule: A printed line, such as a column rule.

Runaround: Type set to run around a photo, artwork, or other element.

Running story: Event that develops and is covered over a period of time. For an event covered in subsequent editions of a newspaper or on a single cycle of a wire service, additional material is handled as follows: new leads — important new information; adds and inserts — less important information; subs — material that replaces dated material, which is removed.

Runover: Portion of a story that continues from one page to another. Also called a jump story.

Sans serif: Type without serifs.

Scanner: The popular term for an optical character reader. (See **OCR**.)

Screamer: A large banner headline.

Screen: Printed matter, normally solid in tone (such as a headline or a block of color), lightened by being photoengraved through a screen into a pattern of small dots.

Screening: Processing photographs in order to build up a tiny dot structure on them that will retain ink and allow them to be printed.

Scroll: To move the viewing area on a VDT up or down the text.

Scroll up, scroll down: To move images up or down on a VDT screen.

Search and replace: Computer capability to find a special word or combination of letters and to substitute another word or combination of letters for it.

Second front page: First page of the second section. Also called a split page.

Section page: First page of a pullout section.

Series: Two or more stories on the same or related subjects published on a predetermined schedule.

Serif: A small line that extends at right angles from a main stroke of a letter, such as the horizontal lines at the top and bottom of the letter.

Sidebar: A secondary story intended to be run with a major story on the same topic. A story about a disaster, for example, may have a sidebar that tells what happened to a single victim.

Skel line: Short for skeleton line. One or two lines of identifying copy under a picture, used when a full cutline is not needed.

Slot: The inside of a U-shaped copy desk. The slotman or slotwoman sits in this position and directs the work of copy editors.

Slug: A word that identifies a story as it is processed through the newspaper plant. It is usually placed in the upper left-hand corner of each take of the story.

Software: Computer programs; coded instructions.

Space out: Direction to the printer to add space between lines until the story fills the space allotted for it.

Spike: Six-inch-long nail on which stories are placed for later use or because they are rejected. To "spike it" means to kill a story. Stories put "on the hook" are rejected.

Split run: Making a change in part of a press run of one edition.

Spread: A lead story and all its subsidiary stories constitute a spread. Also, a story that requires a "top head" — that is, one that goes at the top of a column; also sometimes used to designate the head itself. This also applies to any story longer than a short.

Step lines: Headline with successive lines ahead.

Stereotyping: The process used in letterpress printing of making a duplicate metal plate of a newspaper page from a mat; the duplicate plate is flat or curved to fit the press.

Stet: Copy editor's symbol for "let it stand," to restore peviously changed copy.

Stone: The bench or table, with a stone or metal top, on which the pages lie in the composing room while they are made up (hot metal).

Stripping: A printer who strips photographic negatives into composite negatives, called flats. Also, offset platemaking.

Stylebook: A book of standard usage within newspaper text. It includes rules on grammer, punctuation, capitalization, and abbreviation. AP and UPI publish similar stylebooks that are used by most papers.

Subhead: One-line and sometimes two-line head (usually in boldface body type) inserted in a long story at intervals for emphasis or to break up a long column of type.

System: A combination of computer hardware and software that performs a specific processing operation.

Tabloid: Small-sized newspaper, usually about 11 by 17 inches.

Take: A page of typewritten copy for newspaper use.

Telephoto: UPI system of transmitting photos by wire.

Teletext: Home information retrieval system using television signals for the transmission of data.

Thumbnail: Portrait-style photograph printed in one-half column space.

Tight: Full, too full. Also refers to a paper so crowded with ads that the news space must be reduced. It is the opposite of the wide-open paper.

Time copy: Copy that may be used anytime. Also called grape, plug copy and so on.

Transition: A word, phrase, sentence or paragraph that moves the reader from one thought to the next.

TTS: Teletypesetter, a system used to produce coded paper tape that is read by an automated typesetter.

Typo: Abbreviation for typographical error.

Underline: Headline placed underneath an illustration.

Universal desk: A copy desk that edits material for all editorial departments of a newspaper.

Update: Story that brings the reader up to date on a situation or personality previously in the news. If the state legislature appropriated additional funds for five new criminal court judges to meet the increased number of cases in the courts, an update might be written some months later to see how many more cases were handled after the judges went to work. An update usually has no hard news angle.

Upper case: Capital letters, so called because in the early days of printing the type characters were picked out by hand from the upper of the two cases. (See lower case.)

UP style: Newspaper style in which many proper nouns are capitalized.

VDT: Video display terminal, a part of the electronic system used in news and advertising departments that eliminates typewriters. Copy is written on television screens attached to keyboards rather than on paper. The story is stored on a disk in a computer. Editing is done on the terminals.

Viewdata: Home information retrieval system using direct link to computer through telephone or cable television lines.

Warm start: Normal starting procedure for a computer system at the start of a new workday or at the close of an old one. Directories are automatically purged of some entries during a warm start, according to overall computer programming.

Wicket: Kicker-like element placed to one side of a headline.

Widow: A line of type containing only a few characters, as at the end of a paragraph.

Wooden head: A dull and lifeless headline.

Wrapup: Complete story. Wire services use a wrapup to contain in one story all elements of the same story sent previously.

Appendix D

NEWSPAPER STYLE*

CAPITALIZATION

Capitalize a title preceding a name, but lowercase it after a name.
Mayor Smith will meet Gov. Johnson.
John Smith, mayor, will meet Bill Johnson, governor.

Lowercase a title standing alone.
The mayor will meet with the governor.

Place long titles after the name.
Jim Blayne, executive assistant to the mayor, spoke first.

Lowercase occupational or false titles.
janitor John C. Jones
included rookie left-handed pitcher Bill Wills
The speaker was defense attorney John K. Paul.

Capitalize Union, Republic, and Colonies when referring to the United States or when used as part of the name of a specific foreign governmental body.
Republic of Korea, French Fifth Republic

Capitalize Congress, Senate, House, Cabinet, and Legislature when referring to United States or a specific individual state body.

The building in Washington (or a state capital) is the Capitol. The city is the capital.

Capitalize committee in full names.
The Senate Judiciary Committee met at noon.
The House Ways and Means Committee recessed.

Lowercase committee standing alone. Lowercase subcommittee in all cases.
The committee recessed early.
The Senate Judiciary subcommittee on rules meets tomorrow.

Capitalize complete names of organizations.
State Junior Chamber of Commerce
Interstate Commerce Commission

Lowercase commission standing alone.

*Adapted from The Associated Press *Stylebook* by permission. The examples have been added.

Capitalize Supreme Court, 6th U.S. Circuit Court of Appeals, Juvenile Court, District Court.

It is Juvenile Court Judge William Sanders and not Juvenile Judge William Sanders.

Capitalize Social Security Administration and Social Security Act when referring to the U.S. system.
He received Social Security payments.

Lowercase social security when used in the general sense.
He advocates social security for the aged.

Capitalize Army, Navy, Air Force, Marines, Coast Guard, and National Guard when referring to those of the United States. Lowercase soldier, sailor, and leatherneck, but capitalize Marine and Coast Guardsman.

Capitalize holidays, historic events, ecclesiastical feasts, fast days, special events, hurricanes, and typhoons.
Mother's Day, Labor Day, Battle of the Bulge, Good Friday, Passover, Christmas, Halloween, National Safety Week, Hurricane Hazel, Typhoon Tilda, New Year's Day, New Year's Eve.

Lowercase "new year" when used as follows.
What will the new year bring?
At the start of the new year...

Capitalize specific geographic regions.
Middle East, Mideast, Middle West, Texas Panhandle, Orient, Chicago's South Side, Lower Manhattan

Capitalize ideological and political areas.
East-West relations, East Germany

Lowercase mere direction.
The car traveled west toward the county line.

Capitalize political parties.
Democratic Party, Democrat, Republican Party, Socialist, Communist, Independent

Lowercase generic political terms when standing alone.
democratic form of government, republican system, socialism, communism, party

Capitalize Red when used to refer to a political, geographical, or military unit.

Capitalize names of fraternal organizations.
Knights of Columbus, American Legion, Lions Club

Capitalize God, the Father, the Son, the Son of God, the Redeemer, the Holy Spirit, Allah, but lowercase he, his, him, who, whose, whom. Capitalize Bible, Koran, Talmud, and all names of the Bible and all names of all organized religious movements. Capitalize Satan and Hades, but lowercase heaven, hell, and devil.

Capitalize Civil War, War Between the States, Korean War, Revolutionary War, World War I, World War II, Vietnam War and Revolution (when referring to the Revolutionary War or the Bolshevik Revolution).

Capitalize the names of races (Caucasian, Chinese, Negro, Indian), but lowercase red, black, yellow, and white. Use racial identification only when pertinent. Use black or Negro. Do not use "colored" to identify race.

Capitalize a common noun when used as part of a formal name, but lowercase when standing alone.
　　Hoover Dam, Missouri River, Bibb County Courthouse
　　dam, river, courthouse

Capitalize Empire State Building, Hyatt House (hotel), Rainbow Room, Wall Street, Pershing Square.

Capitalize trade names and trademarks.

Coca-Cola, Deepfreeze, Xerox, and Coke should be used only when referring to the specific product.

Lowercase street, road, and avenue when plural.
　　Broad and Main streets

Capitalize names of organizations and expositions.
　　Boy Scouts, Red Cross, World's Fair, Utah State Fair

Capitalize and place in quotations titles of books, plays, poems, songs, movies, operas, and works of art.
　　"Tom Sawyer," "My Fair Lady," "Mona Lisa"
Exception: Don't put the Bible and books that are primarily catalogs of reference material in quotations.

Such words as a, an, in, of, and the are capitalized only when the first or last word of a title.

Capitalize the first word of a quotation when the quotation comes after a comma or colon and makes a complete sentence.
　　He said, "Omit needless words."

Capitalize fanciful nicknames.
　　Tigers, Sunshine State, Old Glory, the Windy City

Capitalize decorations, medals, and awards.
　　Silver Star, Purple Heart, Pulitzer Prize, Nobel Prize in physics, Medal of Honor (Congressional Medal of Honor is incorrect.)

Capitalize City Council, County Commission, Department of Education, etc., when the reference is to a specific body. Lowercase if condensed to council, commission, or department.
　　The City Council voted...(meaning a specific city)
　　The County Commission...(meaning a specific county)
　　The Department of Education...(meaning a specific department of education)

ABBREVIATIONS

In general, spell out names of firms, organizations, and groups on first mention. Abbreviate thereafter if there is a commonly known abbreviation.
　　The Aluminum Company of America closed two plants Wednesday. An ALCOA spokesman said....
　　The American Civil Liberties Union announced Wednesday plans to....ACLU has been an advocate of....

Abbreviate time zones when used with a specific time.
　　...at 9:30 a.m. CDT on Friday.

Spell out when the specific time is not given.
　　Washington, D.C., is on Eastern Daylight Time.
　　Washington, D.C., is in the Eastern time zone.

Abbreviate the names of business firms if the firm in question does so.

Warner Bros., Brown Implement Co., Almalgamated Leather Ltd., Baltimore and Ohio Railroad, Smith and Sons, Inc., J.C. Penney Co., Inc.

In addresses that include the number, abbreviate St., Ave., Blvd. Spell out all others at all times, including Road, Drive, Place, Circle, Lane, Terrace. If the number is not included, spell out Street, Avenue, Boulevard. If the number is given, abbreviate N., S., E., W., N.W., S.E., N.E., S.W. If the number is not given spell out North, South, East, West, Northwest, Northeast, Southeast, Southwest.

100 Cox St., Cox Street
9 S. Gay St., South Gay Street
3 E. Magnolia Ave., East Magnolia Avenue
8 Eighth Ave. S.W., Eighth Avenue Southwest
80 Jefferson Blvd., Jefferson Boulevard

Lowercase abbreviations that do not involve proper names. Those that spell words take periods.

c.o.d., f.o.b., a.m., p.m. Exceptions: 35mm film, 105mm howitzer, mph, mpg. (On first mention spell out miles per gallon.)

Abbreviate versus as vs. (with a period).

Standard abbreviations for states:

Alaska, Hawaii, and states with fewer than six letters are never abbreviated (Idaho, Iowa, Maine, Ohio, Texas, Utah). Abbreviate all other states when they follow cities or towns, military bases, national parks, reservations.

He was born in Boise, Idaho, and moved to Logan, Utah, at the age of 18.
He was born in Amite, La., and moved to Laurel, Miss., at the age of 12.
They lived at Gray Air Force Base, Texas, for three years.

Spell out the names of all states when they stand alone.

He was born in Alabama and moved to Louisiana at the age of 18.

Omit the state after in-state cities unless doing so would cause confusion.

He grew up in Centreville, but moved to London, Ala., at 20.

States that take abbreviations:

Ala.	Neb.
Ariz.	Nev.
Ark.	N.C.
Calif.	N.D.
Colo.	N.H.
Conn.	N.J.
Del.	N.M.
Fla.	N.Y.
Ga.	Okla.
Ill.	Ore.
Ind.	Pa.
Kan.	R.I.
Ky.	S.C.
La.	S.D.
Md.	Tenn.
Mass.	Vt.
Mich.	Va.
Minn.	Wash.
Miss.	W.Va.
Mo.	Wis.
Mont.	Wyo.

Abbreviate United States and United Nations in titles and when used as adjectives.
U.S. Chamber of Commerce, U.N. headquarters, U.S. foreign policy

Spell out United States and United Nations when used as nouns.
The foreign policy of the United States has been....
The membership of the United Nations is divided on the....

Months that may be abbreviated in news stories are Jan., Feb., Aug., Sept., Oct., Nov., and Dec.

Always spell out March, April, May, June, July.

Abbreviate months only when used with calendar date.
John went to Chicago in January and returned Feb. 3.
The Battle of Iwo Jima started in February 1945 when Marines stormed....
The Battle of Iwo Jima started Feb. 19, 1945, when Marines stormed....

Do not abbreviate days of the week.

Do not abbreviate any proper name unless the person or organization named does so.

TITLES AND NAMES

The full name of a person normally is used only once in a news story, and that is on first mention.
John J. Jones of Reform received the Navy Cross today. Jones, a retired bank clerk, was cited for gallantry in action in 1942 during....
Betty Jane Smith is $1,000 richer today, thanks to her good eyesight and her honesty. Smith found a gold coin in....

Titles normally are used on first mention, either before or following the name.
President Josiah P. Buford of Topps University has called for a....
Dr. Josiah P. Buford, president of Topps University, has called....
Dr. Josiah P. Buford opposed the plan. The Topps president said that....

Do not abbreviate president, vice president, association, detective, department, deputy, assistant, commander, manager, general manager, secretary, treasurer, professor, district attorney, attorney general, superintendent when used before a name.

Titles that should be abbreviated when appearing before the name include Sen., Rep., Gov., Lt. Gov., the Rev., Dr. and military titles.

If an abbreviated title is used, it is always placed immediately before the name and the full name is used.
Right: Lt. Gov. George E. Jones said Tuesday that....
Right: Gov. Walter C. George went to....
Wrong: Lt. Gov. Jones said....

Spell out and lower case all titles used after the name or standing alone.
The lieutenant governor told members....
The senator urged his colleagues....

Courtesy titles are Mr., Mrs., Miss, and Ms. Mr. should be used only in conjunction with Mrs., but courtesy titles for women can be used on second reference.
Wrong: Mr. John J. Smith left ....
Right: John J. Smith left ....

Courtesy titles may occasionally be used when a story involves both a husband and a wife and the title is needed for clarity.

Right: Mr. and Mrs. John J. Smith left....

Use Ms. only if you know that it is preferred by the individual. If you don't know, use Mrs. for a married woman and Miss for a single woman. If a married woman's given name is not known and her husband's is, use Mrs. or Ms. after first mention (but following the rule above on Ms.).

Mrs. Frank C. Young told the Auburn Woman's Club Tuesday....

If a woman has a formal title, such as Dr., Professor, President, Chairman, it may be used in place of the courtesy title.

Military title abbreviations:			
General:	Gen.	Admiral:	Adm.
Lieutenant General:	Lt. Gen.	Vice Admiral:	Vice Adm.
Major General:	Maj. Gen.	Rear Admiral:	Rear Adm.
Brigadier General:	Brig. Gen.	Commodore:	Commodore
Colonel:	Col.	Captain:	Capt.
Lieutenant Colonel:	Lt. Col.	Commander:	Cmdr.
Major:	Maj.	Lieutenant Commander:	Lt. Cmdr.
Captain:	Capt.	Lieutenant:	Lt.
First Lieutenant:	1st Lt.*	Lieutenant Junior Grade:	Lt. j.g.
Second Lieutenant:	2nd Lt.*	Ensign:	Ensign
Sergeant Major:	Sgt. Maj.	Seaman:	Seaman
First Sergeant:	1st Sgt.*	Seaman Apprentice:	Seaman Apprentice
Sergeant First Class:	Sgt. 1st Class	Seaman Recruit:	Seaman Recruit
Specialist Five:	Spec. 5	Master Sergeant:	Master Sgt.
Corporal:	Cpl.	Technical Sergeant:	Tech. Sgt.
Private First Class:	Pfc.	Airman First Class:	Airman 1st Class
Private:	Pvt.	Airman:	Airman
		Chief Petty Officer:	Chief Petty Officer

*Spell out 1st, 2nd at the beginning of a sentence.

PUNCTUATION

The Comma.

Use in a series but omit before the conjunction at the end of the series.

The colors were orange, red, pink, blue and yellow.
Bill, Bob, John and Charles made the trip.

Do not use a comma before "of."

They were Dan Jones of Chicago, Bill Smith of Kansas City and Mrs. J.C. Wade of Detroit.
They were Dan Jones, Chicago; Bill Smith, Kansas City; and Mrs. J.C. Wade, Detroit.

Use before a conjunction when it joins two independent clauses.

Fish abounded in the lake, and the shore was lined with deer.

Use to set off attribution.

She said, "We will go."
"We will go," she said, "if the weather is good."
The work, she said, is exacting.

Use to set off phrases or words in apposition or contrast.

Wisconsin, the favorite, won easily.

Omit the comma before Roman numerals, Jr., Sr., the ampersand, and dash; in street addresses, telephone numbers, and serial numbers, and after Co., Inc.
John Jones II and William C. Ivey Jr. attended the party.
Smith & Co. owned the building.
She claimed — no one denied it — that she was the owner.
She lived at 4423 N. 30th St. as a youngster.
Her telephone number is 887-7741 and his is 887-7742.
The serial number of the rifle is 996724R.

Use in a number of more than three places.
There were 999 shirts.
They had 1,000 handkerchieves.
9,999 knives, 11,213 forks, 210,121 spoons

The comma indicates the briefest pause of all punctuation marks. The tendency is to use fewer commas. However, the comma sometimes is indispensable to meaning.
a. What's the latest dope?
b. What's the latest, dope?
a. The Democrats, say the Republicans, are sure to lose the election.
b. The Democrats say the Republicans are sure to lose the election.
a. Do not break your bread or roll in your soup.
b. Do not break your bread, or roll in your soup.

The Semicolon.

Use to separate phrases containing commas to avoid confusion.
Attending were six college students: B.M. Smith, an author; R.J. Jordan, a veterinarian; and Paul C. Hackett, a high school English teacher.
Attending were Bill Ray, Detroit; Jack Smith, Chicago; and Bob Jones, Aspen.

Use to separate statements of contrast and statements too closely related.
The draperies, which were ornate, displeased me; the walls, light blue, were pleasing.

The Dash.

Use to indicate a sudden change.
"I think you should not—but who am I to offer advice?"

Use to mark a summing up at the end of a sentence.
Ambition and hard work—these are the ingredients of success.

Otherwise, use the dash sparingly. Commas frequently serve the purpose better.

The Hyphen.

This is one of the most abused and least correctly used marks. Hyphens are joiners. Use them to avoid ambiguity or to form a single idea from two or more words.

Use the hyphen whenever ambiguity would result if it were omitted.
The president will speak to small-business men. (Businessmen normally is one word.)
He recovered his health. He re-covered the leaky roof.

Use when a compound modifier—two or more words that express a single concept—precedes a noun. (Exceptions: don't use with an adverb ending in "ly" or with the adverb "very.")
first-quarter touchdown, bluish-green dress, full-time job, 40-hour week, better-qualified woman
But: easily remembered rule, very costly week

Adjectival use must be clear.
    the 6-foot man-eating shark (This is about a fish.)
    the 6-foot man eating shark (This is about a person eating.)
    the 3-year-old girl, the 6-foot-2 player
    the 6-foot-2-inch player, a 20-foot ladder
    The girl was 3 years old.
    The ladder is 20 feet long.
    The player is 6 feet 2 inches tall.

The Apostrophe.

Use in contractions.
    don't, rock 'n' roll

Use in omission of figures and in plural of figures and letters.
    '90s, '90, class of '22, four A's

Do not use the possessive when it is more natural to do otherwise.
    The wheels of the cars (not the cars' wheels)
    The roofs of the barns (not the barns' roofs)

To form the possessive of a singular noun not ending in s, add 's.
    the church's needs, the girl's toys, John's hat, the fox's den

To form the possessive of singular common nouns ending in s, add 's.
    the hostess's invitation, the witness's answer
Exception: If the next word starts with s, add only the apostrophe.
    the hostess' seat, the witness' story.

To form the possessive of a singular proper name ending in s, add only an apostrophe.
    Agnes' book, Dickens' novels, Williams' plays, Moses' laws

To form the possessive of a plural noun not ending in s, add 's.
    women's rights, men's suits, children's toys, alumni's contributions

To form the possessive of plural nouns that end in s, add only the apostrophe.
    the churches' needs, the girls' toys, the horses' food, states' rights

Quotation Marks.

The comma and the period always go inside the quotation mark. Other punctuation is placed according to the construction.
    "I won't go," he said. "I must stay here."
    Why call it a "gentlemen's agreement"?

NUMERALS

In general, spell out numbers below 10. Use numerals for 10 or more.

Use numerals exclusively for ages, court districts, dates, election returns, dimensions (depth, height, length, width., percentages, speeds, clock time (except for noon and midnight), temperatures (except for zero), highway numbers, military units, political divisions, ratios, proportions, and decimals.

In distances, spell out through nine.

For ordinals (first, 1st, second, 2nd, etc.., spell out first through ninth when they indicate sequence in time or location but starting with 10th use numerals.

first base, First Amendment, first in line, First Street, Ninth Ave, 15th Street

Use 1st, 2nd, etc. when the sequence has been assigned in forming names.

1st Congressional District, 2nd District Court of Appeals

For uses not covered by the above list, spell out whole numbers below 10 and use figures for 10 and more.

The woman has three sons and two daughters.

He has a fleet of 10 station wagons and two buses.

They had 10 dogs, six cats and 97 hamsters.

They had four four-bedroom houses, 10 three-bedroom houses and 12 10-room houses.

AGES:

Jane, 3, won the race.

The calf was 4 days old.

3-year-old girl,

2-day-old cat,

woman in her 30s

HIGHWAYS:

U.S. Highway 29, U.S. Route 29 or U.S. 29, State Route 14 or Route 14, whichever is appropriate.

Interstate Highway 85 on first mention, I-85 on subsequent mention.

TIMES:

He drove it in 2:30:21.64. (hours, minutes, seconds, hundreths)

CLOCK TIME:

9 a.m. Tuesday, 9:15 a.m. Tuesday

8 tonight or 8 p.m. today. 8 p.m. tonight is redundant, as is 5:30 p.m. o'clock.

Appendix E
INSTRUCTIONS FOR MYCRO-TEK 1100 VDT SYSTEM

1. Turn on the terminal by pressing the red rocker switch just below the screen until the light comes on.

2. Give the terminal a few seconds to warm up.

3. Press the yellow "FORM" button and then a small "l." The "FORM" command brings the editorial form onto the screen. No other function can be performed on the screen until the editorial form appears.

4. Certain categories of the editorial form must be filled in before a story can be entered onto a disk.

    a. NAME: A name or number should go here.

    b. DSK: A letter or number designation is needed here.

    c. SLUG: One or two words describing what is being entered.

    d. VER: A number should go here; number 1 if it is the first version; remember to use numbers only, not letters.

    e. DATE: Numbers should be used to fill in the entire category. For example, if the date is September 8, 1981, the category should be filled in as 090881.

5. Once these categories are filled in, you are ready to type your story. Keep in mind the following things:

    a. You may type without having to return the cursor to the end of the line; the system will do that automatically.

    b. **DO NOT MOVE THE CURSOR WITH THE SPACE BAR.** Use the cursor control keys to move the cursor. The space bar creates space characters when it is pressed.

    c. Paragragh indentions are indicated by pressing the tan "M-SPACE" key at the beginning of each paragragh. The "END PARA" key should be pressed at the end of each paragragh, including the last one.

CLEARING THE SCREEN

1. To clear the screen of all words and letters, including those in the editorial form, press the red "CLR ALL" key and then the "RETURN" key.

2. Remember that if you clear the screen of copy which has not been entered onto a disk, that copy will be erased and cannot be retrieved.

ENTERING A STORY

1. Once a story has been typed on the screen, it should be entered onto a disk. First make sure all the necessary editorial form categories are filled in properly. (See step 4 in "Getting on the system.")

2. Press the following keys: "VDT ON LINE", w, "RETURN."

3. By pressing the small "w," you have entered your story onto disk 1. You may, however, want to enter your story onto a disk other than disk 1. You will need to know the controller slot your disk is in.

If it is in the second slot, the command you will give to enter your story onto that disk is "VDT ON LINE, w2, RETURN." For slot 3, the command is "VDT ON LINE, w3, RETURN."

4. When the entry command is given, the cursor will leave the screen for a few seconds. When it returns to the top left, the story has been entered and you may go on to another function of the system.

ERROR MESSAGES

If the cursor does not return to the top left, something is wrong. The system will usually tell you about it by sounding a bell and then giving you a message along the bottom line of the screen (known as the message line). Here's what to do if you get the following messages:

WRONG DATA TYPE: The cursor will show you what needs to be changed in the editorial form, usually in the last parts of the name and slug categories. Delete what you have there.
NUMS ONLY: This means there are letters where numbers should be in the editorial form. The "STYLE," "VER." and "DATE" categories may have only numbers in them.
DUP FILE: Another story with exactly the same editorial form is already on the disk. You need to change any item in the editorial form.

KILLING A STORY

Once you have entered an edited version of a story onto the disk, you may want to delete the original version from the menu. Such a procedure is known as killing the story. Killing may be done in several ways.

1. Call the story you want to kill onto the screen. Issue the following command: VDT ON LINE, k, RETURN if the story is on disk 1; VDT ON LINE, k2, RETURN if the story is on disk 2; VDT ON LINE, k3, RETURN if the story is on disk 3; and so on.

2. If you know the exact slug or name of the story, you may kill a story without calling it onto the screen. Type the slug or name of the story into the appropriate editorial form category. If the story is on disk 1, issue the following command: VDT ON LINE, k, RETURN; VDT ON LINE, k2, RETURN if the story is on disk 2; VDT ON LINE, k3, RETURN if the story is on disk 3; and so on.

3. For the procedure for killing stories directly from the menu, see the section on direct menu commands.

UPDATING, INITIALIZING

Killing a story does not erase it completely from the disk. A story may be erased in one of two ways: updating or initializing. Updating means erasing from the disk only items which have been killed. Initializing means erasing all items from the disk. Both procedures require special commands which only system managers should know.

EDITING ON THE SYSTEM

Define Mode

In order to edit efficiently on the VDT system, the editor must be familiar not only with the cursor control keys but also with the define modes. The define mode allows an editor to identify any block of copy so that certain editing functions can be performed on that copy. There are four ways of defining copy:

DEF WORD: Pressing this key will define single words; successively pressing the key will define a string of words until there is a period or an end paragragh mark.
DEF SENTENCE: This key will define all characters between periods, even if the cursor is located in the middle of a sentence. Pressing the key again will define the next sentence, and so on.

DEF PARA: This key is used to define all material between the end paragragh marks. Successive paragraphs may be defined by pressing this key again.

DEF BLK: Put the cursor at the point where the defined copy begins and press this key. Move the cursor to the end of the copy to be defined, and press this key again. All of the copy in between these two points will be defined.

A DEFINE COMMAND can be negated by pressing the letter "n."

Inserting

1. When the copy you want to insert is to replace copy already there, it may be typed over the original copy if it has fewer characters than the original copy. The original characters will be erased and replaced by the new copy.

2. When the copy you want to insert is in addition to the original or has more characters than the copy you want to replace, the "INSERT CHAR" key must be used through the following procedure.

a. Place the cursor at the point where the inserted material is to begin.

b. Press the "INSERT CHAR" key; sixty-four characters of space will appear at that point.

c. Type the material you wish to insert. If it is more than sixty-four characters, type until you run out of space and wait for a moment; sixty-four more spaces will automatically appear.

d. When all the material to be inserted has been typed, the remaining space may be removed by pressing either the "INSERT CHAR" key or the right arrow cursor key.

Deleting

1. Material may be deleted by typing over it with new material.

2. Individual characters may be deleted by pressing the "DELETE CHAR" key. Holding this key down will delete characters successively.

3. Larger blocks of copy may be deleted by using the following define keys.

a. Define the block of copy which is to be deleted.

b. Press the letter "d." The defined copy will disappear from the screen.

c. **DO NOT USE THE "DEL CHAR" KEY WITH THE DEFINE KEYS.** Doing so can freeze the copy in the define mode, and you will lose the editing you have done on your story.

4. Another way of deleting blocks of copy at the beginning or end of a story is to use the red "CLR" keys.

a. If you want to remove a large amount of copy at the beginning of the story, bring the cursor to stand at the first space after the copy which is to be deleted. Press "CLR TOP" and "RETURN."

b. If you want to remove a large amount of copy at the end of your story, bring the cursor to the last point in the story that should not be deleted. Press "CLR END" and "RETURN."

Moving copy

1. Define the copy which is to be moved.

2. Move the cursor to the point where the copy is to be moved.

3. Press the "m" key.

4. The copy will move to that point. You may continue editing the copy.

Copying material

1. Define the material which is to be copied.
2. Move the cursor to the point where you want another copy of the material.
3. Press the "c" key.
4. The material will be automatically inserted at this point. This function is especially useful when working with copy which must have several sets of parameters. Once a set of parameters has been placed at a point in the story, it may be copied at other points in the story where needed.

Boldfacing and uppercasing copy

1. To have copy set in boldface, define the copy and press the "b" key. The defined copy will begin with an upperrail (UR) symbol and end with a lowerrail (LR) symbol.
2. To have copy set in all capital letters, define the copy and press the "u" key.

GETTING A HARD COPY

You may get a hard copy of any story which has been entered onto a disk. You cannot get a hard copy of something not entered into the system. The story you want to get a hard copy of should be called up on your screen. (See the section on calling up stories from the menu, if necessary.)

1. Make sure the hard copy printer and interface are turned on and the "ON LINE" button on the printer has been pressed. A small red light beside the button will be shining if the button has been pressed.
2. Give the system the hard copy command by pressing the following keys: "VDT ON LINE, h, RETURN."
3. The small "h" alone assumes that your story was on disk 1. If the story had been on disk 2, the command would have been, "VDT ON LINE, h2, RETURN." For a story on disk 3, the command would be "VDT ON LINE, h3, RETURN," and so on.
4. This command takes a few seconds to be accepted by the system. After it has been accepted, a few more seconds will elapse before the printer begins printing.
5. When the printer has finished, press the "FORM FEED" button on the right side of the printer. This will advance the hard copy so that it can be torn off at a perforation. Do not try to rip the copy out of the printer. This will tear up the paper feed and could damage the machine.
6. For another procedure for getting hard copies, see the section on direct menu commands.

MEASURING COPY

The VDT system is programmed to tell you how long a story will be if it is set in 8-point type. The length of the story is also determined by the width of the column in which it is set. The system is set up to measure copy in several widths.

1. In the style category, fill in the number which corresponds to the column width in which you will want your copy set. Use the following guide for this category:

    a. For 9-pica-6-point columns, put the number 1 in the style category.
    b. For 13 pica columns, use the number 2.
    c. For 18 pica columns, use the number 3.
    d. For 21 pica columns, use the number 4.

2. Press the orange "COPY FIT" key.
3. The length of the copy will appear in the INCH category of the editorial form.

For a variety of reasons, an editor may want to measure only part of a story. The system will also help in this regard.

1. Fill in the style category as described above.
2. Define the portion of copy which is to be measured.

3. Press the orange "COPY FIT" key.

4. The measurement will appear in the message line at the bottom of the screen.

5. You may perform whatever function you wish with the defined copy, or you may negate the define command by pressing "n."

6. An alternative to this procedure is to insert an end of text (ETX) symbol at any point in the copy by using the green "ETX" key. When the "COPY FIT" button is pressed, the system will measure the copy from the beginning to wherever the ETX symbol is located.

PARAMETERS

Parameters are a way of telling the typesetter how you want your copy set. Editors who know how to use parameters can have a great amount of flexibility in working with their copy. For a fuller explanation of what parameters mean, see the layout and design section of News Editing. To build a set of parameters, take the following steps.

1. Press the tan "SUPERSHIFT" key.

2. Press the tan "SET MEAS" key. After this you need to type four numbers. The first two represent the number of picas wide your column is; the second two represent the number of additional points. For example, a 9 ½ pica column would have "0906" after the "SET MEAS" designation.

3. Press the tan "SET LEAD" key. After this you need to type three numbers representing the amount of space you want between the lines of copy. The first two represent the space in points; the third will either be a five or a zero representing a half or whole point. For example, a 10 †- point leading would be "105."

4. Press the tan "SIZE" key. After this you need to type two numbers representing the size of type you want the copy to be set in. Eight-point type would be "08."

5. Press the tan "FONT" key. After this you need to type one number corresponding to the typeface you want. This number will depend on the kind of type that is in the typesetter. The number 1, for instance, usually means regular type; the number 2 means boldface; and so on.

6. Press the "SUPERSHIFT" key. *THIS IS A VERY IMPORTANT STEP.* A set of parameters must be surrounded by supershift designations. If one of the supershift commands is left out, the typesetter will not work properly, and the omission may cause some damage to the typesetter. It is always a good idea to check your copy before you send it to the typesetter to make sure that all parameters have supershifts surrounding them.

TYPESETTING A STORY

1. Once you have edited a story and put parameters on it, you are ready to send the story to the typesetter. If you have inserted a set of parameters into an edited story, you will need to enter the story onto a disk before you can send it to be typeset.

2. To send a story to the typesetter, give the following command: VDT ON LINE, t, RETURN for a story on disk 1; VDT ON LINE, t2, RETURN for a story on disk 2; VDT ON LINE, t3, RETURN for a story on disk 3; and so on.

3. For another procedure for typesetting stories, see the section on direct menu commands to follow.

MENUS

Calling up a Menu

A list of stories on any particular disk is called a menu. In order to know what is on a disk, you will want to call up a menu on your screen. From this menu, you may call up any story on the disk. Here's how to do it:

1. Press the following keys: VDT ON LINE, m, RETURN. This command will give you the menu for disk 1. If you want a menu for disk 2, the command is "VDT ON LINE, m2, RETURN;" for disk 3, "VDT ON LINE m3, RETURN;" and so on.

2. The entire menu will be read onto your screen and then will go automatically to the beginning. If the menu takes up more than one screen, you may look through it using the blue "SCROL" or "PAGE" keys.

Calling up a Story

1. When you have found the story you want to see, bring the cursor down to beside the line and press the following keys: "DEF BLK, r." This is a basic command and does not change according to the disk number.

2. The menu will leave the screen and the story you want will soon appear.

3. If you want to call up a story directly without calling it from the menu, fill in the editorial form on your screen with the exact information you find in the "SLUG" entry or some other entry in the story's menu line. Next, press the following keys: "VDT ON LINE, r, RETURN," if the story you want is on disk 1. If it is on disk 2, the command should be "VDT ON LINE, r2, RETURN;" for disk 3, it should be "VDT ON LINE, r3, RETURN;" and so on.

4. If you want to look at the next story on the menu list without going back to the menu, press the following keys: "NEXT FILE, r."

5. If you want to look at the previous story on the menu list without going back to the menu, press the following keys: "PREV FILE, r."

Recalling the Menu

1. If you want to bring the menu back after you are finished with a story, press the following keys: "CURR FILE, c."

2. A menu may contain only 180 items, although a disk may have many more than that. These extra items will be listed on the supplemental menu. To get that menu on your screen, press the following keys: "NEXT FILE, c." To get the first menu back, press the following keys: "PREV FILE, c."

Direct Menu Commands

An editor may want to kill a story, get a hard copy, or send a story to the typesetter without having the story on the screen. These commands may be issued directly from the menu. To do this, the following steps should be taken.

1. Begin with a clear screen. Type an asterisk in the "XTS:" category of the editorial form.

2. Call up the menu you want to work with. When the menu reads out onto the screen, all of the items on the disk will be included, even those which have previously been killed. The killed items will have a stationary cursor beside them, but they may be treated in the same manner as any other item on this menu.

    a. If you want to kill an item not already killed on the menu, bring the cursor to stand beside the item. Give the following command: "DEF BLK, k." A stationary cursor will appear beside the item.

    b. If you want to get a hard copy of an item on the menu, bring the cursor to stand beside the item. Give the following command: "DEF BLK, h."

    c. If you want to send an item on the menu to the typesetter, bring the cursor to stand beside the item. Give the following command: "DEF BLK, t." (You do not need the disk number for any of these commands.)

Searching a Menu

If you want to find a certain item or items on a menu, you need not scan the menu looking for it. If you have the proper information, you can ask the system to conduct a "search" for the stories that you want. This function of the system is especially helpful in working with wire stories, which are often sent in several parts and are often updated. The following instructions describe some of the ways in which you can ask the system to search a menu.

   1. If you know the slug or name under which a story or set of stories is entered on the menu:

      a. Write that slug or name in the proper categories in the editorial form. What you write must be exactly the slug or name in the system.

      b. Give the system the following command: "VDT ON LINE, m, RETURN" for a search of the menu on disk 1; "VDT ON LINE, m2, RETURN" for a search of the menu on disk 2; "VDT ON LINE, m3, RETURN" for disk 3; and so on.

      c. The items which the system finds in its search will appear as a menu on your screen. You may call any of those items to your screen as you would call them from a full menu.

      d. If you want a long menu (the first three lines of each item) of the items found in your search, you need to give the following command: "VDT ON LINE, l, RETURN"; for disk 2; "VDT ON LINE, l2, RETURN"; and so on.

   2. If you want all the items entered under a particular disk designation (such as sports) or on a particular date, the procedure is the same as above. Fill in the proper information in the editorial form and give the short menu (m) or long (l) menu command.

   3. If you know only part of a slug, such as the first two or three letters, but are not sure about the exact spelling of the full slug, you can still conduct a menu search. Fill in the first two or three letters which you know are in the slug; then fill out the rest of the category with asterisks. When the menu command is given, the system will search for all the items whose slugs have the first letters which you filled in. The name category of the editorial form may be used in the same way.

COMPILING

The procedure for compiling the parts of a wire story is somewhat complicated, but it is not particularly difficult once it has been learned. The key to the procedure is keeping one part of the story on the terminal screen while calling up another one.

Two-take Stories

   1. Conduct a menu search, asking for a long menu of the items you want. (See the section on searching a menu). If two items come up in the menu, the first containing the beginning of the story and the second saying "1st add," you are working with a "two-take" story. Use the following procedure for putting them together.

   2. Type the story number of the first item in the name category of the editorial form.

   3. Give the following command: "VDT ON LINE, r, RETURN." If you are working on Disk 2, the command would be "VDT ON LINE, r2, RETURN"; for Disk 3, "VDT ON LINE, r3, RETURN;" and so on.

   4. The first take of the story will be read onto your screen under the menu items.

   5. Give the editorial form command, "FORM l." This command will clear the editorial form and allow you to complete the next step with a smaller chance of errors.

   6. Type the smaller number of the second take into the name category of the editorial form.

   7. Give the same command as in step 3.

   8. The second take of the story will be read onto the screen under the first take.

   9. Delete the menu items.

   10. Go to the end of the first take and delete all non-story items at the end of the first take and the beginning of the second take. The last paragraph of the first take should be followed immediately by the second take.

   11. You now have one story on your screen and can begin editing it.

Multiple-take Stories

   1. Conduct a menu search asking for a long menu of the items you want (see the section on sear-

ching the menu). If several items appear on the menu, you are working with a "multiple take" story. You will need to piece this story together on the screen.

2. Look through the long menu to find the latest (or the most recent) lead of the story available. A menu item which says "2nd lead" will be later than the one that says "1st lead."

3. When you have found the latest lead, you will need to call it up on the screen without losing the long menu which you already have. To do that:

      a. Give the editorial form command, "FORM, l." This command will clear the editorial form and allow you to complete the next step with a smaller chance of errors.

      b. Type the story number of the latest lead in the name category of the editorial form.

      c. Give the following command: "VDT ON LINE, r, RETURN." If you are working on Disk 2, the command would be "VDT ON LINE, r2, RETURN;" for Disk 3, "VDT ON LINE, r3, RETURN;" and so on.

      d. The latest lead will read onto your screen under the menu items.

4. Read through the instructions on the top of this story carefully. What they say will determine your next step. The instructions should tell you what this latest lead substitutes for. If it is a "1st lead," it will substitute for the top paragraphs of the main body of the story. In that case, you will want to call up the first take of the main body of the story. Using the number in the name category of this first take, repeat steps 3a and 3b.

5. A "2nd lead" or subsequent lead, however, may be substituting for a previous new lead. In that case, you will need to call up the previous new lead so that it reads out under the latest lead. Again, you may do this by using steps 3a, 3b and 3c.

6. Once you have the latest lead, any previous leads you need and the first take of the main body of the story on your screen (in that order), you may call up any subsequent takes, additions, or substitutions which are listed on the long menu. Use steps 3a and 3b for this process.

7. Follow the instructions contained within each of the takes to compile your story.

8. Delete all menu and non-story items.

9. You now have one story on your screen and should begin editing it.

MEMORY FUNCTIONS

Each VDT has a certain capacity for storing information so that it can be called upon when needed. This capacity is not unlimited and should be used judiciously, but an editor can find that it saves a great amount of time. One thing should be kept in mind about the terminal's memory: it will be erased when the terminal is turned off.

Storing

1. To store something in a memory terminal, define the copy that is to be stored.

2. Press the "STORE MEM" key and then a two-digit number, anything from 00 to 99. Two items cannot be stored at different times under the same number.

3. When the copy returns to full intensity, it has been stored in the terminal's memory system.

Calling Up Memory

1. Place the cursor at the point where the stored items are to begin.

2. Press the "USE MEM" key and then the two-digit number under which the item is stored in the terminal's memory system.

3. The stored item will be inserted automatically at that point.

SEARCHING A STORY

The Mycro-Tek system, like many other systems, adds an editing feature unique to electronic editing systems — searching for a story automatically for a particular set of letters and numbers. This system has four search operations: the simple search, search and delete, search and replace, and search and decide.

This system has four search operations: the simple search, search and delete, search and replace, and search and decide.

Search

If you want the system to search for a particular item in the story, take the following steps:

1. Press the yellow "SR" key.

2. The cursor will move to the message line of the screen. Type what you wnat the system to search for.

3. Press the "EXECUTE" key.

4. The cursor will stop at the first item that corresponds to what you typed and the message "DECIDE" will appear in the message line. If you want to make any changes at this point, you may do so.

5. Once you have made any changes, or if you have made none, you may continue the search operation by pressing the "EXECUTE" key.

6. The cursor will stop at the next item which corresponds to what you typed in Step 2. Each time you press the "EXECUTE" key, the cursor will go to the next corresponding item. It will continue each time the "EXECUTE" key is pressed, until all the items are found.

Search and Delete

If you want to delete a set of characters or numbers from your story automatically, take the following steps:

1.Press the "SR" key.

2. Type into the message line what you want to delete.

3. Type a slash mark after the item.

4. Press the "EXECUTE" key. The cursor will read through the story and automatically delete the item you have typed.

Search and Replace

If you want to replace one set of characters with another, the system will do this automatically if the following steps are taken:

1. Press the "SR" key.

2. Type the item you want replaced in the message line, followed by a slash mark; then type the item with which you want it replaced.

3. Press the "EXECUTE" key. The system will automatically replace the first item with the second one.

Search and Decide

If you want to check an item in the story and possibly replace it with another, the system will help you do this if you take the following steps.

1. Press the "SR" key.

2. Type the item you want the system to search for and type a slash mark.

3. Type the item with which you may want to replace the first item.

4. Type two slash marks immediately after this second item and then the letter "r."

5. Press the "EXECUTE" key.

6. The cursor will stop at the first item in the story which corresponds to the first item you have typed. The message "DECIDE" will appear on the screen. At this point you may do one of two things:

a. If you want to replace the item with the second one you typed, press the letter "r."
The system will then search for the next item corresponding to the first one you type.

b. If you do not want to replace the item, press the EXECUTE key. The system will then search for the next item corresponding to the first one you typed.

HEADLINES

When you are working on stories on the VDT for which you will be writing a headline, you will need to create some space at the beginning of the story for writing the head. This is called building a headline form. To do this, you should take the following steps before you call up any stories on your screen.

1. Clear the screen and put the cursor in the position immediately below the editorial form.

2. Hit the "RETURN" key four times.

3. Place the cursor on the first return arrow. Strike the "INSERT CHAR" key and type the following: Head order:. Using the "SPACE BAR," move the cursor to near the right margin of the screen. Hit the "END PARA" and the "INSERT CHAR" keys.

4. Place the cursor on the next return arrow down on the screen. Hit the "INSERT CHAR" key, and again using the "SPACE BAR," move the cursor to near the right margin of the screen. Hit the "END PARA" and the "INSERT CHAR" keys.

5. Repeat step 4 for a third and fourth line.

6. Delete the four return marks.

7. Define the entire form usng the "DEF BLK" key. Store it in the terminal's memory using "00."

Once you have stored the headline form in the VDT memory, you may call it up at any time until the terminal is turned off.

Writing a Head

Once you have created some blank space at the top of your story, you are ready to write your headline with the help of the VDT system.

1. Press the orange "HEADFIT" key.

2. The word "HEADFIT" will appear in the message line of the terminal, and the cursor will be on the left. Enter the style of headline you want the system to measure by typing an "s," an equal sign (=), and a number corresponding to the style. The system is programmed to count in the following styles:

1=bodoni bold
2=bodoni extra-bold
3=futura demibold
4=helios
5=helios bold

3. Press the "SPACE BAR."

4. Enter the point size of the head you want the machine to measure by typing a "p," "=," and the number corresponding to the size of the head. For example, to get the system to measure a thirty-point headline, you would type "p=30."

5. Press the "RETURN" key.

6. The cursor, which will have returned to the upper left of the screen, should be brought down out of the editorial form to the first blank line available so that there are four zeros next to the word "WIDTH" in the message line.

7. You are now ready to begin writng your headline. Keep the following things in mind.

a. The four numbers next to the word "WIDTH" in the message line keeping a running measurement of the line in the head which the cursor is on. The first two numbers represent picas and the second two numbers represent additional points.

b. You may delete or insert just as you would in editing copy. When deleting, however, it may be best to use the "SPACE BAR" in order to maintain the space you have created.

c. When you have completed one line of the head and want to go on to the next, press the "RETURN" key.

d. When you are in the headfit mode, you are not locked in. You may scroll or page through your story and perform any editing function while writing the headline. As long as the word width appears in the message line of the screen, the system will measure the headline you are writing.

8. When you are through writing your headline, you should take the system out of the headfit mode. You can do this by pressing the "HEADFIT" key.

Appendix F
INSTRUCTIONS FOR
HENDRIX 6100
VDT SYSTEM *

Journalists are no longer intimidated by the video display terminals in the newsroom. Beginning reporters in college classrooms also discover that the VDT can become an asset in their task of organizing information into understandable form. Perhaps the first frustration for most journalists is the inability to "touch" their copy. Reporters who have been accustomed to rolling a sheet of newsprint into a typewriter, rapidly composing a story, making corrections with a thick-lead pencil, and dropping the copy into a basket discover an almost inhuman aura surrounding the VDT. Adjusting the focus and brightness on the cathode ray tube replaces the insertion of copy paper. Story composition is accomplished by following a blinking light across a TV screen. And at the touch of one key, a finely polished piece of copy disappears into a computer's memory or onto punched teletypesetter tape in a form unrecognizable to the veteran journalist.

But there are benefits, too. And even the crustiest news veterans admit there is a good chance the new technology may improve news writing. At the least, most professionals admit that a good reporter operating under the traditional method of copy preparation remains a good journalist under the new one.

All journalists agree that a larger responsibility is placed upon the reporter in the new system. He or she has greater "CONTROL" over the copy by being the only person to type it. The reporter has the major role in producing error-free copy. This is not to say that the editing function is eliminated from newspapers and magazines. But the printer who formerly retyped the reporter's copy is out of a job in the new system. Copy editors read a reporter's copy in a manner similar to the traditional method, but they do it on a VDT and make changes in the copy electronically.

The challenge for the beginning reporter or copyreader, then, is to become proficient with the mechanical operation of the VDT as soon as possible and to build speed on the machine. Any new procedure slows production at first, but most student journalists learn to operate a VDT very rapidly. They find the operations very similar to those of an electric typewriter with a few handy additions. And they discover the challenge of finding short cuts in composition and copyreading an enjoyable learning experience.

These instructions have been prepared to assist student journalists in understanding the operation of the VDTs manufactured by Hendrix Electronics, just one of the many vendors marketing VDTs today. The vocabulary used is keyed to the Model 6100 Editing System "User's Handbook," 1973, and edited to include the features of the Model 6200 System.

CATHODE RAY TUBE CONTROLS

The monitor of a video display terminal is focused and adjusted like a home television screen. The two controls for the Hendrix VDT cathode ray tube are just beneath the right-hand base of the terminal keyboard.

The front dial controls the contrast of the characters on the screen. The rear dial controls the brightness of the images. The user should adjust these controls to avoid eye strain.

Turning the brightness control wheel clockwise brightens the cursor and characters on the screen. Counterclockwise rotation darkens the characters.

*By James Crook, University of Tennessee, Knoxville

The monitor should not be operated at high levels of brightness. Abnormally high brightness levels cause the characters on the screen to "bloom" and appear to go out of focus. The phosphor in the picture tube may be damaged after prolonged operation at high brightness levels.

The contrast "CONTROL" is used to obtain a sharper character image. It can be adjusted to suit the operator's viewing, but it should not be adjusted over time for a particular viewer and should be adjusted only slightly for different viewers.

When a user completes work with the VDT, he or she should turn the brightness dial counterclockwise to darken the screen. This lengthens the life of the cathode ray tube.

ELECTRIC TOUCH SYSTEM

A VDT operates in much the same way a standard electric typewriter does. Keys on the board should be touched lightly and not hit with unnecessary pressure. If a key is held down, the VDT will repeat the function assigned to the key. This can work to the reporter's advantage, as in producing a long line of dots, or to his or her disadvantage by inserting unnecessary letters or figures.

A very handy feature of the VDT is its ability to wrap from line to line automatically. This allows the reporter to type rapidly without consideration of hyphenation or ending a line. It is only at the end of a paragraph that the reporter inserts a special "CONTROL" symbol to instruct the typesetting machine to fill the remainder of the line with white space. In order to compose a story quickly, then, a reporter should compose his or her thoughts rapidly without concern for ending a line.

The terminal will hold a story of about 750 words. When the reporter is within about 10 to 15 words of this limit, a red light will appear at the upper left hand corner of the keyboard. The light labeled "MEMORY ALERT" warns the reporter that one short sentence may be added before it will be necessary to output the copy produced to this point. After the copy is removed from the terminal, the reporter can finish the story wth a second output. When the terminal is full, a second red light will appear in the upper left labeled "MEMORY FULL." When this light is on, the reporter cannot insert another character. At this point the reporter will probably need to remove the previous sentence and retype it after outputting the copy in the terminal.

THE CURSOR

A reporter or an editor sitting in front of a VDT watches a blinking rectangle of light move across the screen in response to commands he or she produces on the keyboard. This light, or cursor, indicates the exact spot a command message from the keyboard will be enacted.

The movement of the cursor corresponds to the movement of a typewriter carriage. When the cursor reaches the end of a line on the screen, it automatically moves down to the next line. The VDT accomplishes this task just as an electric typewriter automatically moves the reporter's paper up a doublespace.

The reporter has a number of commands at his or her fingertips to move the cursor around a story rapidly.

A configuration of five gray keys at the bottom right side of the keyboard is used to move the cursor to a spot on the screen visible at one time. Four of these keys have arrows on them indicating the direction in which they move the cursor. The key in the center moves the cursor to "HOME" position 8 that is, to the upper left of the screen.

Editors must remember that not all of a story may be visible on the screen. For this reason the key "HOME MEMORY" is very valuable for saving time in rapidly jumping to the top of a story. This key allows the editor to jump to the top of a story to read the lead paragraph again, for example. And, for a similar purpose, the key marked "END OF TEXT" will allow the editor to jump to the end of the last sentence of the story without using the gray keys, which would accomplish the same task more slowly.

It is important for reporters and editors to identify short cuts in the operation of a VDT. Many functions can be accomplished in more than one way. The challenge is to prepare copy as rapidly as possible and to reduce errors that creep in with awkward commands.

CONTROL KEY

Just one key on the Hendrix VDT is color coded. The red key at the left of the keyboard is labeled "CONTROL." The red color is used to show that the key is intended to be used with those keys on the keyboard that have red printing at the top.

The key works like the "SHIFT" key. That is, when the red "CONTROL" key is held down with one finger and a key with red printing is touched, the editor gets the function printed in red. If the red key is not held down, the editor obtains the function printed in black.

An example of the use of the "CONTROL" key is shown by the keys marked "SENT REMOVE" (in black) and "PARA" (in red). When the editor removes a sentence, it is not necessary to use the "CONTROL" key. However, if the editor removes an entire paragraph, he or she may hold the "CONTROL" key and touch the key marked "PARA" (in red). The entire paragraph will blink on the screen. The editor may read the paragraph a second time if necessary before deleting it. By holding the "CONTROL" key and touching the "PARA" key a second time, the editor will remove the paragraph from the terminal.

Other examples of dual functions on one key include the two "BLOCK" keys, the "INSERT" and "C CASE" keys, and the "INPUT" and "OUTPUT" keys.

If a key has only red printing on it, it may only be used with the "CONTROL" key. When the key is pressed without simultaneously touching the red "CONTROL" key, a high-pitched "beep" will sound. This alarm signal is sounded only to remind the editor of the color code. An example of this occurs with the use of the "CLM" (clear memory) key at the upper left hand corner of the keyboard.

Other brands of VDTs use different names for the "CONTROL" key. One manufacturer calls the key a "Super Shift Key."

CONTROL SYMBOLS

The reporter composing a story on the VDT for the first time must learn the control symbols that replace the actions required on a conventional typewriter.

An immediate difference is apparent when the reporter discovers it is not necessary to stop typing at the end of a line. On the VDT the reporter is able to continue typing and the machine will wrap the lines automatically.

The only control symbols necessary, then, are those needed to indicate the beginning and the end of a paragraph. The "EM" key is used to mark the beginning of a paragraph, and the "RETURN" key indicates the end. In each case a control symbol will appear on the screen. This symbol is required by the computer to provide white space at the beginning and end of each paragraph.

Other control symbols are unnecessary unless the reporter wishes to have a special construction in the story. When the reporter finishes the story, he or she should touch the "BELL" key. This symbol serves as the traditional thirty-dash or number sign ending for a news story.

Another difference involves the traditional amount of space left between sentences by a typist. It is not necessary, and in fact is a poor idea, to space twice at the end of a sentence. This causes too much white space within the standard newspaper column width. Reporters should space once between sentences.

Bylines are centered by touching the "QUAD CENTER" key before typing the byline in caps and lower case letters as the newspaper style indicates. For lines of type to be set flush left, the reporter should touch the "QUAD LEFT" key before typing the line. For lines to be set flush right, the procedure is the same, using the "QUAD RIGHT" key. In each case the lines of type should be followed by the "RETURN" symbol.

Transposing blocks of type is quite easy on the VDT. Two keys with two functions each replace the scissors and the paste pot that are used with the traditional editing method. Each key is labeled "BLOCK." The procedure is easy if the reporter takes the steps in order.

At the beginning of the sentence, paragraph, or group of paragraphs to be moved, the reporter should touch the key marked "BLOCK START." This key is marked in red to be used with the "CONTROL" key. When this key is touched, a small symbol will appear at the location of the cursor. It will resemble a "P" with a subscript number "1." The reporter should then move the cursor to the end of the block and repeat the process using the "BLOCK END" key. This function is controlled by the same key and is identified by black printing. The reporter has now defined the block to be moved.

At this point the reporter should read over the block again to be sure the correct number of lines is included. By moving the cursor between the two symbols, the reporter then transfers the block to the memory of the computer by touching the "BLOCK SAVE" key. The block disappears and remains stored in the memory until it is recalled. The reporter then moves the cursor to the spot where the block is to be inserted and touches the "BLOCK INSERT" key. The block appears at this spot in the story, and all succeeding paragraphs will move down in order.

MOVEMENT OF COPY

A reporter sees only seventeen lines of copy on the VDT at a time. A terminal will hold about sixty-five lines of copy, however.

The "HOME MEMORY" key allows the reporter to jump quickly to the top of the story. The "END OF TEXT" key permits rapid movement to the end of the story.

If the reporter wants to move to the the middle of the story, this is easily accomplished by using either the "ROLL UP" key or the "ROLL DOWN" key at the lower right side of the keyboard. These keys advance or reverse the story a line at a time when touched lightly. Rapid movement is accomplished if either key is held down.

INSERT MODE

One of the chief advantages of editing with a VDT comes with the ease of inserting paragraphs, sentences, or words in the middle of a story. This is accomplished without disturbing the copy.

To insert material, the reporter should first place the cursor at the exact place at which the new words appear. Then the reporter should touch the "INSERT" key. When this is done, a small red light will come on directly above the "INSERT" key. This tells the reporter the terminal is in the insert mode. As long as the light remains lit, the reporter may insert material. This insert light will go out when the gray cursor keys are touched or when the "INSERT" key is touched.

If the reporter attempts to insert material without touching the "INSERT" key first, the new copy will replace the original copy. In some cases this may be desirable. In other cases the reporter may have to replace the missing words.

As a reporter inserts copy in the middle of a story, the VDT automatically moves the remaining copy toward the end of the story. When the new copy is inserted, the left margin automatically wraps when a gray cursor key is touched.

REMOVING COPY

Checking a reporter's story for redundancies or wordiness is an easy task on the VDT. An editor quickly removes a single character or punctuation mark, a word, a sentence, or a paragraph. And in an equally short time, the editor can kill an entire story. The challenge is, of course, to remove the exact amount of copy necessary without destroying the content of the story.

Three keys at the lower-right side of the keyboard allow the editor to delete material quickly.

The "CHAR REMOVE" key is used to delete a single character or punctuation mark and close up the story to leave no extra white space in the line.

The "WORD REMOVE" key will remove a series of characters. Since the computer that controls the VDT cannot spell, it will remove any strings of characters and punctuation marks that are not separated by a space.

The "SENT REMOVE" key performs the same function for a string of characters and spaces between two periods. Therefore, if a sentence has an abbreviation (such as, Ave.) in the middle, the "SENT REMOVE" key will delete the first part of the sentence up to Ave. Then the editor needs to move the cursor to the second half of the sentence to remove the remaining part. The computer defines a sentence as any series of characters between two periods.

The "PARA REMOVE" key is labeled in red. This tells the editor to use it in conjunction with the red control key. The "PARA REMOVE" key deletes all material between two "EM" symbols in the copy.

The Hendrix VDT has a safety device on the "WORD REMOVE," the "SENT REMOVE," and the "PARA REMOVE" keys in the form of a blinking mode. Each time the editor touches one of these keys, the material to be deleted blinks until the key is touched a second time. If the editor has a change of opinion about the characters to be deleted, he or she can stop the procedure by touching any character on the keyboard except one of the "REMOVE" keys. This stops the blinking and the cursor may be repositioned.

When the editor has completed work on a story, a punched-tape version of the edited story may be produced, or the story may be retained in the directory of the computer. Then the editor may kill the story from the VDT screen by touching the "CLM" key in the upper left-hand corner of the keyboard. The key is printed in red, indicating the need to touch the "CONTROL" key at the same time. All copy in the terminal blinks in warning to the editor. All copy is killed if the procedure is followed a second time. If the editor decides not to kill the story at this time, it is saved by touching any other key on the keyboard.

CHANGING CASE

Changing a character or word from upper- to lower-case is easily accomplished by using the "C CASE" key at the lower right of the keyboard. The reporter will notice it is printed in red and used jointly with the red "CONTROL" key.

To capitalize a lower-case letter, place the cursor on the letter and touch the "C CASE" key while holding the red "CONTROL" key down. The same procedure works for making a capital letter into a lower-case letter.

This key is especially helpful when an entire word or paragraph needs changing. The "C CASE" key and the red "CONTROL" key may be held down for repeating the function.

STRIKING OVER

Unlike typewriters, VDTs accommodate strike-overs. In fact, in many cases an editing change can be accomplished most easily by merely "typing over" an error.

Strike-overs work best on single characters or punctuation marks. However, it is possible to strike over entire words when the desired word has the same number of characters as the word to be replaced.

A common errror made by beginning editors is to attempt to move the cursor around the screen by touching the "SPACE BAR." Unlike a typewriter, the "SPACE BAR" inserts space and replaces copy already on the screen. When the story appears in hard copy, the editor finds large amounts of unwanted white space in the story. The editor must remember that every black space placed on the screen by the "SPACE BAR" is developed by the phototypesetter and produces a white space in the story.

This is why reporters are advised to make a single space between sentences when writing a story on a VDT.

INPUT MODE

To place a reporter's story on a VDT, an editor must use the keys marked "INPUT" at the upper right of the keyboard. These keys cause the "INPUT" lights above and at the right of the keys to send messages to the editor.

Only one VDT in a system can be connected to the tape reader at one time. Therefore, a series of instructions must be followed to use the reader.

An editor first touches the "INPUT SELECT" key. This turns on one of the lights directly above the key and one of the lights on the right side of the key. If the "BUSY" light is on, the editor should touch the "INPUT SELECT" key again (and again) until the "BUSY" light goes off. This indicates to the editor that the reader is free to be used.

Second, the editor touches the "INPUT RESERVE" key, which is labeled in red, along with the red "CONTROL" key. If no other VDT is connected to the reader, the red "MINE" light will come on. This indicates a connection between the editor's terminal and the reader.

Third, the editor loads the reporter's story or punched tape into the reader.

Fourth, the editor returns to the VDT and touches the "INPUT START" key. The tape is fed through the reader and the reporter's story appears on the screen for editing.

Fifth, the editor turns off the red "MINE" light the same way that it was turned on   8by holding the red "CONTROL" key and touching the "INPUT RESERVE" key.

After editing the story, the editor follows the procedure for the "OUTPUT MODE" (see next section). In a large newspaper system, the editor inserts a code that sends the story directly to the newspaper's central computer. There it is stored for future decision making or is sent directly to the phototypesetter with production codes for type size and column width.

OUTPUT MODE

After editing a story, the editor sends the piece to the computer, where it is identified in the directory. The editor may also reproduce the story on a TTS tape with the punch or a hard copy with the printer. The editor uses the keys marked "OUTPUT" at the upper right side of the keyboard. These keys cause the "OUTPUT" lights above and to the right of the keys to send messages to the editor.

Only one VDT in a system can be connected to each output device at one time. Therefore, a series of instructions are used for the editor to use the punch or the printer.

An editor first touches the "OUTPUT SELECT" key. This turns on one of the lights above the "OUTPUT SELECT" key. If the "BUSY" light comes on, the editor touches the "OUTPUT SELECT" key again (and again) until the "BUSY" light goes off. This indicates to the editor that the output device is free to be used.

Second, the editor touches the "OUTPUT RESERVE" key, which is labeled in red, along with the red "CONTROL" key. If no other VDT is connected to the output device, the red "MINE" light will come on. This indicates a connection between the editor's terminal and the output device.

Third, the editor touches the "OUTPUT START" key. This will cause the punch to produce a TTS tape version or the printer to produce a hard copy of the reporter's story. In the UTK system, the punch is identified as Output Device No. 1 and the printer as Output Device No. 2.

Fourth, the editor turns off the red "MINE" light by means of the same procedure used in turning it on.

In a large newspaper system, the editor skips the TTS tape step and sends the story directly to the central computer or to the phototypesetter. Reporters often produce a hard copy of a story for personal reference.

In producing a paper tape of an edited story, it is best to fold the output tape into six-inch lengths so it will not tear when fed through the phototypesetter. It is easy to spot the side of the tape as it comes from the punch. The tape will curl upwards if the top of the tape is facing up.

DIRECTORY OPERATION

Five commands are available to the reporter or editor through the operation of the directory in the Hendrix system. They enable the journalist to:

S: Save a story in the directory.
C: Copy a story from the directory to the screen of a VDT.
M: Move the "original copy" of a story from the directory to the screen of a VDT.

K: Kill a story in the directory.
N: Rename a story in the directory.

Each of these commands will be described here.

After writing a story, a reporter saves it in the directory for editing at some future time. The reporter touches the "DIRECTORY" key at the upper right of the VDT. Then he or she moves the cursor down to a blank line identified by the letters "A-Q." In the left column, the reporter types an "s" and touches the "EXECUTE" key directly below the "DIRECTORY" key. This places the story in the sixteen-thousand-character directory. The directory will display the first 55 characters of the story, the VDT number at which the story was written, and the length of the story in characters.

An editor calls up a reporter's story by touching the "DIRECTORY" key to identify the location of the story, typing a "c" in the left column, and touching the "EXECUTE" key. This does not kill the story from the directory but makes a copy of the reporter's work for the editor.

The "original copy" of a reporter's story is moved from the directory by typing an "m" in the left column and touching the "EXECUTE" key. This command will work only if the VDT number agrees with the number in the directory.

A story in the directory may be renamed in order to move it to a VDT with a different number or to kill it. To rename a story, the editor types an "n" in the left column of the directory. He or she then moves the cursor to the name field and types in the number of the VDT being used to edit the story. The editor then touches the "EXECUTE" key. The story is then renamed, and it can either be copied on the editor's VDT by using the copy command or killed.

If a story is to be killed from the directory, the editor types a "k" in the left column of the directory next to the appopriate story and touches the "EXECUTE" key. The story is then deleted from the directory. This command will work only if the editor's VDT number agrees with the number shown in the directory.

FORMATS

Twenty formats provide the capability of storing and recalling frequently used phrases and character combinations, such as datelines, bylines, and phototypesetter commands (such as changes in line length, point size, type size, or leading). A total of one thousand characters may be stored in the twenty formats with no set amount assigned to any format.

Once the formats are stored they will be accessible to all terminals in the system, but, to avoid confusion in storing and recalling formats, only the highest-numbered terminal has the ability to store or alter previously stored formats.

To see the stored formats, the reporter touches the "SAVE FORMAT" key. Any format that has not been designated will have the word "undefined" in it.

To select a format numbered 1 through 10, the reporter keeps the "SHIFT" key in the unshift position, holds the "CONTROL" key down, and touches any key 1 through 0, which corresponds to 11 through 20. To insert a format into a story, the reporter positions the cursor at the point desired and selects the correct format (as described above); the selected format will be inserted at this point with no loss of text.

HENDRIX CONTROLLER-COMPUTER

The editing capability of the Hendrix EDS-6100 is supplied by the Editor System Operating Program in the controller. To operate the terminals, this program must be in the controller and working.

The basic software package consists of two types of programs: loader programs and the editor program.

The loader programs, after they have been incorporated into the computer, normally remain there until they are automatically engaged by the computer for the purpose of loading other programs into the system.

The editor program, which makes operation of the system possible is continuously running at all times if the system has not been shut down.

Normally the only program that has to be loaded into the 6100 system is the editor program. However, if the editor program does not make the system operable, the user may need to load a total of three programs. These include the Bootstrap Loader Program, the Absolute Loader Program, and the Editor System Operating Program.

The first program that must be loaded when core memory is completely empty is the Bootstrap Loader Program. This program must be toggled directly into the core of the computer by using the console switches (see Hendrix User's Handbook, p. A-15). The Bootstrap Loader is used to instruct the computer to accept and store data on paper tape in bootstrap form. It is used to load the Absolute Loader Program, a short paper-tape program.

The second program to be loaded is the Absolute Loader Program. It enables the user to load into core memory data punched on paper tape in absolute binary format. It is used primarily to load the EDS-6100 Editor System Operating Program, a long, paper tape program.

The Editor System Operating Program is the last program to be loaded after the Bootstrap Loader and Absolute Loader have been put into the core memory. This program enables the system to perform its editing functions.

MAINTENANCE

Dust accumulating on the face of the picture tube and the backsurface of the face plate because of static charge on the tube should be removed with household detergent and water on a soft cloth. Fingerprints and smudges should be cleaned off the front of the face plate regularly.

Use a damp cloth to clean the keyboard. Be very careful not to allow liquid or foreign material to get under the dust cover or between the keys.

Air ventilation holes in the monitor and the controller should not be blocked during operation. Inadequate ventilation may cause device malfunction. Terminals must be operated in an air conditioned room.

Static electricity caused by certain fabrics may cause the system to be inoperable at times. Consult the reprogramming section for instructions on how to correct this situation.

RESTART PROCEDURE

When terminals will not operate because of electrical problems, insert the key into the controller and move the switch from the "LOCK" position to the "POWER" position.

If a machine halt occurs which is not the result of a power down condition, the editor should attempt a restart that will save the copy that was being edited. This restart procedure is listed first. If it is not successful, the second procedure should be used.

PROCEDURE I:
Raise toggles number 9 and 1. This prepares the "001002" address.
Next press the "HALT" toggle.
Then press the "LOAD ADRS" toggle and the "001002" address will appear directly above the toggles on the "ADDRESS" register in red lights.
Raise the "HALT" toggle.
Finally, press the "START" toggle.
The terminals should now come to life and a high-pitched "beep" will sound. The key in the controller should be moved to the "LOCK" position. If the terminals do not come to life, the second procedure should be followed.

PROCEDURE II:
Raise toggle number 9. This prepares the "001000" address.
Next press the "HALT" toggle.
Then press the "LOAD ADRS" toggle and the "001000" address will appear directly above the toggles on the "ADDRESS" register in red lights.

Raise the "HALT" toggle.

Finally, press the "START" toggle.

The terminals should now come to life and there should be a high-pitched "beep."
Return the key in the controller to the "LOCK" position.

START PROCEDURE

Insert the key into the controller and move the switch from the "OFF" or "LOCK" position to the "POWER" position.   The Absolute Loader Program should be in the core memory. If the following instructions are not successful, consult the *Hendrix User's Handbook* for the Model 6100 Editing System, (p. A-13, as revised in 1980 when the system was upgraded to the 6200 system).

Press the "HALT" toggle.

Place the 6200 Editor System Program (blue paper tape) in the tape reader. Place the blank leader tape directly over the reader sensors. This program enables the system to perform its editing functions.

Raise toggles 6, 8, 9, 10, 11, 12, 13, and 14. This prepares the "077500" address.

Press the "LOAD ADRS" toggle and the "077500" address will appear directly above the toggles on the "ADDRESS" register in red lights.

Raise the "HALT" toggle.

Press the "START" toggle. This should cause the paper tape to be drawn through the tape reader, and the data will be loaded into the core memory. The tape will stop at the end of the data.

The terminals should now come to life and a high pitched "beep" should sound. Return the key in the controller to the "LOCK" position.

STOP PROCEDURE

Insert the key into the controller and move the switch from the "LOCK" position to the "POWER" position.

Press the "HALT" switch.

Move the switch from the "POWER" to the "OFF" position.

Index

21½–						–21½
21–						–21
1–						– 1
20–						–20
2–						– 2
19–						–19
3–						– 3
18–						–18
4–						– 4
17–						–17
5–						– 5
16–						–16
6–						– 6
15–						–15
7–						– 7
14–						–14
8–						– 8
13–						–13
9–						– 9
12–						–12
10–						–10
11–						–11
11–						–11
10–						–10
12–						–12
9–						– 9
13–						–13
8–						– 8
14–						–14
7–						– 7
15–						–15
6–						– 6
16–						–16
5–						– 5
17–						–17
4–						– 4
18–						–18
3–						– 3
19–						–19
2–						– 2
20–						–20
1–						– 1
21–						–21
0–						– 0

21½								-21½
21								-21
1								1
20								-20
2								2
19								-19
3								3
18								-18
4								4
17								-17
5								5
16								-16
6								6
15								-15
7								7
14								-14
8								8
13								-13
9								9
12								-12
10								-10
11								-11
11								11
10								-10
12								12
9								9
13								13
8								8
14								14
7								7
15								15
6								6
16								16
5								5
17								17
4								4
18								18
3								3
19								19
2								2
20								20
1								1
21								21
0								0